Globalization

UNU Policy Perspectives

In its series of *UNU Policy Perspectives*, the United Nations University Press publishes studies that are directly policy-related yet based on solid scholarly research and analysis. Its objective is to provide timely expert information and insight on current issues and thereby to promote the useful application of knowledge.

Globalization

The United Nations Development Dialogue

Finance
Trade
Poverty
Peace-building

Edited by
Isabelle Grunberg
Sarbuland Khan

United Nations
University Press

TOKYO • NEW YORK • PARIS

The views expressed in this publication are those of the authors and do not necessarily reflect the views of the United Nations University.

United Nations University Press
The United Nations University, 53–70, Jingumae 5-chome,
Shibuya-ku, Tokyo, 150-8925, Japan
Tel: +81-3-3499-2811 Fax: +81-3-3406-7345
E-mail: sales@hq.unu.edu
http://www.unu.edu

United Nations University Office in North America
2 United Nations Plaza, Room DC2-1462-70, New York, NY 10017, USA
Tel +1-212-963-6387 Fax: +1-212-371-9454
E-mail: unuona@igc.apc.org

United Nations University Press is the publishing division of the United Nations University.

Cover design by Joyce C. Weston

Printed in Hong Kong

UNUP-1051
ISBN 92-808-1051-0

CONTENTS

Prologue

Globalization is bringing us more choices and new opportunities for prosperity. It is making us more familiar with global diversity. But globalization also brings uncertainties. Millions of people around the world experience it not as an agent of progress but as a disruptive and even destructive force, while many more millions are completely excluded from its benefits. One of the great challenges of our time is to realize globalization's full potential while minimizing the risks.

The United Nations has a key role to play in this process. New thinking emanating from the United Nations Economic and Social Council; new partnership with the Bretton Woods Institutions; new contacts with the World Trade Organization; and new ventures with the private sector, the primary actors that drive globalization, are among the significant steps the United Nations has taken recently to revitalize its work in the economic and social fields.

This publication, which contains statements and other materials from the past two years of debate and dialogue in the Economic and Social Council, is intended to bring the Organization's work to a wider audience. It covers the key issues: finance, trade, poverty and peace-building. And it shows a United Nations seeking greater understanding about globalization and exploring ways to reconcile the imperatives of global markets with the socio-economic needs of the world's people. Furnished with adequate resources and authority to meet the challenges at hand, the United Nations can be a crucial part of the solution.

Kofi Annan
Secretary-General of
the United Nations

Introduction

Globalization, Governance and the Role of the United Nations in Economic and Social Affairs

By Isabelle Grunberg[1]

Why is globalization not improving the lot of millions of the world's poor?[2] What kind of governance is needed for globalization with a human face? What kind of architecture for the world financial system, what kind of framework for global trade? What rules of the game to protect the weak and the poor? This book aims to illuminate these questions by presenting some of the most important debates that took place at the United Nations, especially the Economic and Social Council (ECOSOC) in the years 1998 and 1999, covering the themes of globalization, financial architecture, trade, poverty, global indicators and the nexus between secu-

---

1 Many thanks are due to Sarbuland Khan for comments and suggestions on this Introduction.
2 Because of the effects of the Asian crisis, the number of poor people is now rising once again in most developing countries. The global total of those living on less than $1 a day, 1.2 billion, is the same as in 1987 (*World Bank Economic Outlook*, 1999). According to the Food and Agriculture Organization, the number of chronically undernourished people in developing countries has increased from 822 million to 828 million between 1996 and 1999.

rity, economic and social affairs. This overview analyzes the policy environment and highlights the strengthened role of the United Nations in the new context.

One world—with a governance gap

As we start a new century, globalization is changing our image of the world. States are increasingly faced with a reality that knows no boundaries. Many products are assembled in one country from parts made in several other countries, to be sold in a different set of countries. All the while, the decision-making and management is based in yet another country—and the research and development in another one. These networks of production and distribution treat individual countries as provinces of a same world unit. The "one-world" image also increasingly describes the experiences of many citizens world-wide, especially with the growing use of the Internet and the world-wide web.

Thus, world affairs are less and less the sum total of the inter-dependencies that link individual countries with each other. Many global dynamics simply ignore boundaries. The erosion of the nation state means that governments are becoming more and more powerless. And weakened governments may spell the end of governance. Many applaud this erosion of governance—indeed, many see it as a main attraction of globalization. These are the true anarchists—perhaps more so than the masked youth that smashed windows at the WTO meeting of Seattle in 1999.

Yet there is a powerful rationale for why we need governance. Individuals and firms produce a mixture of public and private goods. Firms, for example, produce public goods in the form of higher employment and growth. Adam Smith pointed out that the seemingly private goods that entrepreneurs are driven to produce is often turned into something that benefits everyone—by the famous operation of the invisible hand.

In many other areas, however, there is simply no invisible hand. And one does not need to be an idealist to realize it. The *Financial Times* regularly reports on the growing danger that business executives face when traveling abroad. "The widening gulf between rich and poor, and a growing sense of disenfranchisement and militancy among those who are losing out, means that business travelers' security is becoming more precarious", warns the newspaper.[3] Yet, what incentives does an individual firm have to deal with poverty and disenfranchisement? It would be like

---

3   "Caught in Capitalism's Crossfire", *Financial Times*, 6 December 1999, p. 10.

Don Quixote tackling the windmills instead of watching the bottom line. Chances are, business executives who read these news pieces will think of hiring more body guards rather than trying to deal with the substance of the global problem. And with only weak governments left, the situation does not look promising.

Cyberspace is vaunted as the ideal market place, free from governmental interference. Yet, many people are deterred from buying on line by worries about payment safety, the bona fide of the vendor, or the lack of legal recourse if a transaction goes sour. And more and more on-line businesses are seeking help in protecting their names or innovations. Without rules, this market place will not live up to its full potential—and so it is with many other market places.

Another reason why we will miss governance—why many *already* miss it—is that governance provides a framework for the exercise of democracy. Democracy guarantees self-determination, and people who do not determine their own fate have their fates determined by someone else. Perhaps that is why anti-globalization demonstrators threw a Boston tea party in Seattle.

So globalization weakens traditional patterns of governance without replacing them with alternative forms of governance where people would feel in control, and where public goods would be adequately provided.

But does that mean a globalized world needs global government? In theory yes. In practice, the idea of a global government is unappealing—because it would be so difficult for such a government to be responsive and accountable to so many; because people still cherish their national identities; and because there are such disparities of wealth and power worldwide that the "illusion of sovereignty" is seen by many poor countries as the last rampart against assimilation and subordination.

Governance in an era of globalization should perhaps concentrate, instead, on common rules and common objectives—and a number of sectoral, inter-governmental regimes that are being built by tradition or negotiated by treaty. Hence, even though the world really looks like a global village, for operational purposes, we have to bring governments and nation-states back into the picture—because up to now, there are little viable alternatives for governance and the exercise of democracy.

Governance in economic and social affairs

The mandate of the United Nations in economic and social affairs is to promote "higher standards of living, full employment and conditions of economic and social progress and development; solutions of international economic, social, health and related problems; international cultural and educational cooperation; universal respect for, and observance of, human rights and fundamental freedoms for all without distinction as to race, sex, language or religion."[4]

This role is discharged by two main kinds of activities: norm and standard-setting; and operational activities.[5] *Operational activities* are a major mandate of the United Nations Development Programme and other Funds and Programmes such as UNICEF, the United Nations High Commissioner for Refugees, the United Nations Fund for Population Activities, the World Food Programme, etc. *Norm and standard-setting activities* are the purview of the General Assembly, the Economic and Social Council and their subsidiary organs. Many funds, programmes and specialized agencies combine the two kinds of activities. The ILO, for example, evolves a body of international norms and standards related to work and employment, and also conducts actions in the field, against child labor, for example.

When the United Nations was created, a number of pre-existing institutions, such as the Universal Postal Union became affiliated with it. The Bretton Woods institutions—the IMF and the World Bank—also formally became part of the United Nations family.

The International Monetary Fund was set up to facilitate international payments and thereby international trade and ultimately for "the promotion and maintenance of high levels of employment and real income and for the development of the productive resources of all [member states]."[6] The original role of the IMF is the maintenance of a stable monetary system, in particular through lending to cover temporary balance of payment deficits.

The International Bank for Reconstruction and Development (part of the World Bank Group) was established to promote the international flow of capital for productive purposes and to assist in financing the reconstruction of post-World War II economies. It now concentrates its lending in developing countries for productive projects or to finance reform programmes.

The World Trade Organization promotes free trade by helping to negotiate and enforce multilateral trade rules, in particular by facilitating the settlement of trade disputes.

This quick review of the mission statements of the main global organizations currently managing international economic and social affairs

---

4 Charter of the United Nations, article 55 of Chapter XI, "International Social and Economic Cooperation"

5 For the role of operational activities in providing global public goods, see Inge Kaul, Isabelle Grunberg and Marc Stern (eds): *Global Public Goods: International Cooperation in the Twenty-First Century*, New York: OUP, 1999.

6 IMF Articles of Agreement, Preamble.

shows that their deliberate aim is to advance and promote globalization—through higher levels of trade and investment for the IMF, the World Bank and the WTO, through the coordination of economic, social and human rights policies for the UN per se. Globalization in turn was expected to deliver higher degrees of welfare for all. We are at a critical juncture where this link, the expectation that globalization creates higher welfare for all, is called into question—and hence the current turmoil within these organizations.

Turmoil and change in global institutions

Recently, the World Bank, the IMF and the WTO have been urged to pay more attention to the impact of globalization on people and the environment. The turning point came at around the Fiftieth anniversary of the Bretton Woods institutions in 1994. Another important landmark was the World Summit on Social Development, held in Copenhagen in 1995. Its final Declaration urged international lending institutions to re-adjust structural adjustment programmes and ensure that budget cuts were not made at the expense of social programmes, education, health—and ultimately the men, women and children who need these services (see Box 1).

Since then, the World Bank's Managing Director James Wolfensohn steered more lending toward the social sector. In 1999, the IMF announced the creation of the Poverty and Growth Facility jointly with the World Bank. Disbursement of this Fund would be made in accordance with a Poverty Reduction Strategy Paper. And there are attempts to incorporate labour and environmental norms into the agenda of the WTO.

These trends are a vindication of the multi-faceted approach to development advocated and practiced by the UN, as remarked by the US Ambassador Alan Larson, Assistant Secretary of State for Economic and Business Affairs, at the Special High-Level Meeting with the Bretton Woods Institutions of April 29, 1999 (see chapter II):

"From the early work of Jim Grant at UNICEF in pointing to the possible negative effects of structural adjustment on the most vulnerable members of society, to the recent Copenhagen Social Summit which in a sense codified key elements of social development, the UN has been a leader .... It was the UN's Agenda 21 that put forth a program for achieving sustainable development, a concept originated in the UN by the Brundtland Commission."

The UN Development Agenda

Indeed, the major UN conferences of the 1990's succeeded in shifting the focus of the global agenda from economic reform and "sound fundamen-

---

Box 1

Structural adjustment with a human face

Commitment 8 of the Final Declaration of the World Summit on Social Development, Copenhagen, 1995

"We commit ourselves to ensuring that when structural adjustment programmes are agreed to, they include social development goals, in particular eradicating poverty, promoting full and productive employment, and enhancing social integration.

To this end, at the national level, we will:

(a) Promote basic social programmes and expenditures, in particular those affecting the poor and the vulnerable segments of society, and protect them from budget reductions, while increasing the quality and effectiveness of social expenditures;

(b) Review the impact of structural adjustment programmes on social development, including, where appropriate, by means of gender-sensitive social impact assessments and other relevant methods, in order to develop policies to reduce their negative effects and improve their positive impact; the cooperation of international financial institutions in the review could be requested by interested countries;

(c) Promote, in the countries with economies in transition, an integrated approach to the transformation process, addressing the social consequences of reforms and human resource development needs;

(d) Reinforce the social development components of all adjustment policies and programmes, including those resulting from the globalization of markets and rapid technological change, by designing policies to promote more equitable and enhanced access to income and resources;

(e) Ensure that women do not bear a disproportionate burden of the transitional costs of such processes.

At the international level, we will:

(f) Work to ensure that multilateral development banks and other donors complement adjustment lending with enhanced targeted social development investment lending;

(g) Strive to ensure that structural adjustment programmes respond to the economic and social conditions, concerns and needs of each country;

(h) Enlist the support and cooperation of regional and international organizations and the United Nations system, in particular the Bretton Woods institutions, in the design, social management and assessment of structural adjustment policies, and in implementing social development goals and integrating them into their policies, programmes and operations."

tals" to "sustainable human development"—or at least to ensure that the two are more compatible. Some of the major UN conferences of the 1990's are listed in Box 2. Their development goals, were ratified at the highest level by almost every single country in the world—and were the result of an intense process involving, not only policy makers, but civil society representatives, experts, citizens, academics and business people. The global conferences have not only established common goals, but chartered plans for their implementation by outlining specific policy proposals and assigning responsibility to various actors of the international system. The Earth Summit, for example, led to four international treaties, on climate change, biological diversity, desertification and high seas fishing. The World Summit on social development pledged to make measur-

---

Box 2

Major United Nations Conferences

- World's Summit for Children, New York, 1990
- UN Conference on Environment and Development, (the "Earth Summit"), Rio de Janeiro, 1992
- World Conference on Human Rights, Vienna, 1993
- International Conference on Population and Development, Cairo, 1994
- World Summit for Social Development, Copenhagen, 1995
- Fourth World Conference on Women, Beijing, 1995
- Second UN Conference on Human Settlements, Istanbul, 1996
- World Food Summit, Rome, 1996

able progress in the areas of employment, education, social integration, the rights of minorities and gender equality. It also aimed to protect the family and lift out of poverty half of the world's poorest people by 2015. Other conferences addressed the welfare of children, the importance of reproductive health, nutrition and food security, human rights or the challenge of urbanization.

Most recently, the United Nations has urged a broader paradigm of globalization with a human face—a process of global integration that takes a more comprehensive and human-centered approach and addresses social issues directly instead of leaving them entirely up to the market. This was a major message of the series of *Human Development Reports* that was started in 1990 by the United Nations Development Programme: growth does not guarantee development. Two countries may have the same GDP per capita, yet offer starkly unequal conditions of life for their peoples.

But long-term policy trends also explain why the United Nations may be called upon to play an even larger role in global economic and social affairs.

The end of debt-led development?

As part of the recent discussions on a new financial architecture, it was noted that developing countries that import capital should more carefully monitor the accumulation of *debt-creating* financial flows (as opposed to direct investment), as this accumulation could sow the seeds of another Asian crisis. The same thinking could also apply to international development assistance. Perhaps it is now time to reexamine the model of 'debt-creating international aid'—in other words, of multilateral loans, as opposed to grants or technical assistance. The impetus for this has been the "silent debt crisis," which has hampered development efforts and sucked resources away from expenditure on health, education, sanitation or infrastructure. Much new lending by the IMF, at least, is to allow countries to honor previous loans. Existing debts will be partly relieved by the strengthened HIPC initiative agreed upon at the Group of Seven meeting in Cologne in 1999. But a debt write-down would be meaningless if we kept into place the debt-creating system that caused the problem in the first place.

The reason so much debt overhang has accumulated is that the projects that were financed did not turn out to be as profitable as foreseen. Or, in the case of programme lending, these programmes did not yield the expected growth that would have allowed a country to repay. This problem will only get worse as the World Bank and the IMF concentrate lending on social programmes. By definition, social programmes yield diffused benefits, as opposed to commercial lending, which produces tangible monetary returns.

As a result, a certain amount of "debt fatigue" is striking—or at least, some weariness about the current model of debt-led development. Witness this statement by Ms. Heidemarie Wieczorek-Zeul, Federal Minister for Economic Co-operation and Development on behalf of the European Union at the Special High-Level Meeting with the Bretton Woods Institutions of 29 April 1999:

"International financing is only one aspect of financing for development. In fact, in many of our partner countries, it plays a secondary role to domestic financing. Unless sufficient domestic financing for productive investment is available, development cannot be sustained in the long term *without accumulating again an excessive debt burden.* To enhance domestic financing, efforts must be undertaken, firstly to stabilise state revenue by means of a fair system of taxation and efficient tax administration, and secondly to mobilise more domestic capital by means of a functioning, private sector-based financing sector that is subject to effective bank supervision." [emphasis added].

Developing countries should indeed strive to raise resources internally. But there is still a place for international public financing. Once donor countries no longer delude themselves into thinking they are giving aid by giving loans, then perhaps they will focus on increasing ODA—official development assistance. These questions should form the core of the next major conference, scheduled for 2001, on Financing for Development.

All these trends are combining to highlight the relevance of the approach used by the United Nations in development and in economic and social affairs. To face this challenge, the organization has undergone an extensive reform process, and in particular a process of revitalization of its Economic and Social Council.

The UN's role in economic and social affairs

A comprehensive plan for UN Reform was set forth by Secretary-General Kofi Annan in 1997 and is currently being implemented. In the economic and social sphere, the plan includes some of the following: consolidation of the Secretariat's capability into an integrated Department for Economic and Social Affairs; creation of the post of Deputy Secretary-General, to concentrate, among other things, on development issues; and consolidating the activities of the UN in the field, in particular via the creation of the UN Development Group and "UN houses" in member countries. In addition, the United Nations embarked in an ambitious effort at field-level coordination around a Common Country Assessment and a UN Development Assistance Framework.

The reform sought to adjust the United Nations to a changing world, improving linkages and coordination—within and outside the organization. This went beyond enhancing the UN's place in cyberspace or the Public Relations machinery. Previously, the Cold War made it difficult to streamline the UN system and increased the temptation to simply create a new body without scrapping the older one. In addition, there are now thousands of inter-governmental organizations, and even more non-governmental ones, many with mandates that overlap that of the UN. Avoiding overlap outside the organization also means strengthening linkages.

The emphasis on coordination meant that the Economic and Social Council would have an important role to play in the operation of the new United Nations.

Revitalizing the UN's Economic and Social Council, 1998–1999

The Economic and Social Council is the main UN body specializing in economic and social affairs that derives a clear mandate and identity from the UN Charter. It ranks as one of six Principal Organs, together with the Security Council or the General Assembly. The blueprint for UN reform singled out, as an "immediate priority", "to enhance the essential policy management and coordinating role of the Economic and Social Council, " by streamlining its subsidiary bodies and evolving new methods for its work" (for more details about ECOSOC, see Box 3).

Simultaneously, the General Assembly launched a comprehensive effort in 1996 to revitalize the United Nations in the economic and social fields, in particular by giving ECOSOC a clear mandate to follow up on the implementation of the decisions taken by world leaders at the major UN Conferences of the 1990's.

And finally, the Presidents of the Council themselves, Ambassadors Juan Somavia of Chile, followed by Paolo Fulci of Italy, took a number of initiatives to revitalize the Council. Among the innovations that took place in these two years were:

- High-level meetings with the governing bodies and executive heads of the Bretton Woods Institutions (Chapter II of this book)
- The practice of issuing short, action-oriented Ministerial Declarations instead of the lengthy resolutions and conclusions of the past. An example is the outcome of the high-level segment of 1999 dedicated to poverty (Chapter IV of this book).

Box 3

The Economic and Social Council of the United Nations

The main functions of the Council are:

- to serve as the central forum for discussing international economic and social issues, and for formulating policy recommendations addressed to Member States and to the United Nations system;
- to make or initiate studies and reports and make recommendations on international economic, social, cultural, educational, health and related matters; to promote respect for, and observance of, human rights and fundamental freedoms;
- to call international conferences and prepare draft conventions for submission to the General Assembly;
- to coordinate the activities of the specialized agencies, through consultations with and recommendations to them, and through recommendations to the General Assembly and Member States;
- to consult with non-governmental organizations concerned with matters with which the Council deals.

The Economic and Social Council is comprised of 54 members, who serve for three years. Each year, eighteen new members are elected. Decisions are taken by a simple majority of members present and voting.

The Economic and Social Council generally holds one four-week substantive session each year, alternating between New York and Geneva. The session includes a high-level special meeting, attended by Ministers and other senior government officials, to discuss major economic and social issues. The year-round work of the Council is carried out in its subsidiary bodies—commissions and committees—which meet at regular intervals and report back to the Council.

- Higher-level participation in ECOSOC debates, and in particular the agreement, in 1998, on a Ministerial Communique on market access for developing countries (Chapter III of this book)
- Reactivation of article 65 of the United Nations charter, which provides for ECOSOC to assist the UN Security Council at its request (Chapter V)
- Initiation of a comprehensive monitoring system to follow up on the UN Conferences of the 1990's, in particular by agreeing on a common set of indicators (Chapter VI).

The outreach effort is enhanced by the broader use of information technology, and the stronger coordinating function is symbolized by the refurbishment and resumed use of the Chamber dedicated to the Economic and Social Council in the Secretariat building. All of this contributes to what President Fulci has called a "renaissance" of ECOSOC— and of course it is fitting given the Italian flavor of that Presidency.

What the book is about

The book gives the reader access to some of the key debates that took place in this context, to some important Reports that were prepared by the Secretariat or other bodies to illuminate these debates, and to key resolutions of the Economic and Social Council or the General Assembly. At the beginning of each chapter, an editors' overview summarizes the issues and briefly describes the nature of the documents reprinted; when necessary, individual documents or sub-sections are preceded by a "Note of Introduction". What is provided is not necessarily an official record of these documents. Reports as well as debates have been occasionally shortened and edited to make them suitable for a book of this length.

The realities discussed in these debates, the decisions taken, are of concern and interest to all the world's citizens. It is hoped that this book will promote a better understanding of these issues, as well as a better awareness of the role played by the United Nations in finding common solutions as the new Millennium unfolds.

1

Globalization with a Human Face: The General Assembly Debate

September 1998

C ONTENTS :

Overview

Overview

On 17 and 18 September 1998, the General Assembly held a high-level meeting on the theme of "Social and economic impact of globalization and interdependence and their policy implications."

The discussions aimed at laying the ground work for a systematic examination of the challenges of globalization, and how the United Nations can be pro-active in addessing these challenges. Indeed, globalization is a multi-issue phenomenon, and the United Nations is the multi-issue, participatory organization *par excellence*.

One of the challenges of globalization is the growing gap between democratic will and policy outcomes—the increasing difficulty experienced by many governments, in the face of severe domestic and external constraints, in carrying out effective policies and obtaining results. In issues such as migration, environmental degradation or the AIDS epidemic, states taken individually can do little more than control the symptoms. Getting at the cause demands coordinated international action.

The discussion highlighted the concerns felt by many developing countries, that they did not always experience the much-vaunted benefits of globalization but certainly experienced its risks, in particular in the wake of the Asian crisis. With hindsight, it is interesting to note that some of these misgivings were forerunners of the objections raised by developing countries at the Ministerial meeting of the WTO in Seattle: the demand for more voice in decision-making; for a timely implementation of the liberalization commitments made by developed countries; and for more time and capacity to allow them to plan and project the future costs and benefits of their multilateral commitments.

In the course of the debate, specific dysfunctionalities were highlighted in the present system. The volatility of financial flows is preventing many countries from enacting policies necessary for human development. Both financial crises *and* the threat of financial crises bring about policies with a deflationary bend. Economic openness increases the vulnerability to external shocks, and financial instability increases the volatility of trade and competitiveness.

The constraints on policy-making exercised by the private sector (in the form of short-term financial flows) are compounded by the multi-sectoral exercise of conditionality: for example, unilateral trade liberalization is sometimes required of countries above and beyond those that are negotiated multilaterally. In addition, developing countries are on the receiving end of massive flows of capital reacting to decisions or trends occurring elsewhere. Major countries need to internalize these ripple effects when making decisions.

Concerning the potential benefits of globalization, they are indeed considerable. But access to these benefits presupposes an existing degree of wealth, or human resource development, that many developing countries simply do not have. Information technologies, for example, require a complex infrastructure and the costs of acquiring these technologies is considerable. Often, people with the skills to use the new technologies emigrate abroad. Hence, human resource development is a key precondition for access to the benefits of globalization. Similarly, resources are often lacking to ensure that growth is compatible with environmental sustainability.

The policy recommendations that emerged from the meeting consisted for the most part in making better use of the organizations that already exist, in particular by creating strategic linkages between them and by uniting them toward a single objective: development. Proposals included better macro-economic coordination, a systematic policy study of the contribution of financial markets to development, or the removal of trade barriers against developing country products. Better global governance should go hand in hand with better *national* governance, and current efforts at capacity building at the national level were therefore important.

The General Assembly's discussions took place in the form of intergovernmental meetings as well as informal panels. These discussions are summarized in the first document reprinted here. The second document, entitled "Analysis of the General Assembly debate", while covering some of the same material, goes into further details and highlights some major themes of the discussion. For further analysis, the reader may also consult the Secretary-General's Report of 15 September 1999 entitled "Role of the United Nations in promoting development in the context of globalization and interdependence."

Finally, the General Assembly resolution reprinted here alerts policy makers to the growing marginalization of some developing countries, to the additional vulnerability brought about by globalization, and to the accentuation of income disparities within and among countries. It calls on the international community to address these challenges, and in particular the widening information gap between developed and developing countries.

I. Summary by the President of the General Assembly of the high-level dialogue on the theme of the social and economic impact of globalization and interdependence and their policy implications, 21 October 1998

The General Assembly held a two-day high-level meeting on renewal of the dialogue on strengthening international economic cooperation for development on 17 and 18 September 1998. It proved to be a productive, enlightening and highly relevant discussion in the current international economic environment. The dialogue represented an encouraging further step in United Nations efforts to advance multilateral cooperation on issues of vital importance to all countries.

First of all, the timeliness and relevance of the dialogue was recognized by all. Conceived some time ago, when globalization was generally viewed with optimism and hope, the dialogue on the social and economic impact of globalization and liberalization acquired a new urgency and importance in view of the current far-reaching economic crisis and its devastating social consequences.

Secondly, the dialogue was held in a new spirit of partnership based on mutual interests and shared benefits. This was an unusually frank, constructive and collaborative interaction of policy makers who fully realized that concerted actions on an international scale are imperative for effective national responses to the challenges of globalization. A genuine desire to understand the point of view of others and a sincere readiness to explore ways of addressing multifaceted concerns created by globalization brought about a spirit of understanding that is necessary for a productive discussion on such a complex, somewhat contradictory and, for many, painful subject as the social and economic impact of globalization. Many participants identified common interests, and an encouraging convergence of perceptions on a number of issues emerged as a result.

Thirdly, the debates were informed, analytic and action-oriented. They provided a rich source of potentially valuable ideas and proposals. The opening statement by the President of the General Assembly, the address by the Secretary-General at the closing plenary meeting and the statement by the Deputy Secretary-General at the start of the debate helped to set the direction and orientation for the dialogue and for further progress.

Last but not least, the format of the meeting was a unique innovation in the work of the General Assembly. During the high-level meeting, a creative combination of events took place: a plenary debate in which delegations stated their national positions; two ministerial round tables on national and international responses to globalization that afforded a stimulating and fruitful exchange of views on key aspects of experiences and policies at the national and international levels; and two informal panels which brought together a wealth of expertise, knowledge and perspectives from the private sector, the academic world, trade unions and the civil society at large. Active participation of United Nations entities such as the United Nations Development Programme, the United Nations Population Fund, the International Labour Organization and the United Nations Educational, Scientific and Cultural Organization, as well as the Bretton Woods institutions, significantly enriched the substance and comprehensiveness of analysis and policy advice. Thus, the vast and complex issue of globalization and its social and economic consequences, as well as the required policy responses, were addressed from a great variety of perspectives.

The general thrust of the two-day discussions may be summarized as follows. First of all, globalization is an irreversible process, not an option. It is a positive and not an evil force, but it is also blind and therefore needs to be carefully harnessed. Secondly, national efforts to meet the challenges of globalization, in particular institution-building, are necessary but not sufficient. Action on a global scale, involving multilateral institutions as well as the world's leading economies is imperative. Thirdly, there is a need to move beyond the status quo, in particular by reviewing the current architecture of the international financial system with a view to enhancing its transparency, accountability and participatory character. Fourthly, globalization is a multifaceted process involving many actors. In order to address effectively the issues of inclusiveness and participation, it is necessary to promote a global civil ethic to shape the rules that will ensure that globalization benefits all, including those who are currently marginalized. Fifthly, the United Nations, owing to its universality and broad mandate, provides a unique platform for defining the principles and norms necessary to harness the potential of globalization and for promoting a comprehensive dialogue on globalization around the concept of "global housekeeping".

It was noted that the dialogue was the most recent in a series of innovative events organized at the United Nations in 1998. The special high-level meeting of the Economic and Social Council with the Bretton Woods institutions on 18 April 1998, the 1998 substantive session of the Council, in particular its high-level segment, and the two-day General Assembly high-level dialogue on globalization vividly demonstrated the unique capacity of the United Nations to convoke most, if not all, stakeholders in issues of vital global importance and involve them in a meaningful and productive interaction.

Summary of the intergovernmental meetings

The two-day high-level meeting on the overall theme of the social and economic impact of globalization and interdependence and their policy implications opened with statements by the President of the General Assembly and the Deputy Secretary-General, followed by over 40 speakers, including ministers and high-level officials. On the second day, two ministerial round tables and a closing plenary meeting were held. The discussions were marked by a positive spirit and were informed by a search for constructive solutions.

The participants expressed their views on the key issues outlined below.

Globalization was seen as inevitable. It is driven by technology and markets. But it is not a force of nature, rather it is the result of man-made processes. It must be shaped to serve humanity. To that end, it needs to be carefully managed by countries nationally and through international cooperation.

Globalization facilitates more efficient worldwide allocation of resources, stimulates growth and increases welfare. Yet, it is not a smooth, painless process. For better integration into the world economy, countries need to adopt sound macroeconomic policies and develop effective institutional and legal frameworks and the necessary physical and human infrastructures. Developing countries have the primary responsibility to meet those requirements within their national borders, but international support is of key importance for the success of their efforts.

Although substantial gains have been attained as a result of globalization and successful development efforts, globalization and technological changes have increased uncertainties and exposure to risks, owing in particular to the contagion effect. Income disparities between and within countries have continued to widen. There is a widespread perception that the rapid pace of globalization is accompanied by the growing frustration of Governments which believe that they have lost some control over their economies or their societies. That is particularly so when economies face sudden withdrawals of capital in response to rapid changes in market conditions.

Considerable attention was given to the marginalization of countries and groups of people within countries and to the issues of asymmetry and inequity. For some developing countries, particularly for the less developed and African countries, the costs of globalization at times appear to outweigh the benefits. The devastating social consequences of the current financial crisis including massive unemployment, loss of health and education services and increasing poverty in the affected countries, were of deep concern.

Governments should not overreact and turn to isolation or autarchy, but should maintain an open economy, focus on what they can do to strengthen institutions and structures, and cooperate to stimulate the world economy and stabilize financial markets. Among the national measures to cope with globalization the following were stressed: the high priority of strengthening financial institutions; the need to tackle the private-sector debt; the urgent need to reshape the economy by addressing monopolistic positions; and the promotion of good governance through increased transparency and elimination of corruption.

Attempts to reverse the process of globalization in order to check its negative manifestations, such as the volatility of short-term capital flows, could prolong or exacerbate the problems, adding to the costs stemming from globalization instead of containing them. The institutional causes of the problems that have led to capital outflows should also be addressed. Institutional constraints normally linked to weak capital markets and inadequate regulations should be addressed in order to strengthen the confidence of investors, domestic and foreign, and decrease the volatility of financial flows.

Facing the negative consequences of globalization requires a strategy of both national and international actions. It is important to recognize that a country in crisis has the main responsibility in finding a solution to its own development problems. National responses are normally a combination of offensive measures aimed at benefiting from globalization and defensive measures aimed at minimizing the risk that could arise from globalization. Today, many developing countries may be tempted to focus on defensive responses, but the solution is probably through the adoption of a balanced mix of the two types of measures. National responses to face the costs of globalization need to be supported by adequate international assistance and an improved external environment.

Contrary to the past, problems have emerged not because of current account imbalances but of sudden disruptive changes in the capital account. Moreover, the amount of resources involved are of such magnitude that they have overwhelmed the available funds in the international financial institutions despite strong and additional bilateral support for many countries. Thus, planning for an adequate level of funds to anticipate and prevent future crisis remains a major collective challenge. The issue of moral hazard needs to be addressed to ensure responsible lending decisions.

The pace and sequencing of liberalization of capital flows should be determined by each country in light of its specific circumstances and needs. The United Nations and the Bretton Woods institutions should work together to support country efforts. One possible national response to the negative impact of globalization is to apply liberalization measures related to capital markets in stages. Before deciding on the introduction of a full-scale liberalization of capital markets, it is important to verify whether there are adequate legal and financial infrastructures to cope with the growth process. No single model of liberalization exists; alternative models can be appropriate to different stages of development. Financial reforms in developing countries have sometimes been interpreted only in terms of increasing liberalization of markets. Financial reforms also require the adoption of new regulations for the markets in order to anticipate the negative consequences of new challenges. Similarly, the temporary control of short-term capital flows could be adopted in the case of a country in deep financial crisis.

Measures to correct market failures are needed from national authorities, but the success of those measures in overcoming the crisis will depend on the actions taken by the world's leading economies and multilateral institutions. The threat of a worldwide deflationary spiral must be countered and the current financial turmoil must not be allowed to turn into global economic recession. Swift and decisive actions are urgently needed to counter that possibility. It was pointed out that increased and sustained international assistance is crucial. A dialogue based on mutual understanding and sharing of responsibilities is required.

There is a need to review the architecture of the international financial system. Critical elements of such a system should be transparency, accountability and participation at all levels—national, regional and international. With financial and labour markets inherently volatile, the need for regulation and supervision is obvious, but the institutions necessary for such oversight are clearly not yet adequate to the challenges of globalization. Consequently, decisive steps to accelerate institution-building were urgently needed.

A transparent rule-based trading system is needed to provide a level playing field to allow sharing of the benefits of globalization. Although much progress has been made in the area of trade liberalization since the creation of the World Trade Organization (WTO), significant market barriers still exist. Africa and the least developed countries that face the threat of marginalization need free access to markets. Marginalized countries are the ones most in need of trade, investment and growth generated by globalization. It was recalled that at the high-level segment of the Economic and Social Council in 1998, the need for a more secure and broad-based trading system was discussed. A set of additional coherent measures must be articulated in the area of trade liberalization.

While private capital flows have increased tremendously, these cannot be a substitute for official development assistance (ODA). The level and quality of ODA must be improved. Increased ODA is essential to support national efforts to establish a social safety net and support the poorest and most vulnerable sectors of society. More vigorous debt-relief measures are also needed. An increased level of long-term non-concessional loans from the international financial institutions could act as a stabilizing factor. Balance-of-payment surpluses could be recycled as untied loans and humanitarian aid.

Globalization is not merely an economic process; it must take place in the right social and political context. Social cohesion and social contracts were seen as coming under serious threat. The pursuit of liberalization in the name of globalization not only with respect to capital flows and trade, but also in terms of privatizing social policies, was putting increasing strains on social solidarity. The move away from the universality of social programmes towards targeted social safety nets for the poor and marginalized was seen by some as an unwelcome trend.

The asymmetric distribution of benefits and risks arising from globalization warranted the conclusion of a new contract between developing and developed countries, based on genuine solidarity and shared responsibility, with a view to creating a level playing field where all countries could take full advantage of the process. A central aspect of this contract should be a common vision of universal growth and development benefiting all countries and all individuals.

A major challenge facing policy makers was seen to consist in how to make the policies and measures which addressed the problems in financial markets compatible with strategies which aimed at the eradication of poverty. Addressing poverty, population growth and environmental degradation is crucial in attaining the goals and commitments made at the major United Nations conferences. Sufficient resources exist to eradicate poverty, according to the *Human Development Report* of the United Nations Development Programme. However, the political will to honour the national and international commitments already made is needed.

Market-driven globalization will ensure neither fairness nor social progress. Major joint efforts by all members of the international community are needed to devise norms for globalization to be truly supportive of human development. Common responses have to be built on shared values that reflect the broader aspirations of our global society. It is the role of the United Nations to assume normative leadership and to set the "values agenda" for globalization.

Summary of informal panels

Two informal panels were held, one on the economic and the other on the social aspects of globalization. Eight panellists, representing a wide geographical diversity, provided the meeting with their analyses from the perspectives of non-governmental actors, including the private sector, academia, parliamentarians and trade unions. The salient points of the panel discussions are summarized below.

Globalization means growing interdependence among countries, each finding it increasingly useful to share part of their former power over policies on a reciprocal basis with other countries within a framework of established international organizations. That tendency is driven by strong economic motivation, since there are benefits to be gained in exchange for similar concessions from other countries, and by rapid advances in technology, in particular in telecommunications and transport.

Liberalization of trade and investment has been the hallmark of globalization for the past decades, generating accelerated economic growth. The sustainability of growth should not be seen only for its employment or environmental impact, but also in the context of financial instability. Globalization phenomena should not be considered only for their impact on physical and financial capital flows, but also on human and natural capital, as well as on national sovereignty and cultural diversity, including at the local and community level.

There are, at the same time, problems and risks associated with globalization, including the following:

- Different types of capital flows (foreign direct investment, portfolio investments, borrowing etc.) have very different degrees of beneficial effects. In fact, short-term portfolio investments imply increased volatility and create risks for national balance of payments and foreign-exchange markets;
- Private capital flows are heavily concentrated and some countries are virtually excluded;
- Excessive capital inflows can create problems such as currency appreciation, a rise in asset prices, an increase in money supply and subsequent inflationary pressures.

One of the main problems of globalization is that countries do not have the same access to the global markets. Capital inflows and technological transfers do not necessarily bring benefits to developing countries in the same proportion as to developed countries, unless they are accompanied by the presence of other factors of the production function. The main reason is the current inadequacy of institutions and management capabilities in developing countries. Building up both will take time.

One lesson learned from the volatility of capital markets is that liberalization of trade is not the same as liberalization of capital flows. Freedom in capital movements should not be introduced until national institutions are ready, and a number of measures can be introduced to reduce the mobility of capital in an emerging economy. Liberalization must be compatible with national economic systems. If the liberalization efforts overshoot, they might make a developing country more vulnerable.

Efforts to control the instability of capital movements can be undertaken at different levels as follows:

- Within countries, it is necessary to make an effort to adjust to the globalization process by improving the institutional and regulatory context. Capital-importing countries should minimize internal risks and instability connected with capital flows. Protectionism and isolationism are not valid responses to the challenge of globalization. Rather, it is necessary to tackle the problems at their source. Thus, countries hit by financial crises that are linked to domestic financial imbalances should address those imbalances, such as: large fiscal deficits; inadequate functioning of the banking sector due to lack of banking regulations; and rigidities of exchange rates. In particular, developing countries must speed up reforms of their domestic institutions;
- It is also important to strengthen the decentralization of economic processes at the regional and local level within countries, in order to enhance local capacity to benefit from the advantages generated by globalization and to minimize the effects of crises;
- A global system of support, cooperation and collaboration among countries is necessary in order to reduce systemic risks. It is important to develop, within multilateral institutions, mechanisms of international cooperation and coordination to monitor certain world economic processes, especially as regards the financial system. It is necessary not only to introduce an early warning system, but also to ensure transparency of the markets, since changes in one country immediately affect other parts of the world. The measures include efforts to achieve regional integration and to strengthen international institutions, such as those within the United Nations system, including the International Monetary Fund (IMF), WTO and the

World Bank. It is not necessary to create new international organizations, although the existing ones (like IMF) need to be decisively reformed by adapting their objectives and policies in order to increase their effectiveness and to take account of the longer-term effects of financial instability;

- Governments should introduce measures aimed at improving the environment for foreign direct investment in their countries. It is also essential to coordinate national policies, especially fiscal policies, in order to discourage capital flows generated only by differentials in fiscal treatment.

Recent crises have demonstrated that a global market by itself cannot guarantee stability and order. Mutually beneficial globalization requires an improvement of both domestic and international institutions and the building-up of market management capability. This means that globalization should no longer be a spontaneous process solely driven by the profit motive. It also requires more than only the efforts of developing countries to solve their domestic problems: some form of intervention is needed from global public forces such as international organizations to provide assistance and regulations to reduce the disadvantages of developing countries. Globalization thus requires global governance. A major effort on the international level should be undertaken in order to maximize the opportunities and minimize the uncertainties. Particular attention should be paid to capital flows so that the global financial market does not develop into a "world financial casino".

International organizations should introduce reforms in order to provide early warning, risk assessment and speculation management mechanisms for member countries, particularly for less developed countries. International organizations should also provide more assistance for institutional reforms in developing countries.

The impact of Internet and new information technologies shows that globalization processes in this domain bring a shift of power from countries with technologically less developed information infrastructure to multinational firms with the ability to gather, interpret and react to vast information sources. The United Nations system, through such organizations as the United Nations Educational, Scientific and Cultural Organization, the International Telecommunication Union and the World Bank, can provide support to less developed parts of the world in the information revolution currently under way.

Concluding observations

At the close of the two-day meeting, there was general agreement that the high-level debate had clearly shown the usefulness and value of a timely and comprehensive dialogue, conducted in a constructive and collaborative spirit with ministerial participation, on a most critical issue of globalization that affects the whole of humanity. A common desire was expressed to continue the political dialogue with a view to developing a coherent and effective response to the opportunities and challenges of globalization. The General Assembly will evaluate the experience of the high-level meeting and decide on the appropriate follow-up.

Proposals and suggestions made by delegations

In the course of the dialogue, proposals on possible further steps in addressing the issues discussed at the meeting were made by delegations.

Many delegations argued for the development of reasonable but effective regulation of international money markets so that they would become more open and transparent. It was also suggested that consideration be given to establishing a mechanism to mitigate the unpredictability and dire effects of globalization and to ensure that the opportunities created by it were equally available to all countries. Such a mechanism should be able to monitor and ensure surveillance of capital markets and international financial operations. In that context, an in-depth study of the world monetary and financial system from the perspective of the requirements of development was believed to be of crucial importance.

One delegation suggested that the negative aspects of globalization should be addressed through implementation of the idea of the new development strategy, the core of which was a partnership between recipient and donor countries and the ownership of the development process by developing countries. Another delegation stressed the need to continue to work together to address with increased vigour the troika of poverty, environmental degradation and population growth, while ensuring that developing countries remained at the centre of their own development.

Several speakers underscored the importance of appropriate national policy responses to the challenges of globalization and welcomed the growing convergence of views on what constituted sound policies. It was noted that besides strong macroeconomic fundamentals, a sound institutional and regulatory framework was critical, and that the social dimension, including a better distribution of benefits of growth, must be an integral part of policy responses. In that context, the need to support poor developing countries in their efforts to improve their institutional and management capabilities was emphasized.

Many delegations focused on the need to strengthen multilateralism. It was underscored that the establishment of a global governance that would match the potency and the scope of globalization was possible only through the central instrumentality of a reformed, democratized and fully empowered United Nations. One delegation was of the view that a global dialogue should be launched to implement the goals and objectives of the Agenda for Development (General Assembly resolution 51/240, annex), and that a resumed fifty-third session of the General Assembly could be held to initiate such a dialogue at the ministerial level. Other speakers stated that common responses had to be built on shared values that reflected the broader aspirations of global society, and that the United Nations was the unique forum for defining the principles and norms necessary to harness the potential of globalization. One delegation, recalling the need to enhance international cooperation to deal effectively with emerging crises, suggested the establishment of a peer review mechanism, to function in close collaboration with the IMF and the World Bank, that would enhance oversight of developments in the financial sector in all countries.

It was suggested that an emergency action programme to shield the weakest economies from the consequences of global economic turbulence was needed. The following broad components should be considered on a priority basis: safety-net measures, including emergency assistance; balance-of-payment support to severely affected countries; an immediate increase in the level of ODA; reduction of a significant amount of external debt on an urgent basis, while pursuing serious efforts at a decisive reduction of the debt burden on the least developed countries; compensatory measures to cover shortfalls in earnings from primary commodity exports and from a reduction in remittances; and the immediate lifting of trade barriers affecting the least developed countries.

One delegation suggested the following action: collaboration among the industrialized countries to spur economic growth; debt relief for private sector firms in crisis-affected countries; doubling World Bank support for social safety-nets programmes; activating the IMF emergency fund of 15 billion United States dollars to head off more financial panic; opening markets further to expand trade while putting in place safeguards for labour standards and the environment; and calling a meeting of finance ministers and central bank directors from the G-7 and emerging economies to seek ways to revise the international financial architecture to meet the current challenges.

Many speakers addressed the urgent need for rethinking the existing international financial institutions. It was suggested, for instance, that they should be gradually turned into a more efficient instrument for consolidation of the global financial system, regulation of transboundary financial flows and implementation of preventive anti-crisis measures, including through development, following the WTO example of international rules and standards of conduct for financial market operators, as well as monitoring their compliance. Other speakers stressed the need for much better regulation and supervision of the financial system in all countries, on the basis of a common set of norms and standards, as well as the need for better information and transparency and more effective surveillance. One of the unresolved problems in that regard was how surveillance could be made more symmetric so that it focused not just on the financial system of recipient countries, but also on financial institutions in the capital-exporting countries. The need to enhance the IMF capability to act as a lender of last resort was also emphasized.

Several speakers reiterated their support for the proposed international conference on financing for development.

II. The role of the United Nations in promoting development in the context of globalization and interdependence: Analysis of the General Assembly Debate, 1999

The item on globalization and interdependence received considerable attention in the Committee. This confirmed that globalization is considered to be at the centre of the development agenda, and that many Member States attach crucial importance to the United Nations' role in addressing globalization and its effect on development.

The following observations may be made about the debate:

The urgency of harnessing globalization

A very strong message, primarily but not exclusively from developing countries, was that globalization, in the form it is currently occurring, is inexorably leading to further marginalization of developing countries and to the deepening of inequity. There is a growing realization that the international community must take urgent measures to mitigate the negative effects of globalization and to ensure that its benefits were spread more equitably, lest there would be a serious risk of global backlash and instability. There is still a window of opportunity of several years for shaping required policies and institutions, but time is running out and unless adequate steps are taken globalization may become a divisive, instead of uniting, issue in the global discourse.

The need to broaden the debate on globalization

While overwhelming attention was devoted to the manifestations of globalization in the area of trade, finance and information, speakers agreed with the broader approach taken in the Secretary General's report that also covered social, environmental and other areas. It was emphasized that social aspects of globalization had not been appropriately addressed thus far, nor were their interrelationships with economic aspects. With regard to cultural aspects, there was a concern that globalization could lead to uniformization, and several speakers stressed the need to ensure that the diversity of cultures is preserved. Some delegates also addressed the upsurge of transboundary criminal activities brought about by globalization and called for stronger multilateral cooperation in combating drug trafficking, money laundering and related illegal activities. Several speakers underscored the unique ability of the United Nations to address the various aspects of globalization in an integrated fashion.

The need for improved global governance and international cooperation

It was reiterated that improved global governance was required to harness the benefits of globalization and ensure that globalization has "a human face". The Asian crisis had revealed the urgent need to adjust institutional and regulatory mechanisms to the new realities of globalization. In the view of some countries, the negative impact of globalization on development derived largely from the fact that the current system, institutions and policies are fundamentally biased towards developed countries and thus ensure an increasing concentration of income and wealth in a few individuals, corporations and countries. However, the thrust of the debate was not so much on creating new institutions but rather on the need to modify existing ones to reflect new realities. Particularly important in such modification was ensuring that developing countries play a greater role in global economic decision-making. In particular, a better mechanism of macroeconomic policy coordination was required, one that would not be restricted to a few but involve all countries.

Better global governance also required better coordination of actions of national and international actors to ensure greater coherence between trade, finance, macroeconomic, social and environmental policies. Such coherence should aim at giving special impetus to poverty eradication and other goals agreed at the United Nations conferences of the nineties.

Improved global governance will not be enough, however, in view of the depth of the problems faced by developing countries. Increased international cooperation was essential. There was a strong message that industrialized countries had a responsibility to assist developing countries not only because they undertook to do so at the world conferences, but also because they are the ones who benefit most from globalization. The whole range of issues related to the enabling environment for development, ODA, financing for development and developing countries' access to market and technology was addressed by many speakers.

Governments' role

While recognizing that, in the context of globalization and interdependence, governance at national level could hardly be effective without adequate global governance, several speakers underscored that the greatest efforts to promote development and manage globalization still must be made at the national level. A key challenge was therefore to strengthen developing countries' national capacities so that they could, inter alia, more fully utilize the opportunities provided by globalization. Globalization had placed a premium on human resource development which was a key factor in a country's ability to benefit from new technology. The importance of building basic infrastructure in developing countries was also reaffirmed as was the need for sound national macroeconomic policies. Again, some speakers expressed their concern that a globalized world entailed unacceptable limitations to national sovereignty.

The UN's role

The main message of the debate was, again, that due to its democratic and universal nature the UN was in a unique position for promoting a better understanding of and concrete responses to globalization. Speakers proposed a whole range of actions that the UN should take, ranging from the more general to the more specific.

There was a broad agreement that the UN had a unique responsibility of ensuring that the development goals defined at the world conferences are implemented. Delegations underscored that the UN was indeed the only forum where there could be a holistic, comprehensive consideration of globalization and of its impact and where the interrelations between trade, finance and development issues could be examined. Thus, the UN should be entrusted not only with examining globalization and its developmental impact, but should be given a key role in ensuring policy coherence. It was suggested that the UN should keep the impact of globalization on developing countries under constant monitoring, propose policy responses and appraise their effectiveness. Another proposal was to use the UN's current work on globalization to design a special UN programme to respond to the challenges of globalization, complementing the Agenda for Development.

Many speakers also stressed that the UN had an important role in addressing specific financial, trade and other sectoral issues in their overall context. The Organization could thus make "strategic interventions" in specific areas related to globalization, as it had done with the process on financing for development. The recommendation contained in the Secretary General's report that ECOSOC should commission a study on regulatory gaps, reversible portfolio flows and hedge funds activities received support from several speakers. The UN was also said to be well-placed to launch the discussions on setting rules, norms and standards for global governance that would subsequently be spelled out in specialized forums, such as the WTO, the BWIs and specialized agencies.

Still, there was no clear agreement on how far the UN could go in addressing trade or finance issues without encroaching on other organizations' mandates.

One of the key messages of the debate, on which there was a broad agreement, was that the UN had to intensify its dialogue and strengthen its cooperation with the Bretton Woods Institutions, the WTO and regional organizations.

Another important point was that ECOSOC was viewed as a particularly important forum to address globalization and policy coherence. Delegates welcomed the Council's growing links with the Bretton Woods institutions, supported the SG's proposals to enhance the dialogue of ECOSOC with the WTO and to establish a task force under ECOSOC to make proposals for promoting policy coherence and institutional capacity-building measures. The need to build partnerships with other organizations such as OECD was also stressed.

There was also a broad agreement that globalization should be made a more central issue on the UN agenda. An important consideration in the context of continued reform of the United Nations should be the need to address globalization and to find ways to promote development in that new environment. The General Assembly should be strengthened to achieve that task. The agenda items of the General Assembly could be regrouped to enable an integrated approach more in line with globalization. There is also a need to further reform regional commissions so that they could tackle effectively the diverging demands arising from globalization. The UN's operational activities for development were deemed an important tool to make globalization "with a human face" a reality. They should be planned and executed in a manner contributing to developing countries' integration in global economy. There was a strong emphasis that any strategy to respond to globalization should be responsive to countries' specific needs and circumstances.

Overall, the speakers believed that the UN's work in coordinating the system's activities in the economic and social area contributed to managing globalization. Nevertheless, the work of the various UN forums on globalization should be better coordinated and synchronized in the framework of an overall concerted agenda that would also include forthcoming WTO and UNCTAD X.

A strategy to manage globalization should be flexible, able to adapt rapidly to changes, and innovative. Since not all of globalization's implications are currently known and understood, there was a need for a comprehensive and in-depth study of this phenomenon and ways to manage it. Processes such as the renewal of the dialogue and panels could be useful in this regard.

Science and technology

The UN should take a more proactive role in facilitating developing countries' access to information and communication technology and enhancing their integration in the global information network. The 2000 ECOSOC high-level segment could bring substantial progress in that area, perhaps supported by a group of experts on enhancing the integration of developing countries in the world economy through information technology. At the same time, other speakers stressed that there were more urgent issues to be addressed in developing countries, such as health, education and other basic needs without which access to computers would be a distant dream. The two are inter-dependent: helping developing countries to build their human resource base would also help them access technology.

Overall, an international dialogue should be initiated to develop an international technology architecture more responsive to developing countries' concerns. The continued viability of frameworks for the protection of intellectual property should be examined.

Trade and finance

Integration and liberalization should take place at a pace designed to allow developing countries to withstand competition and benefit from globalization. It should thus take into account levels of development of individual countries and the need for them to build up their national capabilities. Particular caution is needed in liberalizing capital flows. Speakers reiterated the importance of reforming the international financial architecture to better prevent and cope with crises and avoid contagion. This new financial architecture should help ensure that financial flows better respond to the developmental needs of the South. Some speakers underscored the UN's role in leading this reform, others believed that the Bretton Woods Institutions should serve as central forum for discussion on the international financial system. On trade, speakers reaffirmed that the forthcoming Seattle trade negotiations should take into account developing countries' interests, ensure that they are able to take advantage of more open markets, and focus on implementing provisions for their special and preferential treatment.

The challenge of involving civil society and the private sector

A key challenge for global governance and the UN will be involving the private sector in responding to globalization and in promoting globally agreed standards and values. In this respect, speakers attached particular importance to participatory processes at the national level, as well as to dialogues between governments and civil society and the private sector. The Secretary General's Davos initiative to build new partnerships continued to be praised. NetAid was characterized as an indication as to what could be accomplished by enlisting private sector's participation in a good cause. The debate also confirmed that on developing countries' side, there was a renewed emphasis on the need to regulate the activities of transnational and multinational corporations. It was stated that developing countries should be helped to counter unfair practices by multinational companies by appropriate multilateral and national tools and to channel the activities of transnational corporations towards what is of mutual benefit.

Regional and subregional integration and South-South cooperation were believed to be important to face the challenges of globalization.

III. General Assembly Resolution: Role of the United Nations in promoting development in the context of globalization and interdependence

The General Assembly,

Reaffirming the purposes and principles of the Charter of the United Nations, particularly with regard to the role of the United Nations in promoting international economic and social cooperation, including seeking solutions to international economic, social and related problems,

Recognizing the challenges and opportunities of globalization and interdependence,

Expressing concern over the serious risks of marginalization of a large number of developing countries from the globalization process, including in the finance and trade sectors, and the increasing vulnerability of those developing countries that are integrating into the world economy, resulting particularly from the volatility of short-term capital flows and the accentuation of income disparities within and among countries,

Mindful, in the process of trade liberalization, of the diminution of trade preferential margins for developing countries, particularly the least developed countries and small island developing States, and of the need for countries to take measures, as appropriate, in accordance with the rules of the World Trade Organization, to address that diminution with a view to offsetting it,

Recognizing that globalization and interdependence have opened new opportunities, through increased trade and capital flows and advancement in technology, for the growth of the world economy, for development and for the improvement of living standards around the world,

Underlining the need to work on a wide range of reforms to create a strengthened international financial system,

Stressing the importance of promoting the integration of developing countries into the world economy to allow them to take the fullest possible advantage of the trading opportunities arising from globalization and liberalization,

Emphasizing that technical assistance is also vital in enabling developing countries to benefit from the international trading environment,

Underlining the urgent need to mitigate the negative consequences of globalization and interdependence so as to realize the mutually reinforcing objectives of poverty eradication and development,

Reiterating that the United Nations is in a unique position, as a universal forum, to achieve international cooperation in addressing the challenges of promoting development in the context of globalization and interdependence,

Emphasizing that the United Nations system has a key role in fostering greater coherence, complementarity and coordination in economic and development issues at the global level,

Recognizing the importance of appropriate policy responses at the national level by all countries to the challenges of globalization, in particular by pursuing sound macroeconomic and social policies, noting the need for support from the international community for the efforts, in particular of the least developed countries, to improve their institutional and management capacities, and also recognizing that all countries should pursue policies conducive to economic growth and to promoting a favourable global economic environment,

Recalling the outcome of the ninth session of the United Nations Conference on Trade and Development, held at Midrand, South Africa,[1] which provides an important framework for promoting partnership for growth and development in the context of globalization and interdependence,

Noting the special high-level meeting between the Economic and Social Council and the Bretton Woods institutions, held on 18 April 1998, and the ministerial communiqué on market access adopted by the Economic and Social Council at the high-level segment of its 1998 substantive session,[2]

Recalling the widely shared desire expressed during the high-level dialogue of the General Assembly, held on 17 and 18 September 1998, which constituted a renewal of the dialogue on strengthening international economic cooperation for development through partnership, to continue discussions with a view to developing a coherent and effective response to the opportunities and challenges being offered by globalization and interdependence,

Taking note of the report of the Secretary-General on the causes of conflict and the promotion of durable peace and sustainable development in Africa,[3] wherein he identified, *inter alia,* the obstacles to the full participation of the African economies in the globalization process,

---

1   *Proceedings of the United Nations Conference on Trade and Development, Ninth Session, Midrand, Republic of South Africa, 27 April–11 May 1996, Report and Annexes* [United Nations publication, Sales No. E.97.II.D.4], part one, sect. A.

2   See *Official Records of the General Assembly, Fifty-third Session, Supplement No. 3* [A/53/3], chap. IV, para. 5.

3   A/52/871–S/1998/318: see *Official Records of the Security Council, Fifty-third Year, Supplement for April, May and June 1998,* document S/1998/318.

Reaffirms that the United Nations has a central role to play in promoting international cooperation for development and in providing guidance on global development issues, including in the context of globalization and interdependence;

Re-emphasizes the importance of recognizing the needs of developing countries, particularly the special needs of the least developed countries and small island developing States, in the context of globalization, and urges the international community, including the World Trade Organization, to continue to grant more preferential treatment to developing countries, including the least developed countries and small island developing States;

Welcomes the efforts of the United Nations Conference on Trade and Development and the International Trade Centre to help developing countries, in particular the least developed countries and small island developing States, to address their specific concerns within the globalizing economy, in particular through technology-related assistance in the fields of trade, policy, improvement of trade efficiency and policies and trade in services, in particular in electronic commerce;

Emphasizes the importance of recognizing and addressing the specific concerns of countries with economies in transition so as to help them to benefit from globalization with a view to their full integration into the world economy;

Underlines the need to continue to work to ensure the full participation of all the developing countries in the benefits of globalization and also the need to reduce their vulnerability to the negative impacts of globalization and interdependence;

Emphasizes that concerted efforts should be made, through enhanced cooperation and coordination among all the relevant forums and institutions, to minimize the negative impacts and maximize the benefits of globalization and interdependence for the developing countries;

Stresses the importance, at the national level, of maintaining sound macroeconomic policies and developing effective institutional and regulatory frameworks and human resources;

Strongly underlines the importance of an enabling environment for investment, in particular foreign direct investment, market access, good governance, increase in the volume and effectiveness of official development assistance, tackling of unsustainable debt burdens, including through debt conversion measures, flexibility in the Heavily Indebted Poor Countries Debt Initiative and support for regional cooperation and integration as priority areas that need to be addressed in order to achieve sustainable development in all African countries and to encourage the participation of all African countries in the global economy, as recommended in the report of the Secretary-General;[3]

Stresses the need for continued and constructive dialogue in the appropriate forums among developed and developing countries on issues related to strengthening and reforming the international financial architecture;

Recognizes the urgency of working together in developing a global approach to mitigate the negative consequences of globalization and interdependence, taking into account the specific vulnerabilities, concerns and needs of developing countries;

Invites the Economic and Social Council and the Bretton Woods institutions, in their special high-level meeting in 1999, also to address ways and means of optimizing the benefits and minimizing the negative consequences of globalization and interdependence, in particular for the developing countries;

Requests the Secretary-General to prepare, in collaboration with the United Nations Conference on Trade and Development and in consultation with relevant organizations, in particular the World Trade Organization, the International Monetary Fund, the World Bank and the regional commissions, an analytical report, to be submitted to the General Assembly at its fifty-fourth session, that examines the interrelated issues in order to facilitate better understanding of globalization and makes recommendations on, inter alia

[*a*] The role of the United Nations in promoting development in the context of globalization and interdependence;

[*b*] Promoting coherence, complementarity and coordination on economic and development issues at the global level in order to optimize the benefits and limit the negative consequences of globalization and interdependence;

Decides to include in the agenda of its fifty-fourth session an item entitled "Globalization and interdependence".

2

Financial Architecture and Development:

Debates and cooperation between the United Nations and the Bretton Woods institutions

C O N T E N T S :

Overview

Overview

This chapter is devoted to the dialogue and cooperation between the United Nations and the Bretton Woods institutions, with a substantive focus on the financial aspect of globalization: how these institutions have responded to the Asian financial crisis and worked toward a more stable, transparent and equitable financial architecture.

The high-level meeting between the UN Economic and Social Council and the Bretton Woods institutions that took place in New York in April 1998 was truly a historical premiere. There had been no large-scale meeting between high level policy-makers of these institutions, though all three have a mandate to manage economic and social issues on a global scale. Ministers of finance and development cooperation and Central Bank governors represent their countries in the Washington-based Interim Committee of the Board of Governors of the International Monetary Fund, and the Development Committee. While there are regular opportunities for debate at international level among ministers of foreign affairs within the United Nations, and among ministers of development cooperation, as well as among ministers of finance within the Washington institutions, there has seldom been a dialogue between policy makers in the area of finance, foreign affairs and development cooperation, from both developing and developed countries.

Like the United Nations, the Bank and the International Monetary Fund (IMF) are intergovernmental organizations established by agreement among their respective members. Both the World Bank and IMF have their own governing organs, which act in accordance with the organizations' articles of agreement. Although they are independent institutions, they are also specialized agencies of the United Nations under article 63 of the United Nations Charter.

Cooperation between the United Nations and the Bretton Woods institutions has evolved considerably over the past 50 years. While cooperation between the United Nations and the World Bank was initially focused on ad hoc operational collaboration and co-financing at the project level, the increasing convergence of development policies during the 1990s, with an overriding emphasis on poverty eradication, human-centered sustainable development and capacity-building, is leading to a new level of cooperation that involves both the operational and policy dimensions.

With the IMF, cooperation was initially limited to the exchange of views and information on matters of mutual interest, cooperation between the statistical services of the two organizations, and reciprocal attendance and participation in certain meetings. In recent years, in view of the challenges of a globalized economy and, more specifically, in order to take into account the recommendations of major United Nations conferences, collaboration between the United Nations and the IMF has been strengthened in a number of areas, including coordination of assistance in countries emerging from conflict, social aspects of economic reforms, capacity-building, sustainable development, and environmental issues.

The mandate for the high-level meetings was given by the General Assembly, in its resolution on revitalizing the United Nations in the economic and social fields adopted at its fiftieth session (resolution 50/227). It recommended that the Economic and Social Council schedule periodically a high-level special meeting at a time proximate to the semi-annual meetings of the Bretton Woods institutions.

The rationale was to take advantage of the presence of finance ministers and senior officials attending the Bretton Woods institutions' meeting, in order to bring together policy makers in the areas of development cooperation and finance into the Economic and Social Council and to promote a dialogue among them. The meetings were thus designed as an innovative forum where the community of top policy-makers on development would come together.

The theme of the first meeting, held on 18 April 1998, was "Global financial integration and development and recent issues." Essential documents pertaining to this 1998 meeting are reproduced in section I of this chapter.

Indeed, the financial and economic crisis that began in Asia in the summer of 1997 highlighted more than ever before the direct connections that exist between choices in financial and monetary policy (usually handled by the IMF) and the lives and livelihoods of ordinary people (a traditional concern of the UN). According to the International Labour Organization, 4 to 5 million Indonesian workers lost their jobs as a result of the crisis, and 40 million were expected to fall under the poverty line. In the Republic of Korea, one in twenty workers lost their jobs in the nine months between November 1997 to July 1998, and in Thailand, unemployment tripled, from 2 to 6 percent of the active population. Similar trends were felt in Hong Kong and Malaysia, while regions as far away as Latin America and Russia experienced the ripple effects in the form of monetary crises (sometimes leading to devaluations), investment pull out, joblessness and higher prices for imported items such as food or fuel.

As the Secretary-General noted in his introduction to the 1999 meeting, "recent events have underlined as never before the interdependencies between the economic and social dimensions of development".

The path-breaking meeting set the course for a regular dialogue. Indeed, a second meeting took place in the Spring of 1999—its key speeches and summaries are provided in section III.

Efforts to devise new rules to combat financial volatility continued throughout 1998 and 1999. We reproduce in section II the Report of the UN Executive Committee for Economic and Social Affairs entitled *Toward a new financial architecture*. That report, along with a statement of Under-Secretary-General Nitin Desai at the Interim Committee in April 1999 and the General Assembly resolution reprinted in section IV, are illustrations of the fact that the United Nations system intends to contribute as a full partner to discussions of the new financial architecture.

I. "Global Financial Integration and Development"

Special High-Level Meeting of ECOSOC with the Bretton Woods institutions, New York, April 18, 1998

Note of Introduction

The first high-level meeting centered on the Asian crisis and highlighted the two challenges this human tragedy represents for policy-makers: to devise ways to prevent such crises from happening again; and to cope with the current effects of the social dislocation and disarray. To respond to the first concern, the IMF put forward or updated a number of concrete proposals under the generic name of "new global financial architecture." These proposals, which are summarized in the Secretary-General's Note in preparation to the meeting, focus on better information and monitoring at the national and international levels. But reappraisal of past policies are also in order. The previous emphasis on swift capital market liberalization was seen as possibly contributing to the crisis. While global financial mobility is essential, it became just as important to "make global financial integration safe for development."

Equity issues were also raised in the wake of the crisis. The poor seemed to be paying for high-stake miscalculations by financial markets participants, many of which escaped unscathed.

These themes appear in the opening and closing statements of the ECOSOC President, Ambassador Paolo Fulci, as well as in the welcoming address of the Secretary-General. Subsequently, the summary of the discussion provides a glimpse into the variety of other themes that were covered during the conference.

The panelists were Mr. Abdelkrim Harchaoui, Minister of Finance of Algeria and incoming Chairman of the G-24; Mr. Philippe Maystadt, Deputy-Prime Minister and Minister of Finance and Foreign Trade of Belgium, Chairman of the IMF Interim Committee; Dr. Eduardo Fernandez, Vice-Minister of Finance of Columbia; Dr. Fuad Bawazier, Minister of Finance of Indonesia, Chairman of the Group of 77; Mr.

Anwar Ibrahim, Deputy-Prime Minister and Minister of Finance of Malaysia, Chairman of the Development Committee; Mr. James Michel, Chairman of the Development Assistance Committee of the Organization for Economic Cooperation and Development (OECD); Ms. Clare Short, Secretary of State of the United Kingdom for International Development (on behalf of the Group of Ten (G-10) industrial countries); Dr. Antonio Casas Gonzalez, Governor of the Central Bank of Venezuela, outgoing Chairman of G-24.

Global financial integration and development and recent issues
Note by the Secretary-General, New York, April 18, 1998

Introduction

Private international financial flows to developing countries increased from $64 billion in 1990 to $235 billion in 1996 but fell to an estimated $172 billion in 1997. There has been growth not only in the volume, sources and destinations of international flows but also in the agents, types and modes of such flows, resulting in an unprecedented degree of financial interdependence among countries, with dependencies running from source countries to recipient countries and vice versa. This process of global financial integration has been fueled primarily by the liberalization of markets and technological progress.

The experience of East Asia over the past decade has demonstrated the positive contribution that international financial flows can make to development, while the region's more recent experience has revealed the challenges that they can pose. Such experience provides lessons not only for the countries concerned but also for the many other countries that have been affected by recent developments and for countries in the process of becoming integrated into international financial markets.

Discussions might focus on such lessons, in particular the respective roles of national Governments, financial markets and international organizations in addressing global financial integration and its effects. Some of the issues that might be addressed are identified below.

The challenges of global financial integration

The national economic and financial environment

Effective integration into global financial markets requires sound macroeconomic conditions and a sound domestic financial sector. Such conditions are not only conducive to international financial flows but also reduce the threat of financial crises. The meeting could examine the nature of these prerequisites for effective integration into global financial markets.

In the absence of information about local conditions in foreign markets, a change in perceptions can precipitate a disproportionately large reaction in financial markets. The widespread availability of more timely, accurate and comprehensive data and other information about conditions in national economies and within financial and commercial establishments should contribute both to effective economic decision-making by Governments and to the efficiency of financial markets. The meeting could address the extent to which the availability of such information, in and of itself, would reduce volatility in individual markets and contagion across markets, as well as the role of Governments and international institutions in establishing standards for and ensuring the widespread availability of such information.

Monitoring and oversight

Interdependencies among countries create a common global interest in avoiding all potential threats to financial stability. This objective can be served by multilateral mechanisms that monitor all national economic policies affecting international capital flows and other monetary and financial variables. Since neighbouring countries are among those likely to be most affected by a national financial crisis, such arrangements might have a regional as well as an international dimension. The nature and operation of such collective oversight mechanisms could be addressed.

Because unsound practices by banks and similar institutions can pose a threat to the economy at large, developed countries and many developing countries have an array of prudential, supervisory and regulatory arrangements for strengthening competition and the discipline of the market on the financial sector. Many of these arrangements have been enhanced and harmonized among countries in response to the evolution of financial markets. The meeting could consider the nature of the national and international regulatory mechanisms required to take into account the increasing participation of developing and transition economies in world financial markets.

Contingency arrangements

Uncertainty about the future, possible policy weaknesses on the part of Governments and exuberant behaviour on the part of markets make it difficult to eliminate the incidence of financial crises. Such crises need to be addressed as promptly as possible because they become more pronounced (and correspondingly more difficult and costly to resolve) the longer they are left unattended. Moreover, with the continuing expansion of financial markets, such crises as do occur are likely to require a greater effort to resolve than in the past. The meeting could consider whether current international contingency arrangements are adequate in the light of the increasing volume of international financial flows.

Responding to financial crises

Sharing risks and responsibilities

Official measures to reduce the adverse short-term effects and economy-wide threats posed by a financial crisis may result in some private-sector risks being transferred to the public sector, which may encourage private financial entities to take on more risks than would otherwise be the case. In confronting a crisis, Governments and international institutions are faced with a choice: they can allow the crisis to deepen, with the result that those who have taken excessive risks bear the full cost of their decisions but many others will also be adversely affected, or they can mitigate the effects of the crisis, in which case lenders and borrowers may not have to assume the full cost of their decisions but others would also be less seriously affected. Arrangements for the equitable sharing of the costs of resolving financial crises could be addressed.

Protecting vulnerable groups

Financial crises can result in bankruptcies, increased unemployment and other economic hardships. Particularly for vulnerable groups, the suddenness of the crisis is likely to exacerbate these difficulties, and not fully tackling them is likely to lead to broader negative effects, such as crime and heightened political tensions. The meeting could consider ways in which such short-term dislocations and their effects on vulnerable groups should be addressed in the context of major financial crises.

Introduction by the President of the Council, Ambassador Paolo Fulci of Italy

Mr. Secretary-General,
Ministers, Ladies and Gentlemen,

The global economy has already become a reality. It is there for all to see. In the economic field, large companies are feeling the impact of technological progress and new methods of manufacturing. They are always seeking greater efficiency and productivity. They are becoming global, often as part of huge transnational groups. The financial sector is already virtually globalized. Deregulation, the ending of exchange controls, and instant world-wide communication has transformed its operations. In the information field, instant and universal communication of large quantities of data is a new feature of international life.

Globalization brings progress. It should be encouraged. But certainly it also implies some risks. The global economy can be hard on those who do not benefit from its opportunities. Traditional ties of community and solidarity can be undermined. Whole countries and regions can become marginalized. So the gap between the rich and the poor risks growing ever wider rather than smaller.

The recent experience of East Asia (fast economic growth in the last decade, and recent financial crises) is significant, because it shows the positive contribution of financial globalization to development but at the same time, its risks and challenges.

Considering today's excellent turnout, I would urge all of you to keep your comments concise so that everyone can have a chance to be heard. Each and every one of us should keep in mind the Roman historian Tacitus, who could say so much with so few words.

It is now my privilege to invite the Secretary-General of the United Nations, Mr. Kofi Annan, to address the meetings.

Secretary-General Kofi Annan's statement to the special high-level meeting of the Economic and Social Council with the Bretton Woods institutions

Finance is central to the development process, but development finance is also an area where, in recent years, the thinking has changed fundamentally; and where, at the same time, dramatic developments have taken place. There is now universal recognition of the developmental role of private international capital flows. They have brought with them tremendous benefits. Big strides have been made in improving the lives of millions of people.

Yet, as the recent financial crisis in Asia has shown, there are huge risks involved.

There are, as I see it, three main areas of concern in the implications of the recent crisis in Asia. First and foremost, there is the situation of the crisis countries themselves.

One might ask whether the penalty imposed on these countries in terms of lost output and lost jobs is commensurate with the failings of omission or commission they may have had.

I think we are all preoccupied by the harsh toll these crises impose on an entire citizenry. Those hardest hit are usually the most vulnerable. Job seekers who have migrated during the good times; the poor who can no longer pay for the higher priced basic necessities; those groups which are employed in the least organized sectors of the economy. Beyond this is the continuing threat of social strife, breakdown of law and order and loss of self-esteem.

Macro aggregates do not capture the trauma that individuals and families have to undergo as a result of crisis of this nature.

It is not only the countries and their citizens directly concerned that bear the consequences, but the world at large. And here again, I perceive a major area of concern.

The precise impact of the Asian crisis cannot be separated from all other independent developments affecting the world economy. Yet it is becoming increasingly apparent that other developing and transition countries—far removed geographically and even economically from their Asian colleagues—will be affected more severely by the crisis than their developed counterparts. In other words, the collateral damage is greater in developing countries than elsewhere.

A third area of concern can be found in the speed of deterioration and recovery.

A perceived failure to adhere to externally determined standards of creditworthiness can lead to instant loss of international confidence.

There are signs that such confidence can be regained surprisingly rapidly; but not nearly so quickly as it is lost, nor to the same degree. The ensuing short-term losses to an economy not only undo previous gains; they also harm growth prospects in the longer term. And there is a real risk that successes built up over years in reducing poverty will be reversed.

I see these fundamental issues arising from the way the current international financial system itself operates, and they way risks and rewards are balanced.

The question to be addressed is whether we can find ways to preserve the benefits of open financial markets while reducing the risks of crises and designing tools to deal with them that will be less costly in human terms. This is a matter on which our institutions—among many others—should pursue a wide-ranging exchange of views.

The United Nations has a role to play both in easing the impact of such crises and in the longer-term preventive aspects. Short-term concerns can lead to a neglect of the fundamentals of longer-term development. These must be built around human capital investment and broader dimensions such as respect for human rights, institutional development as well as participatory democracy.

When the General Assembly took the decision two years ago to hold this meeting, it could not have known how timely the event would prove to be. The financial turbulence in Asia has presented an enormous challenge to the international community and to the countries directly involved.

However, the ensuing economic, social and developmental—as well as political—consequences of the crisis have served as reminders of the interrelationships between the responsibilities and work of our three organizations. Moreover, the international ramifications are becoming more apparent every day. They are vivid proof of the risks that come with the benefits of globalization. They are also stark evidence that closer cooperation between the United Nations and the Bretton Woods institutions is imperative.

In Washington, the Interim and Development Committees and the Group of 24 consider global financial issues. These intergovernmental mechanisms have different purposes and involve different actors from the processes here in the United Nations. But they are not unrelated. Our organizations share the objective of promoting economic and social progress throughout the world.

We bring to our work different capacities and, in some areas, different perspectives. Yet these differences are rapidly diminishing. The United Nations is no longer constrained by the East-West rivalry of the past, while membership of the International Monetary Fund (IMF) and the World Bank is becoming increasingly universal. Even more important, there is now far greater consensus on the nature of the development process.

Known by relatively few but affecting so many, cooperation between our respective institutions is strongest where it counts most—at the field level. I firmly believe we have made great progress—and continue to do so—in ensuring that the operational activities of the Bank, the Fund and the United Nations system are mutually supportive.

This has been most evident in post-conflict peace-building; but increasingly, the Bretton Woods institutions, the United Nations and the specialized agencies are working together to enhance coherence and impact across the full range of our development efforts.

I look forward to the discussions here today and, even more importantly, to their continuing in the future.

With our overriding commonality of concerns and approaches, it is only appropriate that we should join forces to pursue our common objective. So much more can be achieved by acting together than by acting alone, or separately.

Summary of the discussion[1]

Most speakers noted that globalization was a powerful force leading to new opportunities and challenges. While the focus on the financial crisis was warranted, many speakers stressed the need to consider a response that would take into account several dimensions: effects of the financial crisis on vulnerable groups, human development programmes and other countries; the long-term development perspectives and the strategic integration of social, economic, financial and governance issues; international financial cooperation for poverty eradication and debt relief for poor countries; the architecture of the global financial system; further liberalization of capital flows; and, particularly, prevention of future financial crisis.

Globalization in the aftermath of the East Asia crisis

While it was still premature to derive the full implications of the East Asia crisis, most participants recognized that already many valuable lessons could be inferred. Change in market sentiment had precipitated unexpectedly large reactions in financial flows with damaging collateral effects in several countries which had been, hitherto, characterized as successful economies. It was difficult to know with reasonable accuracy the relative weight of external forces (speculators and perceptions about the sustainability of current account deficits) and domestic factors (adequacy of macro-economic management, micro-economic policies and vulnerability of the financial system) in triggering the capital outflow.

The deliberations at the recent meeting of the IMF Interim Committee had focused on measures to prevent a repetition and avoid the worst consequences and spread of a financial crisis. Five proposals had been considered central in these deliberations:

1. Strengthened domestic financial systems by developing supervisory and regulatory frameworks consistent with international standards;
2. Enhanced IMF surveillance of cross-border flows, particularly short-term flows;
3. More comprehensive and transparent information on economic data and policies; Efforts should be directed at timely data of good quality , particularly to facilitate IMF surveillance; The accessibility of such information to the public and market participants should also be considered;

---

1   Editors' note: Only those themes or ideas that have not been covered by the statements by Mr. Kofi Annan and Mr. Paolo Fulci are summarized here.

4. The timely response of the international community and the IMF had been important and the establishment of the Supplemental Reserve Facility was welcome; While the role of the IMF in catalyzing other sources of financing remained crucial, it was essential to ensure that it had adequate resources for its interventions;

5. Effective procedures to involve the private sector; The latter should more fully bear the consequences of their actions; Equitable burden sharing and reduced moral hazard should be a key objective.

Several speakers stressed that further financial integration was virtually inevitable and that policies should aim at facilitating this process while avoiding excessive volatility. A prudent, phased liberalization of capital markets was preferable. National economies had to proceed at their own pace. Some countries with non-convertible currencies might not be ready to engage in the process. On the question of reduced volatility, it was pointed out that more transparency could help, but would not ensure stability. It was also necessary to look at excessive liability building or over-indebtedness—not only from the point of view of the borrower, but also from the point of view of the lender. Both were responsible for eventual bubbles. It was also important to develop human capacities in developing countries to better integrate into world capital markets, enhance oversight and effectively regulate domestic financial markets.

Delaying reforms was counterproductive: it might help to avoid difficult decisions and hide problems with additional financial flows that provide a false sense of security but that in the end prove unsustainable. In such situations, the IMF involvement would usually lead to painful surgery instead of smooth restructuring or marginal policy changes.

It was encouraging that the rapid response in the East Asia crisis had involved key bilateral actors, the Bretton Woods institutions and the Asian Development Bank. Partnership among them and countries in East Asia had worked well. Some speakers pointed out that much remained to be done to improve the analytical abilities of forecasters to anticipate crises. Enhanced oversight by the IMF should help. Symmetry in surveillance efforts was also important, as the way out of the crisis would be facilitated by sustained non-inflationary growth in developed countries accompanied by open markets. Indeed, expansion of exports from countries affected by the crisis was a critical element in their recovery.

Equity, poverty reduction and international cooperation

The constraints on development brought about by external debt in low-income countries were emphasized by several participants. Despite past efforts at debt relief the problem remained serious. The Heavily Indebted Poor Countries Initiative (HIPC) offered the promise of a faster solution. One country—Uganda—was already benefiting from the initiative and negotiations had started for five others, most of them in Africa.

Many speakers found ODA trends troubling. The gap between the 0.7 percent target and actual flows was widening. It was imperative to reverse the decline and additional efforts should be made by all concerned. In this context, several speakers addressed the issue of aid effectiveness. New approaches had to be considered by donors and recipients to ensure more efficient procedures and that the common objectives are achieved. Aid fatigue was partly due to the perception that ODA was not achieving its objectives, and better information on results and enhanced effectiveness could change that perception.

It was true that private international capital had become key in the development process. However, most participants stressed that the role of international financial institutions also remained essential. The adequate funding of the Bretton Woods institutions and the regional development banks was a critical task for the international community. Globalization and financial integration required more—not less—joint efforts and shared responsibility.

Conclusions by Ambassador Paolo Fulci

One theme running through today's dialogue has been the recognition that globalization has changed the world and that the world must respond. Within this broad framework, our discussions this morning have been driven to a large extent by the repercussions of the so-called Asian crisis. I say "so-called" because it is agreed that we live in an increasingly integrated world and that turmoil anywhere poses risks to all countries around the globe. Nobody, but nobody, can ensure his or her safety from its spillover effects. There is universal recognition that global financial integration is not an option—it is a historical shift. Global financial integration offers great opportunities but also great challenges; it offers benefits but it also poses great risks.

The Asian crisis has resulted in great attention being given to the sharing of risks and benefits in times of financial turmoil. The question of financial burden-sharing in times of crisis is a complicated and technical issue which will have to be addressed in other forums. However, our discussions have also highlighted the need for a sharing of benefits and risks over the longer term. Several speakers have reminded us of the contribution—that is to say, the benefits—of global financial integration to Asia's overall economic success and to the reduction in poverty over the past few decades; but there are also long-term risks—the risk of marginalization, the risk that some countries or individuals may be left behind. There must be a sharing of these long-term benefits and risks. Global financial integration should be to the benefit of all countries and all peoples; and we must all work together to reduce the risks of marginalization. I believe that the discussions this morning have demonstrated, encouragingly, a growing consensus on the means to maximize such benefits so as to reduce these potential risks.

In the short term, there continue to be different points of view about the reasons for the recent crisis and the most appropriate ways of responding to it. Nevertheless, appreciation was expressed for the prompt response to the crisis by the international community, led by the International Monetary Fund (IMF) and the World Bank. At the same time, there was universal recognition that the initial financial crisis has developed wide-ranging economic and social dimensions. There was widespread and deep concern about the adverse consequences of financial crises for vulnerable groups and the profound consequences for poverty. There was unanimity that special efforts need to be made to protect the poor and other vulnerable groups in times of crisis. The alleviation of poverty must remain our ultimate objective, both in the long run and over the short term.

Our discussions this morning have demonstrated that all of us—international institutions and national Governments—still have much to learn about responding to the forces of global financial integration. While many questions remain, we agree that there is a need to strengthen the global architecture, that prevention is better than cure, and that actions are required at both the international and the national levels. The wide-ranging nature of the fallout from the crisis calls for a collective response involving all our institutions to varying degrees. A number of interesting and innovative ideas were presented, demonstrating that this meeting has provided an important opportunity to exchange views on the types of action that need to be taken by us, individually and collectively.

There seems to be universal agreement that more information, greater transparency and improved monitoring are indispensable in reducing the possibility of financial crises. I believe that this meeting has demonstrated, equally, the need to develop the flows of information and transparency between our institutions. There were many references to the need for policy coherence and partnership at all levels, but particularly between our institutions. There was a consensus that greater efforts need to be made to integrate the financial, economic, social and political policies and strategies.

The reason for the Economic and Social Council's originally being conceived by the fathers of the United Nations, the vision and motivation driving recent efforts to renew the economic and social sectors, and the inspiration behind today's meeting have all been focused on a single goal: to make this world a better place to live in for all the people of the planet by giving the developing countries, especially the least developed countries, a better chance to improve their well-being. We must continue to pool all our efforts to eradicate poverty and pave the way towards a future of sustainable development. Development must remain the top priority of the United Nations.

II. "Towards a new financial architecture"

Note of Introduction

The 1999 meeting between the UN Economic and Social Council and the Bretton Woods institutions was preceded by the publication of an important report, reprinted here: "Towards a new international financial architecture: Report of the Task Force of the Executive Committee on Economic and Social Affairs of the United Nations," issued in January. The Report presents a six-point plan to strengthen the global financial system and make it more development-friendly.

Two days before the 1999 meeting, Under-Secretary-General Nitin Desai addressed the Interim Committee on the question of the new financial architecture. His short address points to the range of options that exist on the issue of reform of the international financial system.

Statement by Mr. Nitin Desai, Under-Secretary-General, Department of Economic and Social Affairs, at the Interim Committee meeting, April 27, 1999

Measures to address financial crises

It is universally agreed that, in order to be effective in today's integrated financial markets, national financial institutions need to be strengthened in all countries. Better transparency, supervision and regulation need to be applied, albeit in different ways and to varying extents. At the international level, consensus is evolving on issues such as the need for the industrialized countries to pursue supportive policies in times of financial uncertainty elsewhere; the need to enhance the contingency financing available to countries in difficulties; and the need to improve the institutional framework in which financial markets operate. In these areas, it is necessary to build upon the progress that has been made.

Differences remain on other questions: how to provide liquidity to crisis-stricken countries and the related issue of conditionality; the principles to be adopted regarding capital account convertibility; and the role of regional institutions in the new architecture.

Global crisis, global responsibility

The industrial economies' policies of lowering interest rates have contributed to the improvement in the economic outlook for the crisis countries. This highlights the need for a more systematic and inclusive approach to the solution of financial crises in future. The industrialized countries have a crucial role to play by taking pre-emptive action to break the chain of contagion and similar processes that characterize globalized financial markets.

Providing international liquidity

The management of international liquidity has a special role in preventing contagion and lessening the adverse developmental effects of financial crises. The principle of contingency financing is well accepted, but there is no clear agreement on how to ensure that adequate funds are available at short notice. Ad hoc, case-by-case approaches involving bilateral financing and IMF credits are unlikely to be sufficient. One of the possible solutions would be to create liquidity when required by allowing the issuance of additional SDRs under critical financial conditions. These funds could be destroyed once normal financial conditions are restored. This procedure would introduce an anti-cyclical element into the management of world liquidity, in addition to giving SDRs an increasing role in world finance. A second-best solution would be to allow the IMF to use the market to mobilize the resources required to enable it to provide adequate contingency financing.

A low-conditionality line of credit

The recent financial difficulties were exacerbated in several countries, and even precipitated, by international contagion. When the source of an imbalance is such an international shock, contingency financing should be subject to low conditionality. This principle has been recognized in the Compensatory and Contingency Financing Facility but should be extended to the case of contagion. There are concerns that the conditionality attached to the financing provided in such cases has been excessive; this is undermining its legitimacy and weakening the IMF. In order to restore full confidence in the principle of conditionality, it is necessary to reach a renewed global agreement on how it should be used.

International financial liberalization

It is now generally agreed that capital account liberalization should be gradual, should be applied primarily to longer-term flows, should be cautious with regard to shorter-term and more volatile funds (such as bank credits and portfolio flows), and should be preceded by the development of sound financial institutions (including regulatory and supervisory arrangements). International agreement in this area should include safeguard mechanisms that would allow developing and transition economies to impose temporary disincentives or controls on inflows, particularly in time of capital surges, and on outflows during severe crises.

Making international organizations more democratic

Most of the burden or the economic upheavals of the past two years has been borne by the peoples of the developing and transition economies. Their voices must be more effectively heard and their circumstances more fully taken into account in the collective effort to improve the management of the world economy. The international financial system needs sound and democratic governance and it should accommodate and reflect diversity among countries—in their cultures, in their development aspirations and in their levels of development. The role of the developing and transition economies in the relevant international organizations should be increased and the potential of regional and sub-regional organizations involving these countries should be more fully exploited.

The common element in all the foregoing suggestions is that the response to financial crises should not be addressed just from a narrow technical point of view but from a broader and longer-term development perspective—one that gives priority to the present and future well-being of all individuals, rather than only to short-term financial concerns.

General Assembly's discussions on financing for development

The General Assembly is also preparing for a high-level international event on financing for development, to be held before the end of 2001. The Assembly is currently in the process of deciding on the "form, scope and agenda" of this proposed event. The Bank and the Fund have participated actively and positively in these discussions and Member States have made it clear that they wish both organizations to be fully and actively involved in the preparations for this event, as well as in the event itself. Governments on all sides appear to share the recognition that multilateral decisions on financial matters are largely taken in these and other related institutions. At the same time, Governments also share the view that the United Nations can serve as a forum for developing a political consensus on some broad principles that underlie the decisions taken elsewhere. There is therefore optimism that the event in 2001 will be able to make a positive contribution to enhancing multilateral cooperation in the area of international finance.

Towards a new international financial architecture: Report of the Task Force of the Executive Committee on Economic and Social Affairs of the United Nations, January 21, 1999[1]

The international financial crisis and the need for reform

World events since mid-1997, and its precedents in the 1980s and 1990s, have made painfully clear that the current international financial system is unable to safeguard the world economy from financial crises of high intensity and frequency and devastating real effects. The rapid spread of the current international financial crisis, from East and South-East Asia to other developing and transition economies, and even to the industrialized world, has already led to statements and decisions by the authorities of developed countries, who recognize that it is indeed the most threatening event of its kind in more than half a century. The threat is reflected in the successive substantial downward revisions of forecasts of world economic growth in the last year and a half.

The crisis reflects, first of all, the tendency of financial markets to experience sharp boom-bust cycles. During financial booms, lenders and borrowers underestimate the risks involved in high levels of indebtedness, a fact that only becomes apparent, with particular severity, during the ensuing downswings and panics. This volatility is inherent in the functioning of financial markets. It reflects not only imperfections in the flow of information, but also radical changes in its interpretation and sharp revisions in expectations as new information arrives, shifts that can be severe because of the uncertainty intrinsic to the intertemporal decisions that underlie financial transactions. The liberalization of financial flows among industrialized and some developing countries, floating exchange rates, financial innovations and new communications techniques have increased not only financial transactions, but also volatility in recent decades.

The crisis has also demonstrated, with particular severity on this occasion, that financial crises are contagious; that under panic conditions markets do not adequately discriminate between countries with strong and weak economic fundamentals; and thus that crises tend to spread even to countries with sound economic structures and macroeconomic management. The concentration of participants in international financial markets that apply criteria indiscriminately to all countries is a major basis for contagion. In many cases, financial crises spread because highly leveraged investors, faced with losses in one market and ensuing margin calls, sell good assets in another country; investment banks and mutual funds

---

[1]Originally prepared by the UN Economic Commission for Latin America and the Caribbean.

may also engage in similar behavior in order to raise liquidity in expectation of withdrawals by clients.

Developing and transition economies have been highly vulnerable to financial volatility and contagion. They have been particularly prone to periods of rapid expansion and diversification of financial flows, often followed by abrupt reversals. This pattern has been aggravated by premature and hasty liberalization of the capital account, fragile domestic financial structures, and weak financial regulation and supervision. Extended financial booms build up strong pressures on aggregate domestic demand, which make macroeconomic balances unsustainable during the ensuing financial contraction. They also tend to weaken financial structures, as increasing risks are often underestimated. Under these conditions, the downswing may result in domestic financial crisis, which consumes large amounts of the scarce resources available to development, and severely affects economic activity and investment for several years. The impact of financial crises on the real economy is thus far larger than in developed market economies.

External debt and domestic financial crises generate, in turn, substantial social costs. As it happens, poor sectors of society pay a substantial share of the costs of adjustment to debt crises, whereas they benefit rather marginally from financial booms. The experience of many developing countries in several regions of the world also indicates that the social effects of debt crises continue to afflict countries even after several years of successful economic restructuring and recovery. The Latin American experience since the early 1980s is particularly relevant in this regard. Preliminary evidence suggests that a similar pattern may occur in the East and South-East Asian nations.

Lastly, the recent crisis has demonstrated a fundamental problem in the global economy: **the enormous discrepancy that exists between an increasingly sophisticated and dynamic international financial world, with rapid globalization of financial portfolios, and the lack of a proper institutional framework to regulate it**. In brief, existing institutions are inadequate to deal with financial globalization. This is true of institutions at the international level, which have manifested significant shortcomings in the consistency of macroeconomic policies, and in the management of international liquidity, financial supervision and regulation. It is also true of national institutions in the face of globalization, even in industrial countries. This systemic deficiency and the associated threat of recurring crises in the future have thus underscored the need for a comprehensive reform of the international financial system, geared to prevent costly crises and to manage them better if they occur. The outcome would improve economic and social prospects worldwide.

The need for immediate action

In order to prevent the current crisis from deepening, immediate actions are required from the major industrial countries and from the international community. There is evidence that the world economy is experiencing a major slowdown, which may deepen if inadequately managed. Japan is in its worst recession since the war, much of East and South-East Asia is in depression, Russia is experiencing a major downturn, growth has stalled in Latin America, and the prices of primary commodities and a number of manufactures are falling in international markets. We therefore embrace the declaration of the Group of Seven on the need to confront the threat of world recession, and we applaud the decisions by the central banks of the United States and Western Europe to reduce interest rates in recent months, the important fiscal stimulus announced by Japan and its decision to face up to its domestic financial crisis. Authorities in the industrial countries must nonetheless continue to be alert. Several downside risks still remain, and current policies may prove insufficient to prevent the world economy from slipping into recession. Expansionary fiscal policies may thus be required in other industrial economies, in addition to Japan. It is also crucial that the rules of an open international trading system should operate smoothly, allowing the economies that face adjustment to reduce their deficits or generate trade surpluses with the more vigorous industrial economies.

With the full support of the major industrial countries, IMF should put together contingency funds to assist countries now experiencing crisis or contagion and others that could become the victims of world financial crisis in the future. These include countries that may be affected indirectly by the effects of such crises on trade and commodity prices, particularly low-income African and Asian countries. We therefore welcome the recent declaration and actions by the Group of Seven to guarantee adequate contingency financing, by completing the implementation of the IMF quota increase and the New Arrangements to Borrow, and the commitment to supplement the Fund's resources when necessary. Moreover, as we argue below, it is essential that this new type of contingency financing, which is to be made available **before** international reserves are depleted, should become a stable feature of the new international financial order, and that the availability of funds should be guaranteed without delay when needed. Developing and transition countries experiencing difficulties must obviously be ready to adopt the necessary adjustment policies, as they have generally been doing during the recent crisis.

The reform of the international financial architecture

In the longer term, fundamental reforms of the international financial architecture are needed. The international financial system is an organic whole and requires a comprehensive approach. Reform must therefore encompass a number of interrelated aspects of international liquidity management, global consistency of macroeconomic policies and financial regulation, areas essential to the prevention and management of financial crises, as well as finance for development and the resolution of outstanding debt issues. This report addresses international monetary and financial issues in the first group, but some suggestions on broader and related issues are also provided.

With regard to the first group of issues, it must be emphasized that the present system is badly equipped to prevent financial crises and only partly equipped to manage them. Reforms in this area must be addressed with a sense of urgency in six key areas:

- Improved consistency of macroeconomic policies at the global level;
- Reform of IMF aimed at providing adequate international liquidity in times of crisis;
- The adoption of codes of conduct, improved information, and financial supervision and regulation at national and international levels;
- The preservation of the autonomy of developing and transition economies with regard to capital account issues;
- The incorporation of internationally sanctioned standstill provisions into international lending; and
- The design of a network of regional and subregional organizations to support the management of monetary and financial issues.

It is important to underscore the interrelated character of these reforms. Indeed, it is clear that reliance on any one or a few of these proposals would not generate a balanced world system, either in terms of its ability to both prevent and manage crises or of equitable participation by all members of the international community.

We must emphasize that any reform of the international financial system ought to be based on a broad discussion, involving all countries, and a clear agenda, including all key issues. The process must ensure that the interests of all groups of developing and transition economies, including poor and small countries, are adequately represented. The United Nations, as a universal and the most democratic international forum, should play an important role in these discussions and in the design of the new system.

Improving the consistency of macroeconomic policies at the global level

The crisis has made evident the need to enhance the coherence of macroeconomic policies in industrial countries, in order to avoid both inflationary and deflationary biases at the global level. The design of international institutions and policies must include, in the first place, clear incentives for national authorities in the industrialized world to maintain their economies at close to full employment while at the same time avoiding inflation. This will have favourable effects, not only for these economies, but also for the world at large. It must be emphasized that consistency in this sense should be primarily aimed at ensuring the global coherence of a set of interrelated national policies, rather than the adoption of identical decisions, since, in fact, inflationary or deflationary pressures will not necessarily be uniform at a given time. In order to achieve this objective, a more effective surveillance of national policies by IMF and regional and subregional institutions is necessary. This surveillance must have broad objectives and a preventive character, acting to warn of impending unemployment and growth retardation, as well as of inflationary pressures reflected in the evolution of domestic prices of goods, services and assets or in the deterioration of external balances.

The most appropriate institution or set of institutions to ensure such consistency should be subject to debate. Proposals include granting greater policy powers to the IMF Interim Committee and broadening the Group of Seven to include representatives of the developing and transition countries. The nature of the relative power relations that underlie these organs should be part of the debate. Hence, these proposals should be seen as consistent with the need to strengthen the Economic and Social Council, as indicated in the Report of the Secretary-General, "Renewing the United Nations: A Programme of Reform", to provide political leadership and promote broad consensus on international economic issues. The necessarily broader mandates of this Council would then have to be harmonized with those of the specific body in charge of macroeconomic policy consistency. As argued below, a set of regional institutions whose objectives include macroeconomic coordination and surveillance also offers the advantage of a more balanced world order.

Macroeconomic policies, including decisions by central banks, should be subject to public scrutiny, aimed at ensuring proper balance between their multiple objectives (particularly between employment/growth objectives and inflation/balance-of-payments objectives). For the same reasons, IMF should be also subject to public scrutiny on similar grounds, with effective independent evaluations leading to accountable and pragmatic improvements in policy approaches.

The provision of adequate international liquidity in times of crisis

The management of international liquidity has a special role in preventing and avoiding contagion from financial crises and lessening their adverse economic effects. Whereas these objectives could eventually be best pursued through the creation of a true international "lender of last resort" (i.e., a world central bank), conditions are not ripe for such a bold reform to existing institutional arrangements. It would require, in particular, the surrender of more economic autonomy and powers of intervention in national policies than countries are willing to accept at present. Nonetheless, much can be done to improve the way IMF operates so that, in effect, it moves in that direction. Today, IMF has inadequate funds; it acts more as an organizer of rescues than as a provider of funds; the conditions attached to the use of its funds are not always appropriate to the problems faced by countries in distress; and it has very limited capacity to stop contagion.

Still, the Fund could do much to stem the spread of financial crises. In the first place, where the problem of contagion derives from reduced export demand and prices, it has the authority to make low-conditionality loans through the Compensatory and Contingency Financing Facility (CCFF). The facility should be used more actively, and more resources relative to country quotas should be provided under it. However, the bulk of the demands on the Fund in times of crises will come from countries experiencing capital account problems. Therefore, recent contingency financing mechanisms should become the basis for a stable, low-conditionality facility for countries experiencing financial contagion. Countries that meet certain *ex ante* criteria would be eligible, and eligibility would be examined during Article IV consultations. Low-conditionality funds would then be made available, though at shorter terms and higher interest rates than traditional IMF resources. The corresponding criteria could include indicators such as those associated to current account deficits, the evolution of the exchange rate, the ratio of short-term debt to reserves, and the ratio of short-term and portfolio capital inflows to exports or GDP.

IMF resources should be enlarged in order to enable it to enhance the stability of the international financial system. Three channels can be considered. First, effective and swift mechanisms should be devised to increase its access to official funds in times of crisis. Second, it could be granted authorization to borrow directly from financial markets under those circumstances. Third, and perhaps most importantly, SDRs could be created when several members face financial difficulties. The SDRs thus created would be destroyed as borrowings were repaid. These mechanisms would facilitate the creation of additional liquidity at times of crises, without the painstaking negotiations of quota increases or arrangements to borrow. Moreover, current arrangements to borrow exhibit the shortcoming that they are activated only under systemic threat and after the approval of the suppliers of funds, with the corresponding delays in making new funds available to the Fund and the countries in distress. Indeed, the anticyclical use of SDRs to manage financial cycles should be part of a broader process aimed at enhancing their use as an appropriate international currency for a globalized world.

IMF conditionality is legitimate for drawings that are made when a country is experiencing balance-of-payments problems originating in inappropriate macroeconomic policies, or for the use of funds greater than the automatic low-conditionality facilities mentioned above when facing either an externally-induced current or capital account crisis. However, IMF should restrict itself to the macroeconomic issues that fell within the purview of conditionality in the past. When domestic financial regulation and supervision are deemed inadequate, it could also recommend (or require) a parallel agreement with the international authorities in that area (see section 6 below). Conditionality should not include issues related to economic and social development strategies and institutions, which, by their very nature, should be decided by legitimate national authorities, based on broad social consensus. Indeed, the imposition, under crisis conditions, of structural and institutional changes that do not fit the national situation or the national consensus potentially generates instability—economic and political, national and international. It also tends to undermine the international consensus on which the Fund itself is built. Nor should conditionality cover areas within the purview of other international institutions and agreements, such as the World Trade Organization (WTO). Inasmuch as the Fund currently has no mandate with respect to capital account convertibility—and, as argued below, should not have it in the future with respect to developing and transition economies—, convertibility should not become a requirement for access to Fund resources, either.

Moreover, conditionality should not be used to force the adoption of a specific exchange rate regime by any country. The experience of industrial, as well as of developing and transition economies in recent decades, indicates that a great variety of regimes can be successfully managed under the current world system. They range from currency boards to total exchange rate flexibility, including intermediate regimes such as crawling pegs, exchange rate bands and dirty floats. What should be made clear to national authorities is that the exchange rate regime they adopt should be consistent with fiscal and monetary policies, which vary according to the regime chosen, and that it may require complementary measures. Thus, fixed exchange rate regimes demand a larger amount of international reserves to be viable, and intermediate regimes generally require more active intervention in the management of the capital account.

Therefore, it would appear that the best course of action in this regard is a pragmatic one.

Lastly, in order to avoid overkill, IMF should adopt general practices that allow for automatic reduction of the restrictiveness of an adjustment agreed upon with a borrowing country, if it becomes evident that the contraction of economic activity is greater than originally envisaged in the adjustment programs.

International codes of conduct, improved information, and enhanced financial supervision and regulation

A basic consensus in current discussions relates to the need for international codes of conduct in the fiscal, monetary and financial areas, for principles of sound corporate governance, for improved accounting standards, for greater availability and transparency of information regarding economic and financial data and policies, and for enhanced financial supervision and regulation. These should include international standards to combat money and asset laundering as well as corruption and tax evasion. All these initiatives should be consistent with the provisions contained in the main international human rights instruments adopted by the United Nations, particularly in the International Covenant on Economic, Social and Cultural Rights.

These existing and proposed agreements are part of a laudable process, aimed at creating greater transparency in public policies worldwide. They also play an essential role in risk management and crisis prevention. We therefore welcome initiatives by the Fund, the World Bank, the Organisation for Economic Co-operation and Development (OECD), the Bank for International Settlements (BIS), the International Organization of Securities Commissions (IOSCO) and other relevant institutions in these areas.

The role of financial regulation and supervision in risk management and crisis prevention must be particularly emphasized. A central element of a new international financial architecture is the development of regulatory and supervisory mechanisms that will better correspond to today's globalized private capital and credit markets. Such mechanisms should be global in the sense of including all countries (and particularly source countries) as well as different financial institutions and markets, so as to avoid regulatory gaps and asymmetries. However, due account should be taken of different national financial structures and traditions as regards financial regulation and supervision.

The design of minimum standards for financial regulation and supervision should go hand in hand with global regulation. An important proposal in this area is the recommendation to create a world financial authority–or a standing committee for global financial regulation—in charge of setting the necessary international standards for financial regulation and supervision and of supervising their adoption at the national level. Such an institution could evolve from existing ones, such as BIS and IOSCO. This proposal would require significant expansion of the membership of these organizations. Alternative arrangements include strengthening existing institutions with broader membership, peer review and new regional and subregional organizations.

Minimum prudential standards must be designed not only to cover bank transactions but also, in view of the progressive breakdown of the traditional compartmentalization of the financial industry's activities, to the new actors in financial markets, including hedge and mutual funds. The Core Principles for Effective Banking Supervision of the Basle Committee on Banking Supervision should be worked out more fully as regards international banking and consolidated supervision and become with some urgency an applied standard in all countries taking part in cross-border financial transactions. This would go a long way towards preventing systemic risk at the international level and controlling various risks at the country level. At the same time, a more incremental reform process should also look at standards to prevent restrictive practices and strengthen market integrity in national markets and to foster secure clearance and settlement of the growing volume of international transactions.

In the case of industrial countries, we welcome the Group of Seven declaration of 30 October 1998 on the need to examine "the implications arising from the operations of leveraged international financial organizations including hedge funds and offshore institutions" and "to encourage off-shore centres to comply with internationally agreed standards". In developing and transition countries, the implementation of the Core Principles should go hand in hand with a significant effort to improve domestic regulation and supervision of banks and other financial intermediaries. More broadly, risks related to the growth of credit, to the matching of assets and liabilities as regards both their currency denomination and time profile, and to the valuation of fixed assets as collateral during episodes of asset inflation require careful definitions in line with the Core Principles.

Changes in key macroeconomic variables—interest and exchange rates, in particular—have a large impact on the health of banks, especially in developing and transition countries, where they can fluctuate widely; the unpredictability of these variables needs to be taken into account in devising norms of prudential regulation and supervision. In particular, it suggests that capital adequacy requirements need to be higher in developing and transition economies, and that they should be raised during periods of financial euphoria to take account of the increasing financial risks intermediaries are incurring. Owing to the serious adverse macroeconomic externalities of unhedged exposures of non-financial firms, there is also a good argument for authorities of developing and transition economies to monitor their balance sheets and impose limits or matching requirements on them.

Risk-rating agencies are the main private institutions responsible for providing information to investors. Their performance during recent crises has been unsatisfactory. The inclusion of "subjective" elements in their evaluation of sovereign risks has generated a procyclical pattern of risk evaluation, which has tended to promote first excessive investment in developing and transition economies and then huge and abrupt capital outflows. In this way, instead of attenuating financial cycles—the effect that a good information system should have on markets— they have tended to intensify them. Thus sovereign risk rating should be subject to strict, objective parameters that are publicly known.

Although transparency in information and improved regulation and supervision are certainly important, they are by no means a fail-safe instrument for preventing financial crises, which can also arise from macroeconomic and other factors. Moreover, practices in regulation and supervision tend also to lag behind in a world of constant financial innovations, and they themselves may induce innovations. Furthermore, the information problems that supervisors face should not be underestimated. Therefore, any regulatory framework should give considerable weight to banks' and other intermediaries' own **internal** controls and systems of risk management.

It is clear that the principle of transparency of information should also be applied to international institutions, but evidently different standards should apply to the information generated by these institutions and to their **opinions** on countries' policies.

The preservation of the autonomy of developing and transition economies with regard to capital account issues

Across-the-board liberalization of capital account transactions has been a policy thrust that some developed countries have pursued insistently in recent years in a number of forums, including OECD, WTO and IMF. What they urge is contrary to their own historical experience, which featured long periods of capital controls and very gradual liberalization of their capital accounts in recent decades. Moreover, the current financial crisis has clearly shown that abrupt or premature liberalization of the capital account is inappropriate for developing and transition economies, a fact that is now generally recognized. Strong domestic financial systems, regulation and supervision are essential elements to guarantee appropriate liberalization. However, even with strong fundamentals in these areas, it has proved quite difficult for developing and transition economies that liberalize the capital account to adapt to the conditions generated by volatile international capital flows, which may in fact weaken or destroy those fundamentals. Boom-bust cycles are frequently associated with portfolio and short-term capital flows. Thus, the **composition** and not only the magnitude of flows play an essential role in generating external vulnerability.

Under these conditions, developing and transition economies should retain the right to impose disincentives or controls on inflows, particularly in times of capital surges, and on outflows during severe crises. A flexible approach in this regard is certainly superior to mandatory capital account convertibility. Best practices in these areas should be analysed, to be replicated when appropriate. They could include reserve requirements on short-term inflows, various taxes on capital inflows intended to discourage them, and minimum stay or liquidity requirements for investment banks and mutual funds that wish to invest in the country. They could also include complementary prudential regulations on domestic financial institutions, such as higher reserve or liquidity requirements on short-term deposits into the financial system that are managed in anti-cyclical fashion and upper limits on the prices of assets used as collateral during periods of economic expansion. Mechanisms to guarantee an adequate maturity structure for external (and even domestic) public-sector indebtedness are also crucial complementary tools. Such instruments should be regarded as **permanent**, rather than temporary devices, as long as international financial markets remain volatile and domestic economic structures are weak. Parallel reforms should be oriented towards developing long-term segments of the domestic capital markets.

Considerations regarding the autonomy of developing and transition economies to manage the capital account should therefore be incorporated in the current discussions on broadening IMF mandates to include capital account convertibility, and in possible future discussions on multilateral investment agreements, including the agreement being negotiated in the framework of OECD. It must be clear that any ambitious liberalization of the capital account of developing and transition economies would require equally ambitious reforms in other areas of the international financial architecture, particularly a true and effective "lender of last resort", an issue which, as we have seen, is not a priority in the current agenda.

*Incorporating internationally sanctioned standstill provisions into
international lending and adequate sharing of adjustment*

A standstill on debt servicing is an efficient alternative to disorderly capital flight, once a country faces severe international illiquidity. Capital flight is bad not only for debtor countries, but also for most creditors. Through chaotic exchange rate depreciation and interest rate increases, capital flight worsens the plight of domestic companies and banks, increasing the chance that what is actually a problem of illiquidity may turn into one of insolvency. Domestically, the economic and social costs of adjustment increase. Externally, the probability that creditors as a group may be repaid decreases. Moreover, bailout operations generate significant problems of moral hazard and an inequitable sharing of adjustment. Government guarantees, which are generally sought for the external liabilities of private debtors by international lenders in the renegotiations involved in these operations, increase moral hazard and equity problems. Indeed, they imply that poor sectors of society that did not share in the capital inflows will bear a significant share in adjustment costs, through cuts in social spending.

One way out of these difficulties would be to allow the introduction of standstills on external obligations and capital account convertibility and then to bring the borrowers and lenders together to reschedule debt, while providing financial assistance to support smoother functioning of the economy. Through these "bailing-in" operations, agents in the distressed country have a better chance of surmounting their problems. If financial crises are twin crises—i.e., simultaneous international illiquidity and bank insolvency—, creditors are also likely to recover a larger proportion of the value of their assets through this approach. The costs of adjustment are also more equitably distributed. Article VIII of the Articles of Agreement of the Fund could provide a statutory basis for the application of debt standstills. To avoid moral hazard on the part of borrowers, it may be advisable that standstills be sanctioned by the Fund. They could then be combined with IMF lending into arrears to make up the liquidity needed by the economy to function during the renegotiation of its debt. An alternative would be for the standstill to be declared unilaterally by the debtor country, but then submitted for approval within a specified period to an independent panel, whose sanction would give it legitimacy. This would be the equivalent in the realm of international finance to safeguard provisions in the realm of trade.

To ensure that this mechanism operates properly, two rules are essential. First of all, there should be internationally agreed "collective action clauses" in international lending. We therefore welcome the support given by the Group of Seven to the introduction of such clauses, which are essential for more orderly debt workouts. Their generalized introduction is crucial to avoid "free riding". Secondly, renegotiations should take place within a specified time limit, beyond which either the Fund or the independent panel would have the authority to determine the conditions of the debt rescheduling. Repeated debt renegotiations have, in fact, been one of the most troublesome features of the international financial landscape in recent decades and an underlying cause of the prolonged periods of crisis or slow growth in some developing and transition economies.

Design of a network of regional and subregional organizations to support the management of monetary and financial issues

Most proposals for the reform of the international financial architecture involve strengthening a few international institutions. It can be argued that stronger regional and subregional institutions can play a significant role, in terms of both the stability of the world financial system and the balance of power relations at the international level. The experience of Western Europe, from the Payments Union in the early post-war years to the European Union and the euro today, suggests that regional financial organizations and arrangements can play an essential stabilizing role. More limited experiences at a regional level, including regional and subregional development banks and a few reserve funds, indicate that they can also play an important role in a new international financial architecture, both in crisis management and in finance for development. Strong regional reserve funds would at least partially deter would-be speculators from attacking the currencies of individual countries and thus, among other dire effects, from threatening regional trade and financial relations. They could also supplement IMF funds in times of difficulty. Thus, on both the demand and the supply sides, they could reduce the need for IMF support.

Most regional financial institutions are small, where they do exist, and thus have limited effectiveness, but an investment in their development would certainly pay off in the long run. The design of the new architecture could thus introduce special incentives to develop such institutions. For instance, common reserve funds could be given special automatic access to IMF financing and/or a share in the allocation of SDRs, proportional to the paid-in resources. Indeed, in the long run, IMF could be visualized as part of a network of regional reserve funds, and its operation could then concentrate on relations with these reserve funds rather than on support to specific countries in difficulties.

Moreover, regional institutions and peer review could also play a central role in surveillance, both of macroeconomic policies and of domestic financial regulation and supervision. Indeed, such surveillance and peer review could be more acceptable to countries than that of a single, powerful international institution. It would contribute towards a more balanced globalization.

Complementary actions in the areas of finance for development and outstanding external debt issues

During the current crisis, the focus has been on countries with large financing needs that strain the resources of multilateral institutions. It is important that the attention given to these widely publicized cases and the large volume of IMF and bilateral funds that have been committed to them do not crowd out funding for, and international attention to, the problems of the poorest countries and hence to the financing of the Fund's Enhanced Structural Adjustment Facility (ESAF), the International Development Association (IDA) and the heavily indebted poor countries (HIPC) initiative. Nor should they be allowed to crowd out funding and attention to smaller countries that may be facing financial crises.

The inability of the Fund to mobilize all the resources needed for the rescue of countries in financial distress has required it to arrange financing from other sources, including the World Bank and the regional development banks. These institutions were not designed to provide liquidity to countries facing short-term external financing difficulties. A continuation of this practice would impair their capacity to fulfil their fundamental mission, which is to cater to the long-term development financing needs of countries with inadequate access to private markets.

Special attention should be given to safeguarding the access of the poorest countries to long-term resources, at the Fund, the World Bank and the regional development banks. Accelerated implementation of the HIPC initiative is also a world priority. The development banks could contribute to the alleviation of the worst effects of the crisis by providing financial assistance for the establishment or strengthening of social safety nets in both poor and middle-income countries. Strong protection for the poor during crises, through the design of effective safety nets, is still more a matter of rhetoric than of practice. Development banks also have a clear countercyclical role to play in world financial crises, a role that could be enhanced through innovations enabling them to work more actively to "crowd in" private-sector financing by rapidly disbursing co-financing funds or guaranteeing new debt issues of developing and transition economies. New, more effective rules on guarantees issued by these institutions must be designed to ensure this result.

The interdependence of the components of a new architecture

The goal of redesigning the international monetary and financial system is to harness the potential of private international financial flows to the service of stability and growth in the world economy. In order to pursue this objective effectively, it is important that the various components of the architecture be addressed at the same time. Indeed, these components are interrelated, and putting one or some of them in place in isolation will have limited impact in reducing the disruption caused.

Thus, improvements in supervision and regulation of financial firms are preventive measures that can reduce the incidence of crises and hence the need for IMF resources to cure them. However, since supervision and regulation are far from foolproof, financial crises and contagion will remain problems that need to be dealt with at the international level. Macroeconomic coordination and surveillance are essential to manage both inflationary and deflationary situations, which lie behind boom-bust financial cycles. Regional and subregional institutions could play an essential role as complements to IMF funding and surveillance activities, as well as in surveillance of domestic financial regulation and supervision.

Likewise, new financing facilities and standstill provisions are not substitutes for better regulation and supervision of financial institutions. Rather, all the above measures, along with domestic measures to deal with short-term capital movements, are mutually complementary. Rules regarding internationally sanctioned standstills are also no substitute for the establishment of an IMF facility to deal with contagion. Standstills have the unintended consequence of shutting off borrowers from access to capital markets for some time. Just as countries have legitimate differences in their preferences for integration into international financial markets, they would also differ in their willingness to call a standstill. The least willing are likely to be those whose liquidity crises are to a great extent the result of contagion and which have a high degree of integration into international financial markets. Therefore, a well-functioning international financial system will require both standstills and institutional innovation at the IMF.

Standstills cannot be implemented without regulations on capital outflows. In effect, capital controls will become indispensable when a country cannot meet its external payments because of a run on its currency. Hence, the recognition of the need for diversity with regard to approaches to the capital account cannot be divorced from the establishment of norms to deal with crisis situations. Reliance on any one or even a few of these proposals would hardly bring about the changes needed to both prevent and manage crises or lead to greater equity in power relations. There is an evident need for a comprehensive and well-timed approach, in order to generate more balanced and hence sustainable globalization.

III. "Functioning of the international financial markets and stability in finance for development"

Second special high-level meeting of the Economic and Social Council with the Bretton Woods institutions, New York, April 29, 1999

Note of Introduction

The second special high-level meeting of the Economic and Social Council with the Bretton Woods institutions was held on 29 April 1999. The meeting brought together key policy makers in the areas of development cooperation, foreign affairs and finance, on a topic closely tied to the globalization process.

The discussions, while still drawing the lessons of the Asian crisis, addressed broader issues related to the theme of finance for development, such as the external debt of developing countries. Participants also examined the mechanics of cooperation between the United Nations and the Bretton Woods Institutions, in particular the relationship between two major initiatives aimed at close coordination of development efforts in the field: one of the United Nations, the United Nations Development Assistance Framework, and one of the World Bank, the Comprehensive Development Framework.

The panelists were Carlo Azeglio Ciampi, Minister of the Treasury of Italy, Chairman of the Interim Committee of the Board of Governors on the International Monetary Fund; Tarrin Nimmanahaeminda, Minister of Finance of Thailand, Chairman of the Development Committee; Carlos Saito, Adviser to the President of the Central Bank of Peru, Vice-President of the Deputies of the Group of Twenty-Four (G-24); and Mats Karlsson, State Secretary for International Development Cooperation, representing Sweden as the country chairing the Group of Ten (G-10). The meeting was opened by the Deputy Secretary-General of the United Nations and chaired by the President of the Council.

Functioning of international financial markets and stability in financing for development
Note by the Secretary-General, 29 April 1999

As a result of the special high-level meeting of the Economic and Social Council with the Bretton Woods institutions in April 1998, the General Assembly in resolution 53/172 of 15 December 1998 invited the

Secretary-General to support the Council in the organization of a second such dialogue in 1999. The Assembly in resolution 53/169 of 15 December 1998 suggested that the dialogue address ways and means to optimize the benefits and minimize the negative consequences of globalization and interdependence, particularly for the developing countries. In the light of this request and in order to provide some continuity with the 1998 meeting, the theme selected for the present meeting is the functioning of international financial markets and stability in financing for development. The present note identifies some of the questions that participants might wish to address within this general framework.

Measures to promote recovery in the developing and transition economies

As the fallout from the initial financial crisis in Thailand enters its third year, weak international trade and the negligible improvement in private financial inflows mean that most developing and transition economies continue to face a tight external payments constraint. Such an international economic environment is not propitious for adjustment and economic growth.

In this light, the following questions might be addressed:

- What additional measures should be taken to improve the growth prospects of developing and transition economies, including accelerating the return to former levels of income per capita in crisis-stricken countries?
- How can the vulnerability of developing and transition economies to the contagion processes that operated in 1997–1998 be reduced?

Financial architecture and financial flows for development

The depth and breadth of the crisis and the shortcomings that it has exposed have given rise to numerous suggestions from many quarters for reform of the international monetary and financial "architecture". The Interim Committee of the Board of Governors on the International Monetary System (International Monetary Fund (IMF)) will have discussed a number of such reforms at its meeting in April 1999. For its part, the United Nations Secretariat has identified a set of proposals for reform.[1]

In the light of these and various other proposals, the following questions might be addressed:

- What progress has been made in the reform of the international financial architecture and what remains to be done?

---

1 Report of the Executive Committee on Economic and Social Affairs of the United Nations, entitled "Towards a new international financial architecture", 21 January 1999 reprinted above.

- Will the necessary reforms materialize if the perceived threats to the system diminish?
- What national and international actions can be taken to increase the level and stability of longer-term flows of development finance?

International policy on external debt

At its launching, the Heavily Indebted Poor Countries (HIPC) Debt Initiative of the World Bank and IMF was recognized as a breakthrough in addressing the debt problems of this group of countries. However, the past two years have seen civil society and non-governmental organizations increasingly question international policy regarding the treatment of the external debt of many of the low-income countries. In the past few months, several creditor Governments have floated proposals for deeper and quicker debt relief for heavily indebted poor countries. Meanwhile, the World Bank and IMF have been undertaking a survey of the views of the public on international debt policy and the findings will have been discussed at the Interim and Development Committees in April. At the G-7/G-8 World Economic Summit in Cologne in June, participants are expected to revise their policies in this area.

In the light of these developments, the following questions might be addressed:

- Should there be outright debt cancellation for heavily indebted poor countries?
- What mechanisms should be used to secure the financial resources necessary to provide debt relief, particularly on multilateral debt?
- Should debt relief continue to be seen as a quid pro quo for the adoption of appropriate policies?
- Should the resources made available through debt relief be redirected to human needs, such as basic education and health services, and if so, how?

Economic crisis and social policy initiatives

The World Summit for Social Development in Copenhagen raised expectations that substantial and rapid global progress would be made in rolling back poverty and unemployment and promoting social integration. However, the financial and economic crises have erased much of the progress that was made in reducing poverty levels in South-East Asia in previous years, there has been negligible success in reducing poverty in Africa and Latin America in the 1990s, and poverty rates in a number of transition economies have returned to levels unknown for decades.

Recent experience has focused attention on the need to address the negative social consequences of financial crises and their aftermath. At the same time, greater attention is now being given to the role and importance of the provision of basic social services in the development process.[2] Reflecting this increased determination to meet social needs and objectives, a draft set of "general principles of good practice in social policy" has been prepared by the World Bank and is expected to be discussed by the Development Committee at its April meeting.

In the light of these developments, the following questions might be addressed:

- How can the international goals established at the Copenhagen Summit be better integrated into national stabilization and adjustment programmes?
- What additional measures, beyond those contained in the Programme of Action of the World Summit for Social Development, adopted at Copenhagen, need to be taken at the national and international levels in order to reduce the social consequences of future crises?
- How should international assistance in crisis situations ensure that the social impact is mitigated?

Further cooperation between the United Nations and the Bretton Woods institutions

The second joint meeting between the Economic and Social Council and the Bretton Woods institutions represents one of a number of further steps that have been taken to increase cooperation, at all levels, among the United Nations, IMF and the World Bank. Both Member States and the organizations themselves recognize the need for this cooperation to be further broadened and deepened. In addition to continuing the recent initiatives, some further developments provide additional opportunities for cooperation.

The General Assembly has embarked on a process that is to lead by 2001 to a high-level international intergovernmental consideration of financing for development before the end of 2001.[3] An ad hoc open-ended working group is required to make recommendations to the Assembly at its next session on the form, scope and agenda of such a consideration. Many of the issues being considered under this rubric lie within the purview of the Bretton Woods institutions. The following question could therefore be addressed:

---

2 Report of the World Summit for Social Development, Copenhagen, 6–12 March 1995 (United Nations publication, Sales No. E.96.IV.8), chap. I, resolution 1, annex II.

3 See General Assembly resolutions 52/179 of 18 December 1997 and 53/173, of 15 December 1998. Further information on the financing-for-development process is available on the Internet at www.un.org/esa/analysis/ffd

- How might the Bretton Woods institutions be linked with discussions in the United Nations on financing for development?

In his 21 January 1999 memorandum to the Executive Board, the President of the World Bank proposed the elaboration of a Comprehensive Development Framework (CDF).[4] The objective of the CDF is to develop a comprehensive and holistic approach to the sequencing of policies, programmes and projects and the pacing of reforms at the country level. In the light of this proposal, the following questions could be addressed:

- How will the CDF relate to the United Nations Development Assistance Framework (UNDAF) which is also intended to facilitate the design and coordination of country-driven, collaborative and coherent development programmes?
- How should IMF programmes be related to the CDF and UNDAF?

Opening Statement by the President of ECOSOC, Ambassador Francesco Paolo Fulci

Our meeting this year has attracted participation from Ministers and high-level officials from Capitals even greater than last year. Persistent economic crises in the world continues to underscore the need for a comprehensive view of the reform of the international financial system and of the problems of development. The Economic and Social Council, as envisaged by the founding fathers of the United Nations, appears to be the most appropriate, the natural forum to promote dialogue and build confidence on world economic and social issues. Our meeting is another step forward in this direction.

The issues we shall discuss today, the "functioning of the international financial markets and the stability of financing for development" are all topics very much on the minds of Government leaders and policy-makers everywhere. Financial markets' stability is indeed a "must" for development to advance in an orderly fashion. Never in the past has there been such awareness that no financial architecture can stand unless it is based also on solid social foundations. In the end, the fight against poverty world-wide is much more than a noble ideal of human solidarity. It is an act of enlightened self-interest, probably the best insurance policy to safeguard the well-being of those who are fortunate enough to enjoy it already.

---

4   Available on the Internet at http://www.worldbank.org/cdf/cdf.pdf

Seen in this perspective, it is very disturbing to note that the gap between rich and poor is increasing not decreasing. As it is disturbing to note that the overall Official Development Assistance has just reached its lowest level in fifty years, measured in terms of the GDP percentage of developed countries. This trend is dangerous. It must be reversed. Relief should be given particularly to the poorest of countries, to free them from unsustainable debt levels and to make more resources available to meet the most elementary human needs of their populations. Luckily, encouraging signals in this direction have been received from the just concluded Washington meetings. I am sure we are all anxious to learn more about them directly from the key players, who are with us this morning.

The President of the World Bank, in his press conference before those meetings, stressed very eloquently that "more can be done" in terms of debt reduction and poverty alleviation. I hope, President Wolfensohn, that soon we may say "more *will* be done."

ECOSOC is ready to help in any possible way or manner, especially by raising awareness of the situation. In its July meeting in Geneva the highest priority will be devoted to the goal of poverty eradication. Soon we shall submit to the Council the draft of a Manifesto to Eradicate Poverty, aimed at increasing public attention to this fundamental challenge of our times.

Before concluding, let me recall an important initiative launched by the General Assembly last year: the promotion of a high-level intergovernmental event on the issue of financing for development. The two Co-Vice-Chairmen of the Working Group engaged in preparing the initiative, Ambassadors Sucharipa of Austria and Sharma of India, are submitting a short paper for the information of the participants in this meeting, which I ask now to distribute. Both Ambassadors will be glad to answer any questions you may have for them.

Finally, allow me to draw your attention on the limited time available for our dialogue today. There will be first presentations by our panelists of ten minutes each and then four rounds of questions or observations. Please be brief in your statements, so that all can speak and all get a response. Without further ado, I now give the floor to the Deputy Secretary-General, Madame Louise Frechette.

Summary of the statements and the discussions

LOUISE FRÉCHETTE, Deputy Secretary-General, said the effects of the great financial crisis were still present and it would be a grave mistake to return to business as usual. Now was not the time for complacency. For anyone tempted by complacency, she would note three simple things: the rate of growth of the world economy had been slowing down, and the down-side risks remained significant; in many developing countries, the crisis had reversed, in a matter of months, the social gains of several decades and its impact would continue to be felt for some time; and a large part of the developing world remained on the margins of the global market and could not enjoy the potential benefits of the liberalized world economy.

Faced with that reality, the priorities should be a reversal of the decline in the rate of growth of the world economy; completion of work on the establishment of a new global financial architecture; helping developing countries build the capacity to engage in the global economy on a sustainable basis; ensuring that sufficient resources were available for the task; and continuing the reinforcement of cooperation and coordination among all the stakeholders in the development process.

She said that, although progress had been made in strengthening the international system, much remained to be done to improve the ability of governments and international agencies to reduce instability in private capital markets, and so prevent the recurrence of the kind of crises confronted last year. It would be most unfortunate if the political will to make tough decisions were allowed to fade. The United Nations had put forward a number of ideas for reforming the system.

The issue of governance of the strengthened system was especially important, she said. Neither its design nor its management must be the prerogative of only a few States. Liberalization was not in and of itself sufficient to achieve that goal. Developing countries also needed to put in place the appropriate policies and mechanisms to provide economic security and social welfare for all their people. In turn, the prescriptions offered by the multilateral economic and financial institutions should be supportive of those aims, she said.

The United Nations welcomed the increased attention the Bretton Woods institutions were now giving to social issues. The results of the major United Nations conferences earlier in the decade should serve as the common frame of reference. The achievement of the goals set out by those conferences, particularly those related to the eradication of poverty, should become an integral part of any development strategy.

She said that the role of trade and private investment in the development process was now well recognized, but ODA would continue to play a critical role in many of the poorer countries. It was, therefore, imperative that its decline be reversed and further steps taken to relieve the burden of the external debt of the highly indebted countries.

She welcomed the recent proposals to expand the HIPC Debt Initiative and to further reduce official bilateral debt. She stressed, however, that action on debt should not be taken at the expense of official development assistance, and she welcomed proposals to finance debt relief for the poorest countries by the sale of IMF gold holdings. In addition, she said other new and additional resources should be found to achieve the desired results.

She said that to achieve sustainable development, a holistic approach was required—one that attempted to integrate economic, social, political and environmental goals. That was why, she said, the Secretary-General had launched the United Nations Development Assistance Framework. Noting a similar initiative undertaken by the President of the World Bank, she said all initiatives must complement and support one another.

CARLO AZEGLIO CIAMPI, Minister of the Treasury of Italy and Chairman of the Interim Committee of the Board of Governors of the IMF, said that two days ago the Committee had taken stock of the state of the world economy. It had discussed ways to make countries more re-silient to crises, to better equip them to participate fully in a global fi-nancial marketplace, and ways to make the international community help countries more effectively deal with those crises. Also discussed was the situation facing those countries that were not participating fully in the globalized world—the very poor, the heavily indebted, and those emerg-ing from ravaging conflicts.

Elaborating on the way in which the Committee's work was develop-ing, he said that several innovations had been introduced in a pragmatic way. The meeting had been prepared by a group of deputies, direct col-laborators of the members. That had increased the efficiency of the Committee's work. Discussions had been more lively and more focused. There had been a true and constructive dialogue, even on issues that had come to the Committee's agenda with short notice, such as the unfortu-nate events related to the Kosovo war.

The Committee intended to continue its search for greater efficiency, while involving a broader range of countries in the discussion, he contin-ued. Maximizing efficiency and representation was achieved through the system of constituencies, on which the IMF and the World Bank were based. Such a system could be improved, particularly to take into account the emerging realities of the world economy, but it remained valid, by providing the necessary legitimacy to the actions of the international fi-nancial institutions.

A lot had happened since last year's meeting, he continued. Contagion had spread from one end of the globe to another. Major crises had erupted in Russia and Brazil. Economic activity in some industrial countries had turned out to be weaker than expected. Although the worst of the crisis seemed to have passed, the world economy was nevertheless far from growing at its full potential. Policies had to be geared towards sustainable growth, especially in Europe and Japan, so as to provide a stimulus to the world economy.

The main question now was how to mitigate the impact of crises and how to prevent future ones, he said. After months of discussion in the official and private sectors and in the academic community, several important goals had been achieved by the international financial institutions. A Contingent Credit Line (CCL) had been established by the Fund, to prevent and contain contagion. That facility provided the incentive for countries to pursue sound and sustainable policies to maintain stability. To be eligible, countries had to adopt sustainable exchange policies, implement sound debt management, adhere to international debt standards and involve the private sector in financing their external borrowing requirements.

Significant progress had been achieved in developing, disseminating and monitoring the implementation of internationally recognized standards, he continued, particularly concerning international reserves and related data.

Codes on transparency of fiscal, monetary and financial policies were being developed, through a broad collaborative effort with other international institutions and bodies. The Fund would use those standards in its surveillance activity.

Work was being pursued, in the Fund and in other forums, to devise practical ways to involve the private sector in ensuring stable financial flows towards emerging and less developed countries, he said. The Fund had cooperated closely with the World Bank and the Asian Development Bank to put in place as quickly as possible social sector policies that would limit unemployment, increase income transfers, and broaden social safety nets. At the same time, countries had a responsibility to allocate resources towards education, health and other social services, and not on wasteful military expenditures.

In discussions on architecture and globalized financial markets, those countries that risked being excluded from the global economy should not be forgotten, he said. The Committee endorsed the Fund's continued support under the HIPC Debt Initiative. It had asked the Fund and the Bank to work towards a framework that provided for deeper relief to a broader group of countries, in a way that strengthened the incentives for adoption of strong reform programmes, and fostered the respect of human rights. The Committee also discussed ways in which the IMF could enhance its support for those countries emerging from conflict, including through more concessional resources with longer maturities.

With regard to the human tragedy unfolding in Kosovo, bilateral and multilateral donors were responding to the humanitarian crisis, he said. The international community had to help the affected countries address the damage done to their economies and to sustain the economic reform efforts. In that regard, the international financial institutions would play an important role. The Committee endorsed the need for a rapid, substantial and coordinated response by the international community to the economic consequences of the crisis in the region.

It had also agreed that the financing of balance of payments and budget costs in affected countries should be provided in highly concessional terms, he added. The Committee asked the Fund and the Bank to continue their work in coordinating the international response to the economic impact of the crisis, in close cooperation with other interested agencies and donors.

In conclusion, he said that financial globalization must work in the interest of the people and not vice-versa. At its meeting two days ago, the Committee had broadly endorsed the activities performed by the Fund in such difficult times. It had outlined the direction for its further work. He was confident that those measures, together with the activities of the Bank and the United Nations, would provide the pillars for a stronger, more effective and coordinated action of the international financial institutions.

TARRIN NIMMANAHAEMINDA, Chairman of the Development Committee of the IMF and World Bank and Minister of Finance of Thailand, said he would concentrate on two subjects—international policy for external debt, and economic crisis and social policy. The main concern of the Development Committee was the HIPC Debt Initiative. Progress on that Initiative achieved over the past two and a half years was appreciated. More than $6 billion of debt relief had been provided for seven countries, but it was also clear that the results fell short of what was needed. Thus, it was encouraging to hear creditor nations offer to take additional steps bilaterally to ease debt, and to examine options that would make the Initiative broader, deeper and faster.

Moreover, ministers believed there should be a close link between debt reduction and helping countries achieve sustainable development and poverty reduction, he said. They wanted reforms to have a "pro-poor" growth focus. The Committee also endorsed principles that should guide any changes in the HIPC Debt Initiative. Those included recognition of the need to preserve the integrity of international financial institutions.

New financing for poor countries should be on a grant basis or concessional, he continued. Debt relief alone would not be sufficient to reach the goal of reducing poverty, but trade and aid were also needed. The sharp decline in ODA was viewed with concern.

The Committee's last meeting asked the World Bank to take the lead in developing a set of "Principles and Good Practice in Social Policy", he said. The Bank and United Nations agencies had been in consultation and a paper that included the issues involved in implementation of such principles in individual country settings had been produced. Reflecting on the lessons of the recent financial crisis, the ministers had reiterated the importance of helping countries bolster their social policies and institutions, and stressed the need for the Bank to concentrate on translating broad principles into practical country-specific results. The stress now given to implementation and developing best practices was seen as the Bank's comparative advantage.

Regarding Thailand, he said that social policy must: be consistent with Thai values and culture; be sustainable after the crisis, in fiscal and governance terms; and deepen the reform agenda's emphasis on transparency, people participation and community development. A set of two-track policies were consequently developed. The first track strengthened government programmes, particularly related to alleviation of unemployment. The second track was based on involving civil society and local communities as full partners in social programmes.

In concluding, he said it was clear that sustainable economic recovery for those countries in financial crisis depended on coherent and effective social policies, as much as on economic reform measures.

MATS KARLSSON, State Secretary for International Development Cooperation of Sweden and Chairman of the Group of 10, said that only with an enhanced degree of global economic governance could common objectives be reached. A stable and favourable economic environment was needed to enable each nation to pursue and enjoy its potential. Agreed and evolving norms and rules should ensure benefits from economic integration for all. The partnerships must be based on a sense of common responsibility and solidarity.

This year's "World Development Indicators", which had been released by the World Bank a few days ago, confirmed that, despite a generation of significant progress in the developing world, the international community was not making sufficient progress in eradicating poverty, he continued. The objective of reducing world poverty by half by the year 2015 had been born in the world conferences of the current decade. The consensus on what it meant in terms of practical policy was today greater among nations than before. It had been well developed by the United

Nations, the World Bank and the IMF. Donor nations had drawn conclusions and committed themselves in that respect.

He said that the functioning of international financial markets and stability in financing for development were prerequisites for reaching development objectives. Mobilizing resources for development was still a tough and complex task. Globalization challenged the international community to fight global and regional public "bads". There was also a rapidly expanding demand for the provision of global public "goods", from the mundane everyday issues to knowledge and security, he said.

Continuing, he welcomed the ongoing process to review the international financial architecture, which needed to have a holistic approach with a focus on both macroeconomic and financial issues, as well as on social and structural issues. It was necessary to develop instruments for preventing crises, rather than just measures to manage them. The specific needs of emerging economies and nations with weak institutions must be addressed.

Stable financial markets were needed to facilitate the task of securing adequate financial flows for development, he continued. It was necessary to bring together the competence—which in many countries was divided between ministries of finance, economy, trade, planning, foreign affairs, development and other public bodies—to see what could be done to focus substantial instruments and resources on the development objective. There was also a need to relate more clearly to the private sector. With better institutional cooperation between the United Nations, the multilateral development banks, the European Union and bilateral donors, better partnerships with developing countries could be developed.

Development assistance alone could not create sustainable development, he said. The effects of domestic saving and investment and international trade had a much larger potential. That needed to be more fully recognized in the current process, as well as in the forthcoming round of negotiations in the World Trade Organization (WTO).

Additional debt relief must be an integral part of the total effort to achieve human development objectives. The HIPC Debt Initiative had been a major step forward, but the time had come for its revision. Countries needed to be given options for viable exits from the debt trap. His Government encouraged all creditor countries to cancel all ODA debt. It was crucial that new financing be provided on highly concessional terms, within a framework of a well-defined national debt strategy. He also welcomed the Comprehensive Development Framework recently launched by the World Bank and the efforts of the United Nations, and in particular its Development Group, for a more integrated and strengthened United Nations contribution at the country level.

CARLOS SAITO, Adviser to the President of the Central Bank of Peru and Vice-President of the Group of 24, which represents the interests of developing countries in negotiations on international monetary matters, said that at the Group's meeting on 26 April, three main points were covered: the international monetary system; strengthening that system; and financing for development. On the first point, concern was expressed at the direction the world economy was taking, especially the low rates of growth. Members expressed the need for the industrialized countries to open their markets wider to imports from the developing countries.

As for the strengthening of the international monetary system, he said that there was a need to avoid and contain high crises. Developed and developing countries should develop a working group on the matter. Regarding the Contingent Credit Line, there had to be a clear criteria for its eligibility and it should offer incentives. In addition, the Lender of Last Resort Initiative needed to be studied in greater detail.

The Group was satisfied with the possibilities of ensuring private sector involvement in preventing and resolving crises, he continued. Integration into international financial markets remained a fundamental goal for developing countries. Regarding the liberalization of capital accounts, the specific characteristics of each country had to be taken into account. The operational procedures of development committees had to be improved to enhance their effectiveness.

On the third point, financing for development, proposals for greater debt relief, including the HIPC Debt Initiative, had been discussed, he said. The Group was satisfied at the growing consensus in that area. They agreed that it would require greater resources, the equitable redistribution of the burden and alternative mechanisms for funding. The Group was also concerned at the lessening inflows of ODA. The Fund's granting of additional funds for post-conflict countries was welcome and the Group was gratified with the World Bank's initiatives in that area. Expanding the definition of countries in conflict was also encouraged.

The Group urged the Bretton Woods institutions and donors to provide the resources necessary to build capacity in Africa, he added. Regarding the integrated development framework, concern about planning capacity and costs incurred by lending countries was expressed. The Group agreed with the core principles of promoting social development. The United Nations organs had to coordinate the implementation of those principles. In conclusion, he said that the Group felt that the United Nations initiative for holding a high-level forum for financing for development before the end of the year 2001 was very important.

Discussion

BHARRAT JAGDEO, Minister of Finance of Guyana, speaking on behalf of the "Group of 77" developing countries and China, said that while developing countries were generally pleased with the broad statements on the issues, they were concerned about the design of initiatives to give effect to those statements. They often felt excluded and unable to participate in the design processes. What, apart from existing consultation mechanisms, could the IMF and the World Bank do to ensure that developing countries, and especially small developing countries, could better participate in the processes and thereby gain ownership of the initiatives? he asked.

Developing countries were also concerned about implementation, he said. Countries that did not pose systemic risks did not have access to higher levels at the two international financial institutions. He asked how developing countries, especially smaller ones, could get access to the higher levels of the two institutions, if they felt issues with which they were concerned were not given attention.

The $6 million of debt relief previously mentioned had been committed, but was not all implemented, he said. The HIPC Debt Initiative used a sustainability threshold of debt-to-revenue of 280 per cent. One case about to come before them involved a country with in excess of 400 per cent debt-to-revenue. He asked how that particular case would be handled. Finally, he said he understood that proposals had been made to use service-to-revenue as a measure of sustainability. What were the views of the financial institutions on that proposal? he asked.

HEIDEMARIE WIECZOREK-ZEUL, Federal Minister for Economic Cooperation and Development of Germany, speaking on behalf of the European Union, said that globalization brought with it great opportunities for worldwide development, but also harboured considerable risks. Internal and external peace in the next century depended to a large extent on tackling those risks.

She said that, while a whole range of innovations aimed at increasing transparency and keeping the volatility of financial flows in check had been launched and were now under way, that was not a guarantee of more stability in financing for development. Despite improved rules and supervision of international capital transactions, there would be no guarantee of stable financial flows. Further, only if the appropriate safeguards were established at national institutional level could investor confidence be restored and flows of private capital thus resumed. In addition, flows of private capital were concentrated in a small group of countries and a limited number of sectors within those countries. In particular, poor countries received inadequate financing.

The European Union remained prepared to lend adequate support in times of financial crisis, she said. Countries should not, however, be providing public funds to cover the risks of private investors, nor should they assume the function of the international financial institutions. Above all, it was the responsibility of the IMF to offer liquidity assistance, while the multilateral development banks were responsible for long-term development financing aimed at achieving structural change.

Yet, international financing was only one aspect of financing for development, she said. In many partner countries it played a secondary role to domestic financing. Unless sufficient domestic financing was available for productive investment, development could not be sustained in the long term without an excessive burden of debt again being accumulated. Efforts must be undertaken in both the public and the private sectors to, first, stabilize state revenue through a fair taxation system and efficient tax administration, and, second, to mobilize more domestic capital by means of a private financing sector, subject to effective bank supervisors.

She said financing for development meant that the recipient countries themselves must create the fundamental safeguards needed to ensure that financing would indeed have a positive impact on development. Those safeguards included: rules on competition; financial sector reform; transparency; rule of law; a public spending sector that made adequate provision for society's poor; core labour standards; and democratic control of State action.

ALAN P. LARSON, Assistant Secretary of State for Economic and Business Affairs of the United States, said that the dynamism of the world economy had brought hope to millions of people all over the world, but it had also produced shocks and imposed hardships. It was important to address the political and social foundations of the world economy. Families were a fundamental unit in the economy, and they needed to have confidence that there would be social safety nets. He wanted to know how the United Nations, the IMF and the World Bank could work together to ensure that a high priority was placed on investing in people, job creation, active exchange of information and so on.

What more could be done so citizens could benefit from accessible and accountable institutions? he asked. If the goal was to ensure greater stability in the flow of capital to the emerging markets, how was it possible to ensure stability for investors who wanted to make long-term commitments? What could the international community do to identify and implement policies to make those markets appealing to investors? In terms of fostering democracy, what could be done to give citizens a voice in the decisions that affected their lives? Further, he asked, what more could be done so that families in the poorest of nations could be sure that their countries would benefit from measures aimed at debt relief, environmental protection, child survival and education? The United States, along with many other countries, had made proposals on how to best accomplish those goals.

ANDREI G. SHAPOVALIANTS, Minister of the Economy of the Russian Federation, said that international financial institutions in their present form had proven incapable of preventing crisis. The most serious problem was the fact that assistance after a crisis was granted on the same strict terms as before it. Such an approach needed to be revised and he wanted to know what steps were being planned in that direction.

His country had not received timely financial support after the crisis, he continued. After the first period of recovery, priority should be given to restructuring the banking system. His country was counting on the support of the international community in that respect. He also wanted to know what measures were being undertaken to strengthen the banking system of the countries affected by the crisis. Regarding the international architecture of the financial system, he stressed that it lacked an early warning system and prevention mechanisms in case of crisis. Proposals by seven major industrial countries had sketched the main lines of reform, but further work was needed. It was essential that other interested institutions took part in that work. The report of the United Nations contained interesting suggestions and they should be considered in a careful manner.

HIKMET ULUGBAY, Deputy Prime Minister and Minister of State of Turkey, said that today the world was challenged by abrupt, large-scale cross-border movements of capital, whose effects, particularly on exchange and interest rates, were a major concern for emerging market countries. Capital outflows from emerging market countries had been both cause and effect of numerous recent crises. Those countries had needed substantial financial assistance to redress their external imbalances, and dramatic changes to the present financial paradigm were needed. Otherwise, capital movements would continue to trigger contagious effects, which jeopardized world growth and prosperity.

That was basically the reason the international economic and financial communities should busy themselves with revising the policies and priorities of the financial system, he said. The establishment of the Financial Stability Forum, with some 33 countries as members, was a reassuring sign of growing cooperation and dialogue among the most threatened countries and interested groups. His Government also encouraged the cooperation between the United Nations Commission on International Trade Law (UNCITRAL) and the Bretton Woods institutions for the improvement of insolvency regimes.

He said that the scarcity of domestic savings and inadequacy of voluntary savings in developing countries made it crucial for them to attract a sufficient quantity of foreign savings. Establishing a proper finance system, and carefully sequenced capital account liberalization, was now more important than ever. In addition, reforms aimed at improving social conditions should have a high priority. Investing in human capital, especially education and health, would pay off in the longer term and become the most important pillar of sustainable development. In the next century, the only way for developing nations to achieve sustainable gains would be by establishing an appropriate infrastructure through efficient use of their human resources.

A related issue placed on the agenda by the recent crisis was globalization's effects on social protection, he said. The crisis had illuminated the need for emerging economies to protect their populations against incidental damage due to globalization. Any blueprint for reform must recognize and emphasize the basic nature of the requirements for social protection and the enhancement of human capital.

FRANCISCO SOBERON, Minister, President of the Central Bank of Cuba, said that it was important to discuss more transparency with regard to information, and better banking supervision. He wanted to know what the prospects were for regulating the activities of certain actors in the world financial system. His second question concerned the international strategy for debt coverage. The conditions of the HIPC Debt Initiative had to be clearly spelled out and perhaps extended to middle income economies.

TREVOR MANUEL, Finance Minister of South Africa, said that pronouncing the crisis as over only introduced a new crisis into the debate. Today, the developed countries were awash with capital. He welcomed the initiative taken by the World Bank on the Comprehensive Development Framework and called for wider support for it. While the HIPC Debt Initiative made economic sense, it was necessary to accelerate that process. Debt relief was often too little, too late. In the campaign for debt relief, a sound appeal for higher levels of political and financial commitment from the developed countries was needed. Capacity-building was the way forward.

AHMAD KAMAL (Pakistan) said the visible intensification of dialogue between the Bretton Woods institutions and the United Nations was to be appreciated. Initiatives had been announced to cancel the debt of heavily indebted poor countries, and those were encouraging initiatives, but external debt needed to be addressed in a more comprehensive and holistic manner. Piecemeal responses to selected countries might not contribute to the overall goals of development of developing countries. He asked whether it would be possible to consider a global plan of action for debt cancellation, with a primary focus on heavily indebted poor countries, but which would also aim to reduce the debt of other developing countries.

Regarding greater cooperation for financing for development, he said there had been active participation of the Bretton Woods institutions in the United Nations working group on financing for development. He asked about the possibility of establishing a joint United Nations-Bretton Woods task force to provide inputs to the preparatory process for the impending high-level event on financing for development.

Mr. CIAMPI, Chairman of the Interim Committee, said, in response to several questions, that the recent meeting of the Interim Committee had focused on the problems of the poorest countries. The importance of speeding up all initiatives had been recognized, and the resources were now in place, initiatives were well advanced, and the process was close to practical conclusion.

The Italian Government had decided to write off all aid and commercial credits of countries with a per capita income of less than $300 per year, he said. That initiative would involve $1.6 billion of credits and about 40 countries. The only criteria were respect for human rights and abstinence from conflicts.

On the new architecture, there were two tracks, he said. One was to make the operations of the Interim Committee more efficient, by employing all the possibilities of the existing institutional framework. The second was a proposal for institutional change that was under discussion. At the next IMF meeting in Washington in October, he hoped that some agreement on the proposals would be reached. The criteria for any institutional changes should be greater efficiency, more coordination among all the institutions concerned with connected problems, and more focus on preventing, rather than managing, crises.

JAMES WOLFENSOHN, President of the World Bank, in response to the comments of the representative of Guyana on behalf of the Group of 77 and China, said that he was surprised about access problems. In both the Bank and the IMF there was now a country director responsible for each country, who should be able to ensure adequate access. If they did not, he suggested States call him directly.

On the HIPC Debt Initiative, he said it had been correctly stated that debt services had already been agreed upon for about $6 billion, and $1.4 billion in debt reduction had already taken place. There was a phasing-in process agreed to by each country. He believed that it was on track, and by the end of the year another eight or more countries might have qualified. The owner countries were strongly inclined to increase the initiative. Two years ago the initiative did not exist. Where once it had been hard to sell debt relief to his "shareholders", they were now suggesting increasing it.

MICHEL CAMDESSUS, Managing Director of the IMF, said in response to the statement by Guyana, that no effort was spared to have the smallest countries associated with the Fund's decisions. Almost all decisions, and particularly those adapting or establishing facilities, were taken by consensus. That made the decisions a little long in coming, sometimes, but that was the price for the involvement of all. As a matter of principle he received all ministers and governors asking to see him, he said.

The issue of debt-to-revenue levels was technically complex, he said. Recently, the Fund had suggested modifications adding to the HIPC Debt Initiative, when it was discovered that specific problems had developed. Those would be examined in the next few weeks. Any solution would depend on the resources that could be collected. The HIPC Debt Initiative also required good policies from its beneficiaries. Problems arose when they were relaxed after the granting of the facility. The ratios then deteriorated, but that was due to the policies of the countries concerned.

Assisting countries in establishing good frameworks for foreign direct investment was a high priority in the design of his programmes, he said. As a consequence of efforts to improve those frameworks by many developing countries, foreign direct investment flows remained steady and even improved during the worst of the recent global financial crisis. The Fund also wanted to establish a significantly stronger link between debt relief granted and the allocation of resources released to social purposes, such as education and health.

He added that, in trying to reconcile the necessary strength of the reform effort with the need for early disbursement of support under the facility, they were exploring tranched debt alleviation to make relief available earlier, on the condition that it was allocated to increases in priority social spending.

In response to the statement by the Russian Federation's representative, he had finalized a major financing package to help that country yesterday. In response to the suggestion that the Bretton Woods institutions had not been able to warn about the crisis and thereby perhaps prevent it, he had personally flown to Russia to warn officials about the risks that were arising. A major package had been put in place last year to address the problem. The legislative authority had not approved it, so it could not be put in place as early as hoped. It was now in place.

The Fund was accustomed to criticism, he said. The most frequent criticism he heard was that it was too generous to its most important clients and not generous enough to others. Today, he was hearing the opposite criticism, so perhaps the Fund was on the right path. Every effort was made to comply with a key principle—to be even-handed. Regarding strengthening the international monetary architecture, he referred representatives to a document that was to be distributed containing the Fund's initiatives.

In response to the questions about transparency and supervision, he said that covering funds were not handled transparently enough. The Fund organized a detailed study that concluded that there was a need to adopt rules to compel those funds to practise greater transparency. The United States authorities had just adopted principles similar to those proposed. Appropriate norms needed to be developed to ensure that those institutions, along with the offshore financial centres, were subjected to regulations that would mean a more orderly unfolding of financial transactions in the market.

Regarding the suggestions for expansion of debt relief suggested by the representative of Pakistan, there was support from his members for deepening debt relief for the poorest countries and disbursing it more quickly, he said. However, he had seen no interest or readiness in the membership to include middle-income countries in cancellation of debt.

Mr. SAITO, Adviser to the President of the Central Bank of Peru and Vice-President of the Group of 24, said that, in the last five years, the members of the Group of 24 had discussed most major issues, including those of debt and international liquidity. They had also invited representatives of international monetary institutions. The Group was backing any approach where the United Nations, in concert with Bretton Woods institutions, would take positive steps to improve the workings of international financial institutions. Recurrent crises would have a detrimental effect on the world economy, but the capabilities of coping with them had been improving. Solid economic fundamentals were now in place.

JOHN M. ROBINSON, Vice-President, Policy Branch of the International Development Agency of Canada, said that his country had been a strong supporter of the HIPC Debt Initiative and provided all possible assistance in that respect. Generous, timely and flexible relief was needed. Efforts directed at debt alleviation must be undertaken within the framework of a coordinated programme. Debt initiatives should not be achieved at the expense of development. Macroeconomic and social initiatives were also very important. The United Nations must continue to play a leading role, along with other players, including the Bretton Woods institutions. Another issue of utmost importance was greater coordination. Initiatives needed to be both complementary and mutually reinforcing. With the renewed focus on increased coordination between the United Nations and other international institutions, the regional perspective should not be forgotten.

JUAN CAMILO RESTREPO, Minister of Housing and Public Credit of Colombia, said that the crisis that had begun in July had continued longer than expected, despite the strides made since last year. Now, some of the emergent countries were having trouble restarting. At the spring meeting, in Washington, D.C., a number of decisions had been made, including the adoption of the Contingency Credit Line. Thought should be given to early prevention mechanisms and resources should be made at the earliest possible time. Colombia was one of the standout cases of a country that had a strong macroeconomic policy. Dissemination of information and transparency had been ensured. However, despite its achievements, it would not have access to the Contingency Credit Line, due to its eligibility criteria.

It was urgent to have coordination among fiscal and foreign exchange policies, he said. At the Washington meeting, that had been discussed as part of the Comprehensive Development Framework. Achieving peaceful coexistence in Colombia was his Government's focus.

EVELINE HERFKENS, Minister for Development Cooperation of the Netherlands, said that the decline of ODA had to be reversed. Concerning debt, she advocated faster, deeper and broader relief. When looking at recent proposals, there were great ideas, but there was also the need for financing. Resources were still being wasted due to overlapping and turf battles.

There was vast expertise in many quarters, which must be tapped, she said. That would only be possible if various organizations worked together and ensured that developing countries had access to that expertise. Strong commitments were still not enough. Organizations had to work together with the governments concerned, and also with each other. Too often, a country saying one thing in Washington, while saying another in New York. Homework had to be done in capitals, so one voice could be presented at international meetings. There was now a tremendous amount of consensus among the United Nations, the Bretton Woods institutions and governments on what was to be done. Now, that consensus must be implemented.

IBRAHIM AL-ASSAF, Minister of Finance of Saudia Arabia, said that cooperation and coordination between the United Nations and the Bretton Woods institutions was important to achieve common goals. Regarding debt, he supported the HIPC Debt Initiative. While welcoming progress on many recent proposals, he believed that adequate flexibility should continue to be provided. It was also essential for the products of such countries to have access to the markets of the industrialized countries.

He also welcomed the Comprehensive Development Framework initiative of the World Bank. However, he said that the abilities of the countries that were being helped should not be taxed. Each institution should take the lead in the area for which it was best suited. The Bank and the IMF had been looking into ways to address the issue of Kosovo and he welcomed their efforts, as well as those of other countries. While the international community's response had been commendable, further efforts were needed.

LEIV LUNDE, State Secretary for Development Cooperation, Ministry of Foreign Affairs of Norway, said that his country was firmly committed to providing debt relief and had launched a comprehensive strategy in that respect. Regarding the financial crisis, he said that the major lesson to be learned was that a better integrated approach was needed. Higher priority should be given to structural financial reform, and social and structural issues should be better integrated with the financial approaches to the crises.

Among reassuring developments, he mentioned a promise of the IMF and World Bank to work together in Indonesia. Financial policy had just been discussed in Washington, D.C., and the process of financial reform should be focused. There was a need for a strong role of the United Nations in that area. Evaluation systems should be improved, and a lot could be learned from the World Bank in that respect. Norway fully supported the Comprehensive Development Framework initiative. There was a strong need for United Nations involvement in it. The Organization should work constructively with the World Bank and the developing countries themselves.

MOHSIN NOURBAKSH, Governor of the Central Bank of Iran, said that dysfunctional international financial markets and unstable, unbalanced and fragile financial flows to the developing countries constituted the Achilles heel of the present international economic system. Solutions to those problems must be sought within the framework of legitimate and representative international structures with universal membership, in order to harmonize diverse interests and facilitate deeper integration in the world economy.

The Bretton Woods institutions were expected to have the practical capability to address and solve those problems, he continued. Any reform of the international financial architecture required the strengthening of the institutional capacity of the IMF in designing and implementing sound financial policies, and enhanced representation of developing countries in the institution. Similarly, the World Bank's role in intermediating and delivering financing for development must be strengthened.

Considerable thought had been given to strengthening shareholders support for the IMF, he said. The proposal to transform the Interim Committee into a Council merited serious consideration. In addition, the new architecture of the international financial system must emphasize a social safety net. The World Bank's proposal on the Comprehensive Development Framework represented a positive step, which should be further discussed and developed. Also, closer cooperation between the United Nations and the Bretton Woods institutions could produce positive and mutually reinforcing synergies in developing effective responses to the challenges of globalization.

He said Iran strongly supported the active participation of the Bretton Woods institutions in the proposed ad hoc open-ended working group on financing of development which was mandated to formulate recommendations on the form, scope and agenda of a high-level international intergovernmental forum on financing for development, to be presented to the fifty-fourth session of the General Assembly.

TONY FAINT, Director of the Department of International Development of the United Kingdom, said he welcomed the establishment of the meetings. There had been a sea change in the response to the debt burden of poor countries. Every major creditor State had now launched its own proposals for debt relief and a major step forward was now within grasp.

Global consensus on social policy was a key United Nations task, he said. The Copenhagen Declaration principles should be the keys to the way the Bretton Woods institutions dealt with crises. Social policy should be integrated into the international architecture.

The Comprehensive Development Framework and the United Nations Development Framework must be mutually supportive and relate to the development priorities of individual countries, he said. The emphasis must be to draw in all development agencies, as well as the private sector and civil society, to reduce poverty.

GERARD CORR, Director-General of the Multilateral Development Division of the Ministry of Foreign Affairs of Ireland, said the most difficult aspects of coordination arose because the various institutions did not listen to each other. The present dialogue was therefore valuable. The central thing that had emerged from recent meetings and discussion was that international economic governance and financial architecture were not just macroeconomic issues. Any examination or change had to consider development, poverty reduction and capacity-building. Short-term prospects for recovery were emerging. However, he had been struck by the differences between the predictions of the World Bank and the IMF, and would welcome an explanation of the differing positions.

The recent crisis had started out as a liquidity crisis and had easily become a financial crisis, he said. Thailand's dual track approach to addressing it was most interesting. There must be coherence in responses across the range of development instruments, to the crisis and to development. Flows of development cooperation was a key issue. It was paradoxical that, at a time when much thought was being given to architectural issues, development assistance had declined. Ireland had increased its development assistance flows.

There had been much progress in examining the deepening of the HIPC Debt Initiative, he said. He would like to hear views on how to assess the social component in adjustment programmes, many of which had clearly had a damaging effect in many developing countries.

Ireland welcomed greater cooperation between the United Nations and the international financial institutions, he said. He emphasized that cooperation needed to take into account change and progress, particulary that which occurred following the major United Nations conferences in recent years.

There was now an agreed programme and an agreed link between normative and operational goals. To move forward required sensitivity and common effort.

ABDUL WAHAB OSMAN, Minister of Finance and Economy of the Sudan, said that although the HIPC Debt Initiative was a welcome step, it would not by itself resolve the problems of developing economies, unless additional resources were directed towards solving the problems of those countries. The issues involved included: investment to improve infrastructure and boost production, hence increasing income; social development, particularly education and health; poverty alleviation, including social safety nets for those affected by problems arising from structural adjustment; and capacity-building to cope with the rapid growth of technology in a global economy.

He said countries in conflict or post-conflict situations might never benefit from the HIPC Debt Initiative, and those countries needed resources to solve those conflicts. The recent Security Council report on the situation in Africa pointed to that fact. The Initiative excluded countries affected by conflict, in terms of refugees and interruption of trade. He hoped there would be an international conference on such countries.

DENZIL L. DOUGLAS, Prime Minister of Saint Kitts and Nevis, said that countries of his region belonging to the Organization of Eastern Caribbean States were striving to create a single capital market. Vulnerable island States were especially interested in financial reform, for more and more financial resources were being provided to developing countries through portfolio financing, and less and less development assistance was being channelled to them. If they wanted to avoid marginalization, small island developing States must increase their integration into the world financial system. However, such integration increased the danger of systemic collapse through contagion. The risk was exacerbated by the instability of markets for exports of such products as sugar and bananas, and the continuing threat of natural disasters.

Strengthening financial systems ranked very high among the proposals for reform, he continued. In any new financial architecture the measure of the mechanics of cooperation between the supervisory authorities and the developing countries must be clearly defined. The problem of one country could easily become a problem for all, and assistance was not a purely altruistic endeavour. The transfer of relevant technical resources from rich to poor countries must be clearly defined.

The new financial architecture should specifically address the difficulties of small island developing countries, he said. Through today's forum, the Bretton Woods institutions and the United Nations system were working together to solve the financial crisis. The solution of problems would require broad-based consultations between different key players, and new financial architecture must define clear roles for all of them. The question was what mechanisms were in place and were pursued to link the WTO process to the financial development process, in recognition of the strong linkage of trade, financial and development issues.

Responding to questions, Mr. NIMMANAHAEMINDA, Development Committee Chairman, said that Thailand's efforts in the area of social development were supported by the Bretton Woods family. They were being funded partly by the Thai Government and partly by the IMF. The country had managed to stabilize its economy, and domestic and international confidence had been fully restored. However, much still remained to be done. He was confident that a modest growth rate would return during the current calendar year.

He said that there might be a definitional problem in answering whether the crisis was over or not. It was safe to say that the risk of world recession was now gone and, thus, the risk of a deeper crisis was over. With regard to hedge funds, there had been a number of strong recommendations. Those funds did not have their own money and had to borrow. Therefore, control of their borrowing might be the key and that was the responsibility of the central banks.

Mr. KARLSSON, Chairman of the Group of 10, said that regarding the participation of small countries in decision-making, only in practice could the seriousness of partnership be proved. It started with conceptualization. There was capacity around the world, which should be linked and used. More interaction and the use of technology was necessary. Through that linkage, it could be proved that knowledge was power and that could be transformed into reform.

Besides focusing on conceptualization, he said that there was a need to think about how to discuss issues before coming to decisions, as well as on how to interact before entering the negotiating phase.

WOLFGANG RUTTENSTORFER, State Secretary of the Federal Ministry of Finance of Austria, said the main thing to emerge from recent meetings was a return to a broader picture. Six months ago the discussion was of international financial architecture, but now it was about financial and development architecture. Reform of the development and interim committees would provide for a greater sense of ownership and for a reaffirmation of the political mandate of the Bretton Woods institutions. He sought an explanation of how the Comprehensive Development Framework and the United Nations Framework for Development would not compete, but would be supplementary.

YUKIO SATOH (Japan) said the critical issue of the current crisis was the liquidity of the countries in crisis. What was needed was a strengthening of the IMF resource base and an allowance for quicker loans. Japan welcomed recent action in that regard. Regional cooperation was equally important. Japan had recently announced the provision of $30 billion to Asian countries struck by the crisis, making a total of $80 billion now provided. Japan had also announced measures to increase the level of debt it could relieve.

S.A. SAMAD, Principal Secretary of the Prime Minister's Secretariat of Bangladesh, said that while he agreed that there was a need to develop new global financial architecture, the morphology of that architecture needed to be drawn more clearly, and the Fund should play a key role. The change must evolve from a participatory process, where all players were on a level playing field.

While Bangladesh had no problem with centre stage being occupied by the needs of the heavily indebted poor countries, he said there were other poor countries that had good records, but limited access to assistance. They were being crowded out of the global finance markets. Private capital flows must be induced to reach them. In cases where countries had undertaken structural reform for more than 20 years, it was necessary to provide them with compensatory assistance. He was speaking about the countries of South Asia, including his own. Regarding the new architecture, the Bretton Woods institutions and the United Nations needed to be better coordinated and any overlap should be reduced.

Mr. WOLFENSOHN, President of the World Bank, said that throughout today's discussion, the prevalence of issues of poverty and the need for unifying efforts was evident. Organizational issues also dominated the discussion. The Copenhagen Declaration had stated that countries of the world were committed to ensuring the social and financial environment to achieve development. There was no significant distinction between the United Nations in establishing principles and the World Bank trying to determine the financial policies. The issue was not whether it was the responsibility of the United Nations or the World Bank. In fact, they were doing the same work. It was necessary to build on today's meeting to ensure that the two institutions worked together.

Regarding a Comprehensive Development Framework, he said that the words could be forgotten. The words were not important. It was important to do the work and to address the question of cooperation. It was important to bring together the players in a coordinated partnership. It was important to address the issues of poverty and development. "Let us deal with the substance of the question, and not the form", he said. It seemed to be generally agreed that there was a link between the macroeconomic, structural, social and human issues, which needed to be taken together. The Bank had set forth some ideas to be incorporated in a comprehensive framework for development. Today's discussion had demonstrated a broad consensus on that approach.

Turning to the HIPC Debt Initiative, he said that it was part of the totality of the development process. Additional forms of support for development were important, as well as its human dimension. He was very encouraged by the fact that the world was devoting attention to debt issues, but they should be viewed in context. Representing the World Bank, he was pleased to say that its relations with the United Nations system were getting better and that they were no longer "covered with suspicion". It was necessary to stop worrying about structure and being suspicious of each other and proceed with doing the work, for the crisis really existed and that should create a sense of urgency.

Mr. CAMDESSUS, Managing Director of the IMF, said that concerning the question of whether the crisis was over or not, if he were to say prematurely that it was over, then governments would react and not fully support reforms. A large measure of stability was now returning and it was true that the countries most affected were in a recovery process or very close to it. He was delighted at their determined efforts at reform. Their recovery was faster than expected. Even if reforms were adopted rapidly, however, it would take time to permeate through the system. Indeed, times of transition were dangerous times.

Several statements had pointed to the need to make the Bretton Woods institutions more participatory, he continued. The suggestion about transforming the Interim Committee into a council would give the representatives of developing countries a forum where they could speak about their concerns. That idea was still gaining support. It was a time for the world community to prevent crises, rather than manage them. The Contingency Credit Line was exactly about that and, in fact, it was revolutionary, because instead of reacting to crisis, it devoted resources, with no access limit, to prevent crisis. It was important to create the right incentives for countries to address their vulnerabilities.

The need for comprehensiveness had come under many aspects, he continued. Regarding the HIPC Debt Initiative, it was clear that it could not deliver what it promised without reform in the countries and efforts by some countries to open their markets to developing countries. Also, the trends on ODA must be reversed. It would be too bad to win the battle of debt, if the war of strengthening ODA was lost.

He added that it was important to make sure that all countries adopted, in advance of crisis, the minimal social safety nets. That should be a key part of the principles the World Bank was creating with regard to a social code. It was necessary to properly marry debt relief with social relief. Also, the United Nations family must be better integrated with the Bretton Woods family. Finally, in response to a comment made by the Prime Minister of Saint Kitts and Nevis, he said that the Fund was extremely interested in creating a single currency market in the region.

Ms. FRÉCHETTE, Deputy Secretary-General, said that being concerned about labels was not the spirit in which the United Nations was approaching the new initiative by the World Bank. There was no incompatibility between the goals and principles of the United Nations Development Assistance Framework and those of the Comprehensive Development Framework. A genuine commitment to work together had to be seen and translated into daily behaviour. The history of mistrust that had existed would not be overcome overnight. Tremendous changes were taking place in the United Nations system and in the relationship between it and the Bretton Woods institutions.

Concluding remarks by the President of ECOSOC

From the many interventions I have distilled only a few salient points:

Economic outlook

It is still by no means certain that a recovery is fully underway. Hopeful signs can be discerned, but downside risks are still substantial and growth in the world economy is still fragile. Growth rates are seen as unsatisfactory, particularly in developing countries. For many such countries a crisis situation still prevails with unacceptably low growth rates. If these do not improve, we will not meet our goals for poverty reduction. Consequently, many agreed that measures are needed to accelerate economic growth, especially in developing countries.

Financial architecture

Many noted the positive initial steps that have been taken to address financial crises. While some stability has returned to financial markets, many observed that vulnerability still exists. Complacency would be dangerous. Measures should continue to be taken to strengthen the international financial architecture, keeping in view the need for a holistic approach and the needs and views of developing countries. Particular attention was paid to the need to enhance transparency in institutions, markets, governments and international organizations.

Financing for development and external debt

Many welcomed the new departures in addressing the external debt burden especially of low income and least-developed countries. The political momentum in dealing with debt crises should not be lost but be built upon. Particular concern was expressed about the debt burden in many African countries, especially in view of the very low commodity prices they are facing. Emphasis should be placed on faster, deeper and broader debt relief for all poor reforming countries. It was stressed that these objectives require additional resources and that they should not be at the expense of development assistance. Equally important is to reverse decline in ODA and move toward the 0.7 per cent target. The participants welcomed the General Assembly initiative to convene high-level international event on financing for development and we appreciate the readiness of the heads of the Bretton Woods Institutions to support this process.

Social dimensions

All reaffirmed the principles which had emerged at the Social Summit in Copenhagen. It is clear that the economic crisis has brought the social dimensions of economic policy into sharper focus. This can be seen as an important step forward as it is now recognized that the social pillar is an integral part of dealing with the economic and financial crises. Many saw this as a further opportunity for strengthening and achieving closer cooperation between the United Nations and the Bretton Woods institutions. The recently proposed Comprehensive Development Framework in the World Bank and the UNDAF in the United Nations provide a further opportunity to this end. The Bretton Woods Institutions, the UN system and governments need to build strong partnerships to meet the needs of global economic governance to reach common global goals.

IV. General Assembly Resolution: " Towards a stable international financial system, responsive to the challenges of development, especially in the developing countries."

The General Assembly,

Reaffirming its resolution 53/172 of 15 December 1998 on the financial crisis and its impact on growth and development, especially in the developing countries,

Noting the high-level regional meeting on the theme "Towards a stable and predictable international financial system and its relationship to social development", held in Mexico on 5 and 6 September 1999, in collaboration with the Economic Commission for Latin America and the Caribbean, in order to contribute to the process launched by the General Assembly in its resolution 53/172,

Recognizing that the increasing globalization of financial markets and capital flows have presented Governments, the multilateral financial institutions and the international community at large with new challenges and opportunities for the mobilization of adequate and more stable resources for promoting economic development and social welfare,

Stressing the importance of the provision of adequate financial resources for the development of all countries, in particular developing countries, including through public and private financial flows, international trade, official development assistance, adequate level of funding support for debt relief, in particular the agreement for an overall financing plan for the enhanced Heavily Indebted Poor Countries Initiative, as well as mobilization of domestic resources, and that the comprehensive and integrated consideration of those issues should continue in the framework of the dialogue and collaboration between the United Nations system and the Bretton Woods institutions,

Deeply concerned at the overall declining trend in official development assistance, which is a significant external resource for financing development and an important source of support to the efforts of developing countries, in particular least developed countries to create an enabling environment for eradicating poverty and tackling basic social needs, especially where private capital flows may either be inadequate or unavailable,

Emphasizing the importance of finding a durable solution to the problem of developing countries in meeting their external debt and debt-servicing obligations, in order to release resources for financing their development efforts, and in this context welcoming the Cologne initiative launched in June 1999 and the recent decisions of the International Monetary Fund and the World Bank on the enhanced Heavily Indebted Poor Countries Debt Initiative, which should provide deeper, broader and faster relief, and in this regard stressing the need for fair, equitable and transparent burden-sharing among the international public creditor community and other donor countries,

Noting the establishment of credit contingency lines by the International Monetary Fund, and the efforts to create and strengthen the regional reserves in some regions,

Expressing the need for future multilateral trade negotiations to result, *inter alia*, in increased access to markets for goods and services that are of export interest to developing countries, in particular the least developed countries, as trade is an important source of financial resources for their development efforts,

Mindful of the need that the benefits of the increasing integration of global markets should be extended to all nations and peoples, in particular to the developing countries, especially the least developed among them, and noting that while a number of developing countries have been able to take advantage of globalization of finance, not all countries have benefited from such flows as they may not be available or adequate or are too concentrated to satisfy the need of developing countries, especially the least developed among them,

Noting the desirability of financial regulatory frameworks so that capital mobility should benefit developing economies rather than undermine their development efforts, and noting in particular that short-term speculative capital flows, owing to their highly volatile nature, can often have negative impacts on the long-term goals of developing countries,

Regretting that the recent financial crises led to a significant slowdown in the economic growth of many developing countries and other affected countries and negative impacts in terms of social development, with the gravest impact on the most vulnerable, and in this context noting that while some of the most visible effects of the crises are being overcome in some regions and sectors, continued action on a wide range of reforms needs to be taken to strengthen the international financial system and to adopt as well as implement economic and legal frameworks while reaffirming the need for continued efforts of individual economies necessary to avoid the repetition of such crises,

Recognizing that the recent financial crises have exposed weaknesses in the international financial system, and underlining the urgent need to continue to work on a wide range of reforms for a strengthened and more stable and international financial system, with a view to enabling it to deal more effectively and in a timely manner with the new challenges of development in the context of global financial integration,

Emphasizing that the United Nations, in fulfilling its role in the promotion of development, in particular of developing countries, plays an important role in the international efforts to build up the necessary international consensus on the continuation of a wide range of reforms needed for a strengthened and more stable international financial system responsive to the challenges of development, especially in the developing countries, and to the promotion of economic and social equity in the global economy,

Takes note with appreciation of the report of the Secretary-General,[1] the note by the United Nations Conference on Trade and Development entitled "The financial crisis and its impact on growth and development, especially in the developing countries",[2] the report of the Executive Committee on Economic and Social Affairs entitled "Towards a new in-

---

1   A/54/471.
2   A/54/512/Add.1.

ternational financial architecture", the *World Economic and Social Survey, 1999*[3] and the *Trade and Development Report, 1999;*[4]

Emphasizes the need to renew national, regional and international efforts, in order to promote international financial stability, and to this end to improve early warning, prevention and response capabilities for dealing with the emergence and spread of financial crisis in a timely manner, taking a comprehensive and long-term perspective, while remaining responsive to the challenges of development and the protection of the most vulnerable countries and social groups;

Stresses the importance of having an enabling international environment through strong cooperative efforts by all countries and institutions to promote global economic development, and to this end calls upon all countries, in particular major industrialized countries, which have significant weight in influencing world economic growth, to adopt and pursue coordinated policies conducive to world economic growth and international financial stability and the promotion of a favourable external economic environment for a widespread economic recovery, including the full recovery of crisis-affected countries;

Recognizes the importance of international financial stability, and in this context invites developed countries, in particular major industrialized countries, when formulating their macroeconomic policies, to take into account the priorities of growth and development, in particular of developing countries,

Also stresses the importance at the national level of strong domestic institutions to promote the achievement of growth and development, including through sound macroeconomic policies and policies aimed at strengthening the regulatory and supervisory systems of the financial and banking sectors, including appropriate institutional arrangements both in the countries of origin and destination of international capital flows;

Recognizes the importance of accelerating the growth and development prospects of least developed countries, which remain the poorest and most vulnerable of the international community, and calls upon development partners to carry on their efforts to increase official development assistance and their efforts aimed at strengthened debt relief, improved market access and enhanced balance-of-payment support;

3   United Nations publication, Sales No. E.99.II.C.1.
4   United Nations publication, Sales No. E.99.II.D.1.

Stresses the need for a continued and constructive dialogue in the relevant institutions and forums among developed and developing countries, including at the regional and subregional levels, on the need for the international community to continue to work together in formulating approaches to promote financial stability and on issues related to strengthening and reforming the international financial system, and in this context reiterates the need for broadening and strengthening the participation of developing countries in the international economic decision-making process in order to promote more efficient international financial institutions and arrangements in which all relevant interests can be effectively represented;

Encourages the deepening of the dialogue between the Economic and Social Council and the Bretton Woods institutions in order to promote the wide range of reforms needed in international financial architecture that reflects the global interests of the international community, and in this regard recommends that their next high-level meeting give priority to the consideration of the modalities to achieve a strengthened and more stable international financial system responsive to the challenges of development, especially in the developing countries, and to the promotion of economic and social equity in the global economy;

Emphasizes that the international financial institutions, in providing policy advice and supporting adjustment programmes, should ensure that they are sensitive to the specific circumstances of concerned countries and to the special needs of developing countries and work towards the best possible outcomes in terms of growth and development, including poverty eradication, including through the protection of effective social expenditure determined by each country in accordance with its national economic and social development strategies;

Stresses the need to further define the role and improve the capacities of the international, regional and subregional financial institutions with regard to the prevention, management and resolution in a timely and effective manner of international financial crisis, and in this regard encourages efforts to enhance the stabilizing role of regional and subregional financial institutions and arrangements in supporting the management of monetary and financial issues, in accordance with the mandate of each institution, and requests the regional commissions to provide their views on this matter to the General Assembly at its fifty-fifth session through their regular reporting to the Economic and Social Council;

Emphasizes the need to further develop early warning capacities and modalities to prevent or, as the case may be, to take timely action to address the threat of financial crisis, and in this regard encourages the International Monetary Fund and other relevant international and regional institutions to continue their efforts to contribute to this process;

Underscores the need for the enhancement of worldwide financial stability, including through the provision to the international financial institutions, in particular the International Monetary Fund, of adequate resources to provide emergency financing in a timely manner to countries affected by financial crisis;

Underlines that the opening of the capital account must be carried out in an orderly, gradual and well-sequenced manner, keeping its pace in line with the strengthening of the ability of countries to cope with its consequences, underscores the crucial importance of solid domestic financial systems and of an effective prudential framework, invites the International Monetary Fund, the World Bank and relevant international regulatory bodies to contribute to this process, and in this context recognizes that all countries have autonomy in the management of capital accounts in accordance with their own national priorities and needs;

Reaffirms the need to strengthen international and national financial systems through a more effective national, regional and international surveillance of both the public and private sectors, based, *inter alia*, on the improvement of the availability and transparency of information, as appropriate, and possible additional regulatory and voluntary disclosure measures concerning financial market participants, including international institutional investors, in particular concerning highly leveraged operations, and in this context reaffirms the importance of continuing to work in the relevant forums on questions related to surveillance, transparency and disclosure, regulation and supervision;

Stresses the importance of strengthened collaboration between the World Bank and the International Monetary Fund in specific areas where collaboration is needed, such as the financial sector, while recognizing the specific mandates of the two institutions, and also stresses the need for institutions dealing with financial crises to keep in mind the overall objective of facilitating long-term development;

Calls for the renewal of national, regional and international efforts to promote the greater involvement of the private sector in the prevention and resolution of financial crisis, and in this context underscores the importance of a more equitable distribution of the cost of adjustments between the public and private sectors and between debtors, creditors and investors, and requests the United Nations Conference on Trade and Development to inform the General Assembly at its fifty-fifth session on the work it has undertaken on this matter;

Reiterates its call upon the international community to pursue national, regional and international efforts to contribute to minimizing negative impacts of excessive volatility of global financial flows, reiterates in this context the need to consider the establishment of regulatory frameworks for short-term capital flows and trade in currencies, and invites the International Monetary Fund and the relevant regulatory bodies to contribute to this process;

Underlines the importance that sovereign risk assessments made by private sector agencies be based on objective and transparent parameters, and in this regard invites the relevant national, regional and international regulatory bodies to contribute to the development of appropriate standards to ensure that risk-assessment agencies provide complete and accurate information on a timely and regular basis;

Encourages the continuing efforts of the World Bank and regional development banks to help Governments to address the social consequences of crisis, in particular through the strengthening of social safety nets in developing countries, particularly for the most vulnerable groups, without losing sight of the long-term goals of development;

Requests the Secretary-General to support, including through collaboration with the regional commissions and regional and subregional initiatives, the ongoing work on the identification of measures that will contribute to a more stable and predictable international financial system responsive to the challenges of development, in particular of developing countries, and in this regard requests the Secretary-General to make available the results of those exercises to the General Assembly at its fifty-fifth session;

Also requests the Secretary-General, in close cooperation with all relevant entities of the United Nations, including the United Nations Conference on Trade and Development and the regional commissions, within their respective mandates, and in consultation with the Bretton Woods institutions, to report to the General Assembly at its fifty-fifth session on the implementation of the present resolution under the subitem, "Financing of development, including net transfer of resources between developed and developing countries", with an analysis of the current trend in global financial flows, and of recommendations for an agenda for a strengthened and more stable international financial system responsive to the priorities of growth and development, in particular of developing countries and to the promotion of economic and social equity in the global economy;

Requests the President of the General Assembly to transmit the present resolution to the Board of Directors of the World Bank and the International Monetary Fund, in order to bring it to their attention as an input to their discussions on these matters.

3

Making International Trade Work for Developing Countries:

Dialogue with the World Trade Organization, UNCTAD, and the Bretton Woods Institutions

---

CONTENTS

Overview

The success stories of development—Chile, China, South Korea, etc—did not primarily come about because of particular financial or monetary policies. They came about because of trade and its use towards human development. A wise use of trade and investment allowed these countries to build up their export earnings, their skills, their productive capacities, and ultimately to build a resource base for anti-poverty policies.

This highlights the importance of market access for development. By contrast, finance makes its best contribution when it is the neutral, supportive, invisible grease in the wheels of commerce.

On 6–8 July 1998, the Economic and Social Council assembled again the top executive heads of the Bretton Woods Institutions, this time along with the heads of the World Trade Organization and the United Nations Conference on Trade and Development (UNCTAD). The high-level discussion that followed centred on the theme of "Market access: developments since the Uruguay Round, implications, opportunities and challenges, in particular for the developing countries and the least developed among them, in the context of globalization and liberalization."

The debate was prefaced by a Report jointly prepared by the Secretariats of UNCTAD and the WTO, and followed by a Ministerial declaration, the first ever issued by ECOSOC. The high-level debate attempted to take stock, four years after, of the treaty that concluded the Uruguay Round of Multilateral Trade Negotiations.

That treaty, which was signed in 1994, embodied a bargain between developed and developing countries: developed countries were to gain market access in areas where they had a comparative advantage: advanced tradeable services (including financial services) and intellectual property. In return, they agreed to submit to a process of legal recourse and remedy: the new WTO dispute settlement mechanism. This was an important concession, because rules protect the weak. Those countries with large markets possess a structural advantage in most disputes, because their threats of retaliation carry more weight. Developed countries also agreed to phase out, within ten years, the so-called voluntary restrictions on textiles and clothing that had been in place for decades against developing country exports.

Developing countries thus expected to gain better market access, not only in textile and clothing, but in other agricultural and industrial products.

As tariffs were reduced across the board, however, developing countries also saw the value of their preferential arrangements dwindle—compared to the lower tariffs now offered to all other countries. Also, lower world food prices, projected as a result of the Round, were expected to hurt the export earnings of developing countries. Some projections even anticipated a net loss in the short term for some African economies.

To compensate for this and for the erosion of trade preferences, and to help developing countries take advantage of the further lowering of trade barriers, a number of initiatives were taken. UNCTAD, the WTO, the International Trade Center (ITC), the United Nations Development Programme (UNDP), the World Bank and the IMF agreed on an Integrated Framework for Trade-related Technical Assistance, including for Human and Institutional Capacity-Building, to Support Least Developed Countries in their Trade and Trade-related Activities. UNCTAD, the WTO and ITC are also combining their forces in a joint integrated technical assistance programme for selected African countries, the first phase of which includes four least developed countries.

Four years after the signing of the Treaty, however, many developing countries were somehow disenchanted with the pace of liberalization in developed countries, and with the stringent limitations stipulated in the Trade-Related Intellectual Property Rights agreement.

The implementation of the Uruguay Round agreements is a salient theme of the debate of 6–8 July, which is summarized here by the President of the Council. The historical adoption of a Ministerial Communique, reprinted at the end of this chapter, symbolizes the importance of trade and market access in the development strategies of many developing countries.

I. Summary of the High-level Segment by the President of the Council, 6–8 July 1998

Note of Introduction

The two-day discussion was introduced by two major statements, made by the Secretary-General and the President of the Council, on the broader context of globalization. Then came a "policy dialogue" between the heads or deputy heads of the IMF, the World Bank, WTO and UNCTAD, which, among other things, addressed the challenges posed by the Asian crisis. This was followed by a free-flowing discussion among delegations, or "high-level debate", which concentrated more closely on trade issues, including trade sanctions, the next steps and follow-up to the Uruguay round, and the instruments available to address the situation of developing countries, especially the least developed ones, in the global trading system.

Opening statements

The President of the Council in his opening statement referred to the current economic crisis in Asia which had made it clear that integration into the global market could bring great benefits, but carried serious risks if not managed well. No country was able to remain insulated from the consequences of events occurring elsewhere. It was of paramount importance to develop a global rapid response capacity in which Governments and international institutions together with the private sector, trade unions and civil society organizations could cooperate to effectively forestall crises and address them expeditiously when they occurred. The current strains in the international financial and trading system served to highlight the need to orient the forces of globalization towards greater balance among the imperatives of economic growth, social equity, workers' rights, gender equality and environmental protection. This posed a global challenge to all international institutions and tested the effectiveness of the multilateral system as a whole.

He stressed that by now it was abundantly clear no single international organization or country, acting individually, with its own set of policy measures and its own interpretation of events, had any meaningful chance to help steer the world towards greater economic and social stability. It was necessary to progressively develop an integrated policy outlook reflecting common objectives of the international community. It was not possible to pursue independent sectoral policies to deal with integrated, multifaceted and systemic problems. This and future policy dialogues, the President observed, provided an opportunity for the Council to help develop a shared understanding of issues and devise a broad policy orientation to address them.

The Secretary-General in his statement noted that global conditions today offered unprecedented prospects for peace and security. Yet, the international community seemed ill-equipped to fully harness that tremendous potential. Tremendous wealth existed alongside chronic destitution. People around the world were torn between the hopes engendered by decades of remarkable progress and the fear of future upheavals. Those hopes and fears were global, as were the economy and markets. However, politics were local and there was a widening gap between what citizens demanded and what Governments could deliver. While there was every reason to treasure and nurture the achievements brought about by the international trading system, the Asian crisis was a reminder of how factors such as finance, economics and socio-political forces were working in tandem to shape, and, at times, shake up the world.

The Secretary-General stated that for the United Nations three broad observations were paramount. First, the crisis had had its most devastating effect on the marginalization of society. It threatened to undo years of progress in alleviating poverty and advancing the rights of women. Second, developing countries were less able than their developed counterparts to withstand the fallout of the crisis. Third, interdependence among nations had an essential complement—interdependence among issues. Finance, trade, governance and social equity were intimately linked.

The open, inclusive, global economy was the most promising means of widely spreading the benefits of globalization, the Secretary-General stressed. At the same time, the fear of globalization had to be taken seriously. The challenge for Governments was to show that global imperatives could coexist with local needs. Choices had to be made between the confinement to purely local points of view and the adoption of a more global perspective. One key question was whether the international community would choose to use the institutions at its disposal. There was really no choice, as it would be grievous for the international community to retreat from multilateralism.

Policy dialogue

The Managing Director of IMF stated that the international community must support the adjustment programmes of the countries most severely affected by the Asian crisis. It was also vital that countries with balance-of-payment surpluses recycle those surpluses in the form of untied loans and humanitarian aid to countries in the process of adjustment. As creditors, they should stand ready to grant generous terms for the restructuring of their claims and support economic recovery in Asia through new loans. Above all, those countries should keep their markets open. Countries that pursued strong, progressive trade liberalization, in the context of general economic reforms and market-oriented policies, would achieve growth and increased trade performance. For their part, industrialized countries should liberalize import restrictions. However, they should avoid replacing tariffs and non-tariff barriers with administered protection measures, such as anti-dumping restrictions.

Working with the World Bank, IMF was exploring ways to accelerate public enterprise and financial sector reforms, to improve the assessment of medium-term investments needs and the capacity to absorb external financing, and to identify potential adverse social consequences of reforms. In order to make the world less prone to financial crises, the Fund's surveillance had to become more effective and the transparency of international finance had to be enhanced. IMF could play a central role in crisis prevention by encouraging members to strengthen their macroeconomic policies and financial sectors.

The President of the World Bank stated that the Bank had sought to assist the countries hardest-hit by the Asian financial crisis. The crisis was not localized and issues in South-East Asia had affected all countries in different ways. The World Bank had also focused on the structural and social aspect of the crisis, with particular attention to poverty-related matters. Attempts had been made to deal with the segments of the economy most affected, including rural areas, so as to ensure provision of basic social programming that offered people a sense of hope. There could be no peace and stability without social stability and hope. Efforts were under way in the financial, judicial and regulatory systems to provide a framework essential for the success of the work of IMF. Before gaining access to markets, countries must establish a fundamental economic base, including infrastructure and a capacity to attract foreign investment. Helping countries to build such a framework was one of the essential functions of the World Bank. Also, transparency between borrower and lender countries was necessary in order to avoid the distortions that came from corruption, crime and the diversion of funds.

The Secretary-General of UNCTAD stressed that the Asian crisis had hit the poor particularly hard, in terms of sharp falls in commodities and in the export prices of some goods. The recent financial crises had occurred because the Governments concerned, among others, had failed to manage their countries' integration into the capital markets. Well-calibrated national policies could help manage financial crises, limit their potential for lasting damage and re-establish economic growth. Yet, when an economic crisis became a systemic problem, action was also needed at the global level. The Asian crisis was only the latest in a string of financial crises that had disrupted the global economy since the breakdown of the Bretton Woods system. The international community still needed to learn how to manage such economic turmoil. It would be useful to conduct an honest re-evaluation of the international policy response to assess its achievements and failures. He also noted that it was much more difficult to manage integration into international capital markets than it was to achieve successful insertion into the international trading system. Developing countries should not be pushed or pressured into premature financial liberalization, as this would deny them the option of protecting their economies from international financial instability and volatile speculative capital flows.

The Deputy Director-General of the World Trade Organization, stated that the fiftieth anniversary of the multilateral trading system six weeks before had demonstrated the virtual consensus throughout every region on the validity of open trade and economic integration under the rule of law. More and more, the ground rules provided by the World Trade Organization reached across, into and around other issues and concerns—ranging from investment and competition policy, to environmental, development, health and social policies. The various challenges needed to be faced as constituting pieces of a larger policy that demanded broader and more integrated solutions. Developing countries were increasingly represented in the world's trading system. This reflected the emergence of many of these countries as important trading powers in their own right. Perhaps most significant of all was the establishment of improved binding mechanisms for settling trade disputes. Even the smallest country could now look to the World Trade Organization in defence of its interests on the basis of shared and enforceable rules. Still, a variety of non-tariff measures continued to restrict exports from developing countries, and the fact that national and international product standards were difficult to meet led to reduced exports opportunities for least developed countries. Also, in the field of trade in services, much scope remained for further liberalization.

In the ensuing exchange of the Council with the Managing Director of IMF, the President of the World Bank and the Secretary-General of UNCTAD, considerable attention was paid to the Asian crisis. It was noted, in this regard that, while inadequacies in domestic financial and monetary policies had played a major part in leading to the problems that countries faced in Asia and elsewhere, those problems would not have reached such proportions if lending institutions operating in the international markets had not taken excessive risks. Concern was also expressed about the recent weakness of the yen which posed a crisis within the crisis. This weakness could seriously jeopardize the ongoing recovery in some countries.

With respect to preventing future crises, it was observed that the severity and the speed of the Asian crisis had highlighted the need for rapid global response capacity to prevent and deal with future crises. This would require the strengthening and adaptation of multilateral institutions and greater coherence in policy-making. An honest re-evaluation of the international policy response without any preconceptions or prejudice was also needed. Furthermore, constant vigilance by all countries over all socio-economic parameters had to be maintained. In particular, soundness of the banking system, avoidance of the unsustainable accumulation of short-term financing, and the transparent and accountable character of governance were seen as essential. Also, transparency in international lending and borrowing were crucially important in order to deal with excessive short-term and speculative capital flows and problems of corruption and debt management in the economy. More effective procedures for involving the private sector in preventing and resolving the debt crisis also needed to be established. In addition, in order to reap the benefits of globalization while minimizing its risks, developing countries should continue to liberalize trade and capital controls, paying due attention to sequencing and the soundness of the financial and balance-of-payments situation. At the same time, developing countries should not be pushed into premature financial liberalization. The fruitful dialogue on these issues at the special high-level meeting of the Economic and Social Council with the Bretton Woods institutions, held on 18 April 1998, was widely noted and a call was made to hold similar meetings in the future.

With regard to trade liberalization and market access, it was noted that they should also be seen in the context of poverty eradication, the ultimate goal of development efforts. In this context, ensuring the provision of basic services, creating adequate infrastructure and investing in human development were all necessary prerequisites of a developing country's benefiting from any enhancement of global market access for its goods. It was also noted that numerous tariff—and non-tariff—barriers remained, as well as tariff peaks and escalation, which affected developing countries' exports. Liberalization should continue in these and other trade areas. Furthermore, the international trading system could not be viewed in isolation from other developmental concerns, nor from other related issues. Therefore, the future multilateral trade agenda should aim at broad-based liberalization of trade.

Concerning coherence of the United Nations system, it was stressed that cooperation and coordination within the United Nations system, between the United Nations and the international financial institutions, and between the United Nations and the World Trade Organization were crucial for preparing future trade negotiations and addressing other major challenges. At the same, it was noted that within the United Nations system, a substantial increase of dialogue and working together had already been achieved; the challenge was to build upon the progress made to achieve greater complementarity and coherence in the management of the global economy.

High-level debate

It was generally agreed that liberalized world trade was essential in promoting growth and development and in eradicating poverty.

Full commitment to the multilateral trading system was expressed. The Uruguay Round of multilateral trade negotiations had resulted in a more open, rule-based and predictable multilateral trading system and significant improvement in market access conditions. Full and faithful implementation of the Uruguay Round commitments, which was considered essential for the credibility of the multilateral trading system, was called for.

Regret was expressed about the lack of progress in implementing the provisions on special and differential treatment for developing countries, and a strengthened commitment and concrete action to implement these provisions were urged. In this regard, it was recalled that trading partners must guarantee developing countries full market access, and industrialized countries should consider granting unilateral duty-free treatment to developing countries on a preferential basis. However, a number of developed countries did consider the integration of developing countries into the world trading system one of the primary objectives of their development policies, and therefore granted all developing countries, for almost all the exports of those countries, preferential access to their markets.

It was pointed out that significant tariffs and other non-tariff barriers to market access remained important impediments in many sectors, a considerable number of which were of particular interest to developing countries and least developed countries. The view was expressed that the implementation of the Uruguay Round was incomplete in many key areas of particular interest to the developing countries. It was noted that there was little commercially meaningful integration of textiles and clothing into the multilateral trading system so far, and that subsidizing agriculture in developed countries impeded developing countries' agricultural exports as well as their efforts to attain food security. On the other hand, it was recalled that the unprecedentedly large number of developing countries that actively participated in the multilateral trade liberalization had derived large benefits from it, including in terms of improved access to the markets of developed countries.

The developing of a comprehensive agenda for further trade liberalization that reflected the interests of all members of the World Trade Organization was called for. It was noted that the launching of a millennium round of trade negotiations was crucial for meeting the challenges of a globalized economy and it was argued that negotiations to further liberalize agriculture and services should be placed in a broader negotiating framework that would allow for a balanced treatment of the interests of all members. Support was expressed for a multilateral framework of rules on investment and competition in the services sector and for mainstreaming sustainable development into the multilateral trade liberalization agenda.

Reference was made to the agreement at the second Ministerial Conference of the World Trade Organization to establish a work programme in preparation for the next World Trade Organization ministerial meeting. The developing of a comprehensive agenda for further liberalization, which would reflect the interest of all members and would be able to deliver results in a short time, was called for. Also, all partners were invited to be proactive in setting out their priorities for a multilateral round of trade negotiations.

Measures taken by members of the World Trade Organization that were in contravention of the spirit of the multilateral trade agreements, such as contingency measures (for example, transitional safeguard measures, unilateral rules of origin and back-loading in the implementation of the agreement on textile and clothing), were deplored. Developed importing countries were called upon to faithfully work towards integrating fully the textile and clothing sector into the system. The abuse of anti-dumping measures and the use of discriminatory trade actions were among the actions to be rejected. Some delegations stressed that the taking of unilateral measures as well as the enactment of national laws with extraterritorial effects should be totally excluded as an option of trade policy in regard to the multilateral trading system.

The mandatory reviews of various agreements, such as the Agreement on Trade-Related Aspects of Intellectual Property Rights, including Trade in Counterfeit Goods, the Agreement on Trade-Related Investment Measures and, especially, the Understanding on Rules and Procedures Governing Settlement of Disputes,[1] were seen as being of considerable importance as well. In this regard, it was pointed out that the Disputes Settlement Understanding should, *inter alia*, include greater technical and legal support to developing countries in order to make the World Trade Organization judicial enforcement mechanism more accessible to those countries.

The lack of technical abilities of the developing countries was seen as a major constraint on their efforts to take fuller advantage of the multilateral trade agreements. The importance of the provision of the necessary technical assistance to developing countries was underlined. Many delegations referred to their ongoing support to developing countries in this regard, as well as to the preferential market access granted by them to these countries.

However, it was noted that securing market access did not by itself guarantee actual export revenues. Competitiveness was based not only on

---

1   See *Legal Instruments Embodying the Results of the Uruguay Round of Multilateral Trade Negotiations, done at Marrakesh on 15 April 1994* (GATT secretariat publication, Sales No. GATT/1994–7).

quality and price of products but also on such interrelated factors as good production practices and export financing. Furthermore, comparative advantages were seen as being time-bound and did not guarantee success in the long run.

One delegation pointed out that, while promoting and increasing exports were universally accepted as a means to create wealth, the importance of imports was not often accorded similar treatment. His country, which provided liberal market access, was providing jobs at home and around the globe.

Sound macroeconomic policies and a legal and economic framework that enhanced the growth of a dynamic private sector were seen as essential in improving countries' capacity to trade. Equally important were an enabling environment for investment, good governance, sound competition policy, fostering of human resources in the areas of trade, trade support services, strengthened public institutions focusing on trade, and trade-related infrastructural development.

The view was expressed that a multilateral framework of rules on investment and competition in the service sector should, in particular, provide a stimulant to foreign direct investment. The importance of examining trade issues related to electronic commerce was also emphasized.

Integration of the least developed countries in the global trading system was a priority for all. A number of measures to improve their market access conditions and supply capacity were suggested, such as full and effective implementation of the Plan of Action for the least developed countries adopted at the first Ministerial Conference of the World Trade Organization,[2] as well as the Integrated Framework for Trade-Related Technical Assistance, Including for Human and Institutional Capacity-building, to Support Least Developed Countries in Their Trade and Trade-related Activities, adopted at the High-level Meeting on Integrated Initiatives for Least Developed Countries' Trade Development held in October 1997; provision of duty-free access to all products and removal of all quantitative import restrictions for least developed countries; elimination of tariff escalation; and elimination of time-based elements in the special and preferential treatment granted to least developed countries in multilateral trade agreements.

Recent preferential actions in favour of least developed countries, including through improvements in generalized system of preference (GSP) schemes, were recounted. It was pointed out that least developed countries themselves needed to continue efforts towards creating a sound macroeconomic framework, including transparent and accountable gov-

---

2   World Trade Organization document WT/LDC/HL/1/Rev.1.

ernance, investment in basic social services and openness to trade and investment.

Commitments to assist least developed countries and African countries were reiterated and bilateral initiatives in favour of these countries were brought to the attention of the Council, and the international community was called upon to continue its effort to enhance market access for products of export interest to Africa and to support Africa's efforts towards diversification and building supply capacity. South-South cooperation in trade and other areas should also be supported.

The importance of official development assistance (ODA) was also noted. It was pointed out that ODA ensures external financial flows to countries that have difficulties in mobilizing domestic resources and in attracting foreign direct investment. ODA-financed development in sectors not reached by private flows, and the 0.7 percent target have lost none of their importance.

It was underscored that trade policy had an important role to play in restoring stability and growth in countries affected by the crisis in Asia. Rejection of protectionist measures and a clear commitment to pursue further comprehensive trade and investment liberalization were essential in this respect. The crisis had shown the importance of promoting greater coherence between trade and macroeconomic, social and other policies. In this respect, the United Nations could play an important role in promoting greater awareness of these interactions and developing international norms. Enhanced cooperation between the World Trade Organization and the Bretton Woods institutions was crucial, as was greater cooperation between the United Nations and the World Trade Organization. The World Trade Organization was called upon to reflect on how to better effect a coherence between its activities and the broader needs and concerns of the global economy.

The need for promoting the principle of universality in the multilateral trading system, within the framework of the World Trade Organization, was emphasized. Early completion of the accession process was also called for. Many of the countries negotiating entry into the World Trade Organization expected the next round of negotiations to be open for participation of interested countries irrespective of their application for entry into the World Trade Organization. In this regard, it was noted that countries acceding to the World Trade Organization should not be asked for commitments higher than those made by countries that had joined the organization earlier. Early completion of the pending processes for accession was called for.

At the same time, it was stressed that regional trading arrangements could make an important contribution to a solid and universal multilateral trading system. Such arrangements could help developing countries achieve integration into the world trading system as they had helped them develop and diversify their market bases. However, these arrangements should be fully consistent with the rules and principles of the international trading system and should maintain the basic tenet of open regionalism. The experience gained through such arrangements could benefit the multilateral trading system.

Arguments in favour of making environment and trade policies mutually supportive were also put forward. Reference was made to a recent proposal that the World Trade Organization should convene a high-level meeting on trade and the environment to help overcome the current impasse in discussion and promote the concept of sustainable development in the World Trade Organization agenda.

The adoption by the International Labour Organization (ILO) of a Declaration on Fundamental Principles and Rights at Work was welcomed and proposals for a practical follow-up mechanism within ILO were eagerly awaited. To pursue enhanced social and environmental protection through positive incentives, a number of developed countries had recently started providing, through their GSP scheme, additional preferences to those developing countries that had adopted and implemented internationally agreed environmental and social norms.

It was also noted that trade conditionalities to enforce non-trading objectives, including those related to labour standards and the environment, could undermine the proper functioning of the multilateral trading system.

One delegation referred to the economic blockade of its country by a developed country, which ignored the successive resolutions of the General Assembly condemning that blockade, and called for its total and unconditional elimination.

A few other delegations noted the importance of emphasizing the danger of an excessive recourse to the imposing of economic sanctions on developing countries. Two delegations condemned the automatic renewal by the Security Council of economic sanctions against their countries despite the General Assembly's calls to put an end to the punitive and unilateral economic measures. It was pointed out by one delegation that the Assembly had not adopted those resolutions by consensus.

One delegation raised the issue of the banana trade and expressed discontent with the World Trade Organization ruling that preferential treatment of African, Caribbean and Pacific (ACP) countries contravened the World Trade Organization's principles. The delegate warned that the implementation of the ruling would bring about a reduction in the living standards of the people of the Caribbean Community (CARICOM) and an acceleration of poverty. A fundamental reform of the dispute settlement was needed. In a right of reply, one delegation stated that trade dispute settlements based on rules would always lead to situations in which countries won some rulings but lost others.

Finally, a view was expressed that the United Nations system as a whole, particularly UNCTAD, should continue to play an active role in helping developing countries through, *inter alia.*

- Ensuring a continuum in its work programme between research activities and its capacity-building and technical cooperation functions;
- Providing objective and in-depth analyses of the effects of liberalization and of any proposals for further liberalization;
- Strengthening the capacity of developing countries to participate in trade negotiations;
- Continuing to devote a large part of its work to building and enhancing capacity to trade in developing countries, in particular the least developed countries and those in Africa, and substantially increasing its trade-related technical cooperation;
- Strengthening its information and training services, and strengthening technical cooperation to expand export supply capabilities of developing countries;
- Promoting better coherence among global development, financial and trade policies so that the ability of the developing countries to benefit from increasing trade was not compromised by imperfections in financial markets;
- Ensuring that the structural factors such as debt, inadequate concessional development finance and restrictions on the transfer of technology did not impede the developing countries in respect of their availing themselves of the opportunities presented by the multilateral trading system.

In conclusion, many delegations commended UNCTAD and the World Trade Organization for their excellent joint documentation in preparation for the high-level segment and for their support towards its successful outcome.

II. Ministerial communiqué of the High-level Segment submitted by the President of the Council

Note of Introduction

This is the first Ministerial Communique in the history of ECOSOC. It highlights the concerns of developing countries on issues of market access, and places these issues into the broader context of globalization and liberalization. It aims at making an impact on future multilateral trade negotiations and stresses the continued need for special measures to enable developing countries to take part fully in the global trade system.

"We, the Ministers and Heads of Delegations participating in the high-level policy dialogue and the high-level segment of the substantive session of 1998 of the Economic and Social Council, held from 6 to 8 July 1998, having considered the theme 'Market access: developments since the Uruguay Round, implications, opportunities and challenges, in particular for the developing countries and the least developed among them, in the context of globalization and liberalization', have adopted the following communiqué:

Fifty years ago, the multilateral trading system was established as the result of a process that had begun at the United Nations Conference on Trade and Employment, which was held pursuant to a resolution of the Economic and Social Council, adopted by the Council at its first session, in 1946, in which the Council called for a conference to draft a convention for the establishment of an international trade organization. Over the succeeding decades, the multilateral trading system made an important contribution to growth, employment and stability by promoting the liberalization and expansion of trade and by providing a framework for the conduct of international trade relations. Today, we reaffirm and renew our commitment to uphold and strengthen the system which contributes to the economic and social advancement of all countries and peoples.

The continued marginalization of the least developed countries concerns us deeply. Arresting and reversing their marginalization, and promoting their expeditious integration into the world economy, constitute an ethical imperative for the international community. We will work together towards further enhanced market access for their exports within the context of supporting their own efforts at capacity-building. We therefore welcome the initiatives taken by the World Trade Organization in cooperation with other organizations to implement the Plan of Action for the Least Developed Countries, including through effective follow-up of the High-level Meeting on Integrated Initiatives for Least Developed Countries' Trade Development, held in October 1997. We recognize that full implementation of the Plan of Action requires further progress towards duty-free imports from least developed countries. We also invite the World Trade Organization, the United Nations Conference on Trade and Development (UNCTAD), the United Nations Development Programme (UNDP), the International Trade Centre (ITC), the World Bank, the International Monetary Fund (IMF), the United Nations

Industrial Development Organization (UNIDO) and other relevant organizations to provide enhanced technical assistance to help strengthen the supply capacity of the least developed countries and to help them take the fullest possible advantage of trading opportunities arising from globalization and liberalization.

The Uruguay Round of multilateral trade negotiations resulted in a more open, rule-based and predictable multilateral trading system and in significant improvements in market access conditions. Furthermore, since the establishment of the World Trade Organization, important multilateral negotiations have been concluded that have increased market access for information technology products, basic telecommunications services, and financial services. In addition, the dispute settlement mechanism of the World Trade Organization, which strengthens the rule-based multilateral trading system, provides effective recourse to members with regard to defending their market access rights.

However, significant non-tariff and tariff barriers and high variance, with tariff peaks and tariff escalation, still affect a notable range of products and sectors, particularly ones of export interest to developing countries, including the least developed countries. The degree of market access commitments in trade in services varies considerably. Future trade negotiations should take these issues into account with a view to securing further broad-based trade liberalization for the benefit of everyone. Resort to trade actions in the form of contingency measures, such as anti-dumping duties and countervailing duties, and of unilateral actions should be subject to increased multilateral surveillance so that they respect and are consistent with multilateral rules and obligations.

Important gains in market access for developing countries' exports have been achieved through regional trading agreements which have built upon increased disciplines and tariff concessions resulting from the Uruguay Round. Bearing in mind the primacy of the multilateral trading system, and the importance of open regional economic integration, regional trade agreements should be outward-oriented and supportive of the multilateral trading system.

We stress the importance of effective application by all members of the World Trade Organization of all provisions of the Final Act Embodying the Results of the Uruguay Round of Multilateral Trade Negotiations,[1] taking into account the specific interests of developing countries and in this respect reiterate the need for the effective imple-

---

1 See *Legal Instruments Embodying the Results of the Uruguay Round of Multilateral Trade Negotiations, done at Marrakesh on 15 April 1994* (GATT secretariat publication, Sales No. GATT/1994–7).

mentation of the special provisions in the multilateral trade agreements and related ministerial decisions in favour of developing country members, in particular the least developed among them. The Generalized System of Preferences (GSP) remains a major instrument for further improving market access of developing countries; there is scope and need for further improvement of the GSP, especially for the least developed countries.

We recall that the second Ministerial Conference of the World Trade Organization decided to establish a process to ensure full and faithful implementation of existing agreements and to prepare for the third Ministerial Conference. In this regard, we stress the importance of the submission by the General Council of the World Trade Organization of recommendations regarding the work programme of the World Trade Organization, including further liberalization sufficiently broad-based to respond to the range of interests and concerns of all members of the organization within the framework of the World Trade Organization, that will enable the members to take decisions at the third Ministerial Conference of the World Trade Organization. The second Ministerial Conference of the World Trade Organization also decided that the General Council of the World Trade Organization would establish a comprehensive work programme to examine all trade-related issues relating to global electronic commerce. In this regard, we stress the importance of assisting developing countries in capacity-building and the development of their services infrastructure, in order to enable them to maximize the benefits they could derive from electronic commerce. Countries with economies in transition also need such assistance. We call upon UNCTAD, in collaboration with other organizations, to provide appropriate analytical support and technical assistance to developing countries in this area.

We strongly underline the need to provide technical assistance to developing countries for capacity-building in trade negotiations and in taking fullest possible advantage of the dispute settlement mechanism of the World Trade Organization. We acknowledge with appreciation the assistance given by UNCTAD to developing countries through its policy research and analysis and technical assistance and we invite UNCTAD to continue to provide such support, including assisting developing countries in formulating a positive agenda for future trade negotiations.

We attach great importance to the diversification of African economies and increased market access for their export products. In this regard, we express our appreciation to the Secretary-General of the United Nations for recently putting forward an action-oriented agenda for the development of Africa. Continued efforts are needed to enhance market access for products of export interest to Africa and to support the African economies' efforts at diversification and building of supply capacity.

We are concerned about the financial crisis afflicting a number of countries, with its serious implications for world economic and trading prospects. There is a need for improved measures to address the negative effects of the volatility of international capital flows on the international trading system and the development prospects of developing countries. Keeping all markets open and maintaining continued growth in world trade are key elements in overcoming this crisis. In this context, we reject the use of any protectionist measures. Consideration should be given to the trade financing needs of the countries affected by the crisis to enable them to import essential items. It is important that the momentum towards increased trade liberalization, particularly as regards products of interest to developing countries, be maintained, and be given attention in the work leading up to the third Ministerial Conference of the World Trade Organization. At a broader level, there is a need for greater coherence between the development objectives agreed to by the international community and the functioning of the international trading and financial system. To this end, we call for close cooperation among the United Nations, and multilateral trade and international financial institutions. An important step in this direction was the convening of the special high-level meeting of the Economic and Social Council with the Bretton Woods institutions, on 18 April 1998.

While noting that multilateral trade agreements have contributed to security of market access for members of the World Trade Organization, we recognize that such security is not enjoyed by non-members, including those seeking accession to the organization. We emphasize the importance of attainment of the universality of the multilateral trading system and the need for government members of the World Trade Organization and relevant international organizations to provide assistance to non-members of the World Trade Organization, so as to facilitate their efforts with respect to accession in an expeditious and transparent manner on the basis of World Trade Organization-related rights and obligations. The World Trade Organization and UNCTAD are invited to provide the necessary technical assistance to these countries in this regard.

We welcome the development of a collaborative and complementary relationship between UNCTAD and the World Trade Organization, which augurs well for the multilateral trading system and for effective integration therein of developing countries, including the least developed countries. We also express our appreciation to the secretariats of UNCTAD and the World Trade Organization for jointly preparing their excellent report (E/1998/55) for the high-level segment."

4

Fighting Poverty:
The Overarching Goal

Panels of the Economic and Social Council

March-July 1998

C O N T E N T S

Overview

At first sight, it would seem that poverty would be a matter for individual states to resolve, using the principle of solidarity between the richest and the poorest. Indeed, poverty exists, to a varying degree, even in rich countries.

Yet, no state is an island. Globalization may weaken national solidarity or the means to exercise it, thus creating new forms of poverty, especially among women, children and other vulnerable groups. It may also increase vulnerability to financial crises, or lead to the over-exploitation of natural resources on which the poor depend.

But globalization can also lift people out of poverty, as exemplified by the successful outward strategy of the Asian tigers. Export industries create jobs, and these jobs often pay better wages. Through migration, many poor people can enhance their life choices and opportunities.

Alternatively, globalization, if untapped, may leave poverty unchanged, as in many Latin American countries, and benefit only a privileged section of society.

A commitment to human rights and the right to development has led the United Nations to make poverty eradication a guiding priority of its work—its operational activities, its policy analysis and its intergovernmental coordination. In 1995, the Copenhagen Summit on social development spelt out a comprehensive agenda for poverty eradication, and set a goal of halving absolute poverty (defined as income of less than one dollar a day) by 2015. In June 2000, the General Assembly will hold a Special Session, entitled "Achieving social development for all in a globalized world," to take stock of progress five years after the social summit.

In 1999, the Economic and Social Council, as part of its substantive segment, organized panels on various aspects of poverty eradication, including the following:

- Advancing gender equality and eradicating poverty (16 March 1999, New York)
- Food security, basic infrastructure and natural resources as imperative dimensions of poverty eradication strategies (23 April 1999, New York)
- Ensuring access to fundamental services and putting vulnerable groups first (12 May 1999, New York)
- The role of training in promoting access to work (4 July 1999, Turin, Italy)
- National policies and international cooperation for employment oriented growth: impact on poverty reduction and gender equality (6 July 1999, Geneva)

Among the contributions submitted to all these panels, we have edited a few and organized them around three themes: Understanding poverty; Fighting poverty: the role of economic policy and; Fighting poverty: the role of social policy. The panel contributions reflect the practical experiences of certain countries or communities. They provide a good background to the concluding statement of the President of the Council, entitled "Ten strategic priorities."

I. Understanding poverty

"Poverty: a sociological view", by Abram de Swaan
"Hunger is the main obstacle to overcoming poverty,"
    by Catherine Bertini
"Urban poverty, rural poverty," by Richard Bilsborrow

Note of introduction

Defining and measuring poverty is the first step to any anti-poverty strategy. For issues of measurement, in addition to the existing estimates, the United Nations is coordinating an inter-agency effort to harmonize and improve data collection, nationally and internationally (see chapter V). But poverty also needs to be understood from a sociological standpoint. In his introduction, Abram de Swaan, stresses the interdependencies between the poor and the non-poor. He argues that any solutions to poverty will have to involve the consent of the richer members of society, and that it is therefore essential to understand the costs and benefits of poverty alleviation to them.

"Hunger is poverty", argues Catherine Bertini, Executive Director of the UN World Food Programme, thus singling out a fundamental characteristic of poverty. Hunger also keeps the poor from taking advantage of opportunities that becomes available to them to improve their lot—be it education, work, micro-credit, etc.

In his contribution, "Urban poverty, rural poverty", Richard Bilsborrow provides a first hand account of the many faces of poverty and analyzes recent trends, with particular emphasis on the environmental dimension of poverty.

"Poverty: a sociological view" by Abram de Swaan, School for Social Research, University of Amsterdam

Poverty exists only in relation to property. Where the institution of property does not exist, there may be scarcity, but there is no poverty. Accordingly, there are no poor people without rich people. The poor have been excluded from the resources that the rich exploit and enjoy —property is the institution that ensures that this will remain so. To make the strongest case right away: if you want to understand poverty, study the rich.

By studying the poor, researchers can identify some of the strategies of subsistence and survival, of resistance and rebellion, of sociability and solidarity that have enabled the poor to cope with their lot. Such research, aimed at the poor themselves, is called "bottom up" research. Moreover, in so far as it gives voice to those who are not heard and depicts those who have remained invisible, it does help to awaken society at large, alert public opinion at home and abroad to the victims of poverty that would otherwise have been mostly ignored. In some cases, this form of poverty research may even help to bring about effective initiatives at cooperation, mutual aid and political action.

But it keeps the rich and the powerful out of the picture. And yet, those who do hold property, prestige and power in their society, in one word the elites, are the key actors: they are not only instrumental in the exclusion of the poor, they are also pivotal in obstructing social change, *and* they are indispensable in bringing about social reform.

Indeed, the policies that together make up the western 'welfare state' were put in place, not through collective action by the poor, although that did play a role—but by elected, activist governments, in a coalition with either the workers' organizations or with the equally organized large employers, or with both. Welfare reform, in Europe, was very much an elite project.

This is as true today as it was half a century ago. But at present the scale of the problem has changed. Very long ago, agrarian poverty was a problem of poor relief at the parish level; with industrialization, urban poverty became a problem for big city government, and in the twentieth century, the problem of poverty was dealt with at a national level, by national states—welfare states.

But today, at the eve of the third millennium, the problem of poverty has surpassed the capacities of separate states, it has become a global matter, to be dealt with in a transnational context, through cooperation among states, and by international organizations, in transnational society. This implies that the relation between the poor and the rich must once again be put in different terms, this time as a worldwide problem: the social question today is a global question.

Not only must the relation between the poor and the elites be studied in each national context, the relation between the poor nations and the rich nations must now also be studied in its encompassing, global context. At the national and the transnational level, quite similar questions are to be posed: How can the rich—the elites in poor countries as well as the rich nations in world society—be persuaded to act so as to alleviate poverty in the national context and at the global level?

To answer these questions we must first ask some others: What are the dangers that the poor create for the rich? What are the opportunities that the poor represent to them ?

The poor represent a threat—through contagion (disease), through crime, violence and revolt, through mass migration ('vagrancy'), and ecological degradation. And, the poor represent opportunity—as potential workers, consumers, recruits and voters.

But, this is the key point: within any nation, rich individuals cannot protect themselves on their own against the threats that emanate from poverty in their society, nor separately realize the opportunities the poor also hold for them.

Today, the same applies to the wealthy nations: no nation on its own can protect itself from the dangers of worldwide poverty or singly realize the opportunities that poor nations also represent.

In other, more technical terms, poverty, both at the national and the international scale, creates externalities that cannot be controlled by individual actors. And the alleviation of poverty may cause positive external effects that do not exclusively benefit those who contributed to the effort. In the last analysis, therefore, the problem of poverty is a problem of collective action for the rich: How to coordinate their efforts and prevent some of their peers from profiting without contributing to the collective effort?

In the twentieth century, this problem of collective action was solved at the national level through state compulsion—by a system of compulsory taxes and legal entitlements—the welfare state.

Today, this is no longer sufficient. At present, a structure of transnational social policy is required, a system in which rich nations collaborate among themselves and with poor nations in worldwide collective action to alleviate poverty in global society.

This perspective also requires new avenues of research, aimed at studying the elites: studies of elite perceptions of the poor in the national context and studies of the perceptions of global poverty among the publics of the wealthy nations. Do they realize the dangers and the opportunities that poverty represents? Are they willing to act to alleviate poverty through concerted action? How will they engage in the creation of the necessary 'global public goods,' as the UNDP has called them? And how will they solve the inevitable dilemmas of collective action?

This program of research on elite attitudes is as urgent as the study of the poor themselves. I am privileged to participate in a multinational comparative research program on 'Elite perceptions of the poor' with Else Oyen from Norway, Elise Reis from Brazil and Jim Manor from the U.K. . This new orientation in poverty research presents a promising challenge to the community of researchers and policy-makers.

"Hunger is The First Obstacle To Ending Poverty" by Catherine Bertini, Executive Director, UN World Food Programme

Hunger is poverty. A person who is always hungry is always poor. We can talk about the eradication of poverty all we want. We can never achieve it, if we don't first end hunger.

Hungry people who get cash or a new tool in their hand must do one thing first, before they do anything else, they must eat. So they spend that asset on food. Furthermore, if a chronically hungry person eats for a week or two, this does not address the problem of stunted weight and growth and loss of energy caused by years without adequate food. So, even a good new job may not be as productive for a hungry person as it would be to a healthy person.

Hunger is the first obstacle to ending poverty

The hungry live in rural areas and urban slums, in refugee camps and on farming homesteads. Wherever they are, hungry families live in the gray area between crisis and normality. Their poverty keeps them vulnerable to hunger. And hunger keeps them poor.

Too many people—around 830 million—have neither the energy, the time, nor the resources to benefit from development. Feeding their families dominates their lives. New schools may be built, more sustainable farming practices developed. But when each day is spent finding food for the family, children do not go to school, and farmers cannot take the risk of trying new methods.

And, hunger keeps people poor. Hunger stunts children intellectually and physically and makes them more susceptible to disease and gives them a legacy that stays with them for life. Hunger forces poor families to degrade natural resources. They farm land that is fragile, deplete forests that need to be conserved—creating a spiral of food insecurity and poverty. And hunger aggravates social and political conflict.

Development that does not promote food security for all people—especially women and children—has weak foundations. And those foundations crumble when faced with political, economic or natural shocks.

Development strategies are needed that focus on investing in the poor and in their food security. Only by investing in people and their access to resources can we be sure that they will remain food secure—in the lean season as well as at harvest time, in bad years as well as in good. In this way development becomes pro-poor and anti-hunger. Such a development strategy supports the physical, social and environmental foundations needed to build a future for the world's poor—a future free of poverty.

Physical infrastructure supports food security

Without adequate basic infrastructure or proper natural resource management poor families have little resilience to shocks and cannot build assets for their future.

Investing in basic infrastructure helps build the assets of the poor. These assets can be physical—like a rural road, or human—like a skill. As a family gains assets, it gains resilience and a chance to escape poverty.

Physical infrastructure, such as roads and storage facilities, is important to food security because first of all, food needs to get to people. In the long run, physical infrastructure is also important because it helps markets work better. Well-functioning markets ensure reliable supplies of food at reasonable prices. And markets offer opportunities for employment and income-earning activities—opportunities for the poor to escape poverty.

But many of the opportunities created by the market will be missed unless investments in physical infrastructure benefit the poor directly.

The 1997 Human Development Report states that "a people-centred strategy for eradicating poverty should start by building the assets of the poor."

Investments in infrastructure need to place more emphasis on ensuring that the assets truly are for the poor. Community-managed fish ponds and woodlots, or storage bins for small farmers' co-operatives are good examples of this kind of investment.

Yet physical infrastructure alone cannot lead to less poverty or better food security. A bridge may make the local market half an hour away rather than half a day. But when you have no education, poor health and no energy, all the opportunities the market holds are beyond your reach.

Social infrastructure supports food security

To eradicate poverty, social investments are crucial. Clinics and schools build human assets—better health, better minds, better lives.

Again, it is not enough that clinics and schools exist. Development strategies must ensure that poor families are able to attend clinics, go to school, and learn how to improve their lives.

Sadly, poverty forces families to make trade-offs. Trade-offs between hunger and meeting other basic needs. Trade-offs for who goes to school and who doesn't. And, trade-offs between who eats and who doesn't.

But study after study shows that education is critical to the future economic success of a family and a community. And education for girls has extremely positive results in future earning potential, decreasing hunger, better health, and smaller families.

Good health care, of course, is critical to the well-being of all humans—and is especially important for fragile and developing bodies.

Nutritional infrastructure

Access to the right kind of food for the right people and at the right time of their lives is critical. For instance, hungry children can't learn well. Children who are fed before they begin their day have better results—in test scores, absorption of information, attendance. So when we educate children, we really don't get the maximum from that investment unless we feed them too.

Hungry pregnant women give birth to small, unhealthy babies. Hungry mothers have limited amounts of milk and adequate nutrition to pass on to their children. We do not get the maximum from any investment in health care unless we ensure that pregnant and breast-feeding women are well-fed. Otherwise, hunger is a sad and destructive legacy passed from mother to child, generation to generation. Malnourished children, robbed of essential nutrients, are often condemned to be less productive adults.

Women and food security

Poverty will never be eradicated without the advancement and empowerment of women.

Women are the leading victims of poverty and humanitarian emergencies. And women are the caretakers of household food security. Women produce food, earn income to buy food, and prepare food for their families. Then, women eat last—ensuring their families benefit most from the food they provide.

Social, cultural and economic inequities keep women in a disadvantaged position. Lasting solutions to poverty and hunger cannot come about unless these inequities are removed.

A study by the International Food Policy Research Institute (IEPRI) shows that improvements in women's education and their status over the period 1970 to 1995 account for over 50 percent of the reduction in child malnutrition. The education of girls and positive changes in the position of women in society make a direct contribution to household food security, in addition to a number of other benefits to their families and to society as a whole.

Wherever possible, we must enlist women to help in the planning, managing and monitoring of programmes. For example, strategies to improve natural resource management should reflect the role of women farmers as users and carers of the natural environment.

Working through women empowers them to help build the food security and the futures of their families.

Support in crisis

In addition to the 830 million hungry people who are barely able to gather and consume enough food to survive, millions of people each year find themselves cut off from their traditional supplies of food:

- North Koreans who depend on government distributions, but the government cupboards are bare;
- Kosovans who were forced from their homes and lands, and who are totally reliant on relief agencies for food;
- Indonesians whose thriving economy came to a screeching halt due to drought and economic policies;
- Sudanese waiting for WFP food air drops as they have little food to grow and no safe surface transportation routes.

In these cases, and too many others, the international community provides life-sustaining support through food aid and many other inputs. We keep millions of people alive each day. We have the capacity, the funding, the efficiency, and the political support to do this.

But these situations are almost all temporary, not permanent.

Proposals

Of course, there has been success decreasing hunger worldwide over the years—chronic hunger. The World Bank's own figures show that the numbers of people who are hungry worldwide has decreased, even while population has increased. Economic development and infrastructural development are key to this success.

So, I'd like to present four actions for the future, designed to decrease poverty by addressing hunger:

1. **Physical infrastructure**—Place a major emphasis on development of lasting community infrastructure built around local agriculture production and getting food to the market. For instance, better roads, irrigation, storage, maybe refrigeration, marketing;
2. **Social infrastructure**—Put a high priority on building schools and health clinics, supporting professional staffs there, securing

high enrolments of children, including equal numbers of girls and boys. And providing daily meals in schools and food packages for pregnant and breastfeeding mothers through health centers;

3. **Emergency assistance**—continue the international community's well-regarded efforts in providing emergency food aid and other relief;

4. **Including women**—When we are discussing hunger—or food—or food security, we are implicitly and explicitly discussing women.

Women hold the key to the most significant positive changes that could be created for those families.

We must educate girls and women. We must involve women in the development and management of any and all community projects designed to improve food security.

Working in Partnership

By working in partnership with Governments, with members of the UN family and international financial institutions, with NGOs, and—most of all, with the millions of people striving each day to escape hunger and poverty—together we can address the different dimensions of food security and poverty.

Our poverty eradication strategies must be coherent. Investments in basic infrastructure, in education and health, and in natural resource management must focus on enabling poor people to participate and benefit from the investments.

Through partnerships, we can combine resources to bring poor people to development opportunities. For example, food aid combines with other development resources to alleviate hunger and enable hungry poor people to invest in themselves and in their future.

And by working in partnership with the poor—and especially with women—we empower them to fight hunger and poverty. We empower them to rise to the challenge of building an equitable, prosperous future. We empower them to begin the journey towards a future free of hunger and poverty.

In conclusion

Hunger is the first obstacle to ending poverty. To eradicate poverty, we must find ways to help the poor invest in their future. They cannot do this if hunger saps energy and productivity, if the need to feed the family today leaves nothing to invest in tomorrow. By fighting hunger first, we can prevent a short term food need from becoming a long term disaster of lost opportunities.

Hunger is poverty. To end poverty, we must first end hunger.

"Urban poverty, rural poverty" by Richard Bilsborrow
University of Chapel Hill, North Carolina

Over a billion people are still poor, nearly a third of the world population, despite substantial progress in recent decades. Poverty is highest in Sub-Saharan Africa, and declining since 1980 in most of the developing world except in Africa and Latin America; the incidence of poverty is considerably higher in rural areas, but the number of poor in urban areas is rising with urbanization.

There exist a number of alternative dimensions of poverty—income, consumption, assets/wealth, housing conditions, satisfaction of "basic needs", access to services, malnutrition, morbidity/mortality, subjective perceptions of one's (poverty) status or well-being; these may lead to very different estimates of poverty, and carry with them clearly different policy prescriptions.

There is a thus a strong need for better measurement, and for new and easier methods of data collection. So-called rapid assessment methods allow governments to more cheaply estimate and monitor over time poverty and the effects of policies intended to reduce poverty. See for example the Core Welfare Indicators Questionnaire of the UN Development Programme, World Bank and UNICEF, as a data source for the proposed Common Country Assessment, and Bilsborrow, Anker, DeGraf: *Poverty Monitoring and Rapid Assessment Surveys* (Geneva: ILO, 1998).

Urban poverty

While environmental conditions in most cities in the developed world have improved significantly in recent decades, they may be deteriorating in most Third World cities and towns. Air, water and solid waste pollution are increasing problems in many cities. There is also an impression, supported by scattered but not systematic evidence, that in cities the poor are more likely to be affected by environmental problems, and to live in miserable squatter areas, sometimes far from the central city and its employment opportunities and in other cases next to polluting factories, along polluted canals, under bridges, on public lands, etc. These are populations whose health is directly affected by urban pollution, with poor access to basic services, and which contribute to further pollution. I have seen this first-hand in various cities in developing countries, including

Jakarta, New Delhi, Guatemala City, Guayaquil, Lima, Caracas, and perhaps most dramatically in the fastest growing city in Central America, San Pedro Sula, Honduras while on a UNFPA-FAO consultation in 1994. The areas and populations I saw in the latter in 1994 have been much further devastated by hurricane Mitch. I have been in correspondence with a family which, like thousands of others, lost virtually everything when its home was submerged.

On the other hand, urban housing and infrastructure has been improving over time in many LDC cities, improving the quality of life for millions of the urban poor. Many areas with substandard, provisional dwellings have been, and are being, improved for human habitation over time. I first visited several tugurios and suburbios of Guayaquil in 1973, and then revisited the same areas 20 years later. Houses built of scavenged materials, supported on stilts over polluted canals—with the canals serving as their latrines, electricity illegally pirated from nearby lines, and the nearest bus service a kilometer away by a gravel road—were now upgraded to modern houses with electricity, indoor plumbing, and paved roads. Such improvements have occurred in many places because of the political clout of the urban populations in democratic systems, and the visibility and closeness of the slums to the political leaders.

Yet, millions of the urban poor in LDCs continue to live in conditions similar to those of Guayaquil in 1973, or in worst conditions. Governments and NGOs can better and more cheaply facilitate improvements through decentralization of certain expenditure programs, including public works, schools, roads, etc. This can be done in a much more cost effective way than is often done (e.g., via large, expensive capital-intensive projects, with international funding), with the city government itself providing/subsidizing materials and technical assistance and the local community providing voluntary manpower. Small credit programs could be promoted and managed by local residents, with minimal public funds drawn upon and repaid through a revolving program. NGOs can often play useful roles in setting up such small, local institutions. Their loans can contribute to improve the quality of life of the poor, even in the absence of improvements in employment or incomes.

Ultimately, the latter is necessary, but is linked to economic improvements in the country. Certainly better macroeconomic policies, and in some countries far less corruption, could contribute significantly to this. But in this increasingly globalized world, the economic health of cities will depend also on their international competitiveness. There have been several studies of the factors that determine this, but more research is needed, which will evidently lead to policy implications. Cities that grow economically will attract both internal and international migrants (and therefore human and financial capital) which will lead to further growth, higher employment and higher wages.

Linkages between urban and rural areas have received very little attention. Cities often have "ecological footprints" on the Earth that are huge. The ecological footprint refers to the land area required to supply all the products consumed or used by the city. The ecological footprints of the urban poor are minuscule compared to those of the rich. Unfortunately, the products consumed by the city are often produced at high environmental cost elsewhere, including the loss of soil fertility and erosion in areas where its food is grown, the value of forests (and biodiversity) lost to supply the city with wood for construction and fuelwood, the depletion of the non-renewable and renewable resources it consumes, the cost of drawing down bodies of surface water and underground aquifers—all on the environmental "source" side—and the cost of the pollution including human health costs on the environmental "sink" side. One of the principal ecological footprints is in the consumption of prime farmland by urban expansion and sprawl. Estimates of the ecological footprint of cities are rare, but find it equivalent to 40 to several hundred times the physical area of the city. Mexico City, for example, has grown so much that the forests surrounding it have been largely destroyed, damaging the watershed, which in turn has led to more erosion and landslides, less water retention and faster depletion of underground aquifers, and poorer air quality. Mexico City has also used up most of the once plentiful lakes in its valley, and now draws water from over 200 km away. Parts of the city have sunk up to 30 feet this century due to subsidence. Untreated liquid wastes (including toxic wastes) pour into a small river that flows into a nearby valley where contaminated food is grown for the city, half the solid wastes are not properly collected and disposed of, and its air pollution (especially solid particulates, ozone and lead from gasoline) is almost legendary and harmful to human health. Similar situations exist around many other Third World cities.

Ecological footprints of urban areas need to and can be reduced by better urban planning, including zoning controls to encourage vertical not horizontal growth combined with preservation of green areas; by eliminating direct and implicit subsidies on water, electricity and transportation to encourage more efficient use; by increased recycling of water and solid waste products (which has hardly begun in developing countries, except scavenging by the poorest); etc. A substantial increase in economic and technological assistance from the developed world is needed to stimulate this process.

Rural poverty

Rural poverty is generally higher than urban poverty: a higher percent of the rural population is poor, and a higher proportion of the rural poor are extremely poor. This is true regardless of the measure of poverty used. Indeed, most non-income measures indicate an even higher proportion of rural compared to urban poor than income measures, e.g., measures based on wealth or ownership of goods, housing conditions (including access to electricity and indoor plumbing), access to education and health facilities, and levels of morbidity and mortality.

Rural poverty is also linked more closely to the depletion of the (natural) environment than is urban poverty. It is the poor, with tiny agricultural plots, who are forced to overuse the soil attempting to grow as much as possible for survival; who migrate to rainforests and fragile semi-arid zones in search of land to clear for new agricultural plots; and who overgraze in areas ever more circumscribed by sedentary farmers, creation of national parks, native reserves, and government or private sector export crop plantations.

The preoccupation with rural-urban migration is a reflection of the urban bias of development researchers and demographers. Data compiled by the UN Population Division for its 1999 report for available countries reveal that urban-urban migration is the largest in 10 countries, rural-rural in 4 and rural-urban only in two. Furthermore, rural-rural migration is larger than rural-urban in 11 of the 16 countries. Since rural-rural migration is often associated with the expansion of the agricultural frontier into ecologically fragile regions, and therefore with environmental degradation, it should be receiving much more attention in research and policy.

Government policies contribute directly to rural poverty. First, land tenure policies in many developing countries, especially in Latin America, have led to (or allowed) extreme concentration in landholdings, with 40 percent of the land commonly in 1 percent of the landholdings while 40 percent of the farmers with the smallest plots have less than 5 percent of the land. The latter have no choice but to overwork the land, work off-farm, or migrate in search of land elsewhere. In such countries, until significant land redistribution occurs, all other policies that can be conceived to reduce rural poverty will amount to little more than deceit.

Nevertheless, other policies have also contributed to rural poverty, including a strong urban bias in development policies in most LDCs. This is manifest in pricing policies that keep prices of basic food commodities (produced by the rural poor) low, reducing rural incomes; lack of investment in infrastructure in rural areas, resulting in massive differences in access to educational and health facilities, consumption goods, amenities, and the quality of life in general. Government investment, government employment, transportation and water, schools, health facilities, etc., are all concentrated in urban areas more than in proportion to the urban population. Technical assistance and credit to agriculture have been cut back in many countries and have become almost inconsequential, while agronomy university training is languishing. It is no wonder that people continue to migrate to urban areas even when urban employment prospects are mediocre.

An example is the Ecuadorian Amazon: I have been involved in studies of migrant settler farmers in the Amazon region of Ecuador for the past decade. Following roads built by petroleum companies originally to lay oil pipelines, over a hundred thousand migrants have moved into the region since 1972, devastating much of one of the 11 richest areas of biodiversity in the world. Most of them came from areas of the Sierra or Highlands where they had little land. They were poor before, and continue to live quite poorly, with family incomes less than a quarter of the mean for the country, far from health facilities and markets, living in wood shacks with no electricity or piped water, sometimes far from the nearest road. They have been largely ignored by government policies, apart from an earlier program to survey the plots of land and issue land titles, even if only provisional. Their needs are many, and much could be done to help them at modest cost, but there is little being done, apart from some scattered though successful programs of infrastructure provision, credit and technical assistance by a few NGOs. Some specific policies needed include much more agricultural extension assistance, creation of small-scale industries in towns, reorientation of credit from cattle to crops, and expanded health and family planning services.

Summary and policy issues

There are pressing needs for better data on poverty, on food consumption and adequacy, and on both the environmental conditions in which people live (mainly an issue in urban areas, but not exclusively so) and their environmental impacts. Better data are needed to provide a better basis for policy formulation and monitoring, especially of policies intended to reduce poverty (however measured). Selective policy-oriented research is needed, including studies of the economic behaviour of the poor, of their children's work vs. school attendance and therefore of future opportunities to escape poverty, and of the effects of programs of infrastructure, loans and employment generation, based on well designed surveys of households before and after policy experiments. The results should be widely disseminated internationally, as well as used responsibly within countries to improve policies.

If ecological footprints are considered at the level of persons, it is evident that, from the consumption side, the rich have far bigger footprints than the poor, both within developing countries, and between developed and developing countries. This has evident implications for policy measures at both national and global scales, though there seems ever less political will to face up to this reality with the dominant development paradigm now focused on neoliberal policies.

Certain types of development programs can have significant impacts on reducing poverty, and can often be geographically sited for that purpose, including much physical infrastructure, credit, and even technical assistance. Programs oriented at decentralization, that go beyond the current popular lip service and devolve some revenue raising as well as expenditure and decision-making functions to local communities, are often good ways of ensuring that the poor benefit. In "top-down" programs, those running the show at the top are usually the wealthy, who protect their own interests. In this context, NGOs have often been very successful working at the local level. It is refreshing that bilateral and even multilateral development agencies are now working significantly with NGOs.

There has been too much emphasis on achieving development through grand schemes (related closely to the point above) and through bricks and mortar. Such schemes usually involve high costs in money, in human relocation, and to the environment, and too often provide short-lived benefits. The old Chinese saying seems relevant here, about the value of building a mind: There needs to be more focus on the human capital side of development, a focus which goes beyond the bricks of school buildings and formal education, though that is important and has probably been the most successful use of development aid over the past 4 decades. On-the-job training through experience is also crucial for development. But something more is needed, which explains why some of the NGOs are having far higher benefits per dollar of expenditures than most government or private sector social activities. Institutions need to be created and improved that embody the improved human capital, and multiply its impacts. In this context, a larger (but temporary) input of foreign experts working closely with and training local officials/staff/farmers, etc., during longer periods of stay in LDCs than our usual fly-bys. Those "trained" can in turn then more effectively provide technical assistance and leadership and train people within their own country to be more productive, and to engage in economic activities which are more sustainable in terms of the environment. This requires not just longer-term postings of foreign development personnel in LDCs rather than the typical rotations of people out every 2–3 years (precisely when they are becoming effective); it also requires aid personnel with more technical skills, and fewer bureaucrats. Some international agencies, including the U. S. Peace Corps, have moved in this direction, but much more is needed. A whole new outlook on development, focussing on human capital transfers and strengthening local institutions for development is needed, as well as better technology.

II. Fighting poverty: the role of economic policy

"The case for openness," by T. N. Srivanasan
"Openness plus ODA equals Development, " by Makoto Taniguchi
"The limits of openness" by Dariuz Rosati

Note of introduction

The range of economic policies conducive to poverty alleviation is large. Readers can also refer to the Report of the Secretary-General published on 18 May 1999 in connection with these panels, and entitled "The role of employment and work in poverty eradication: the empowerment and advancement of women."

In this section, panelists address the issue of openness as the best posture to attain pro-poor growth. The case for openness is made by T.N. Srinivasan, who demonstates that the growth created by openness is pro-poor because it allows the poor, who can find new work in export industries, to enhance the value of their main asset—their labour. Srinivasan thus sees the opening of world market as strategic for alleviating world poverty.

Makotoa Taniguchi also advocates economic openness, but contrary to T.N. Srinavasan, he is sanguine about the catalytic effects that official development assistance can have on developing countries, including South-South cooperation. In particular, ODA can be used to improve agricultural development and food security, as exemplified by the current Japanese programmes of development cooperation.

Elaborating on the experiences of transition economies in the past ten years, Dariusz Rosati warns that openness does not necessarily bring about social progress and poverty alleviation. Instead, more emphasis should be put on the non-economic components of growth, including social participation and assent, good government, good infrastructure and social safety nets—a subject to be discussed in the following section.

"The case for openness" by T.N. Srinivasan, Yale University

Poverty is concentrated in a few countries of the world. Of the over 1.3 billion people who lived on less than U. S. $ 1 a day in 1993, nearly two

thirds live in China and South Asia, with China and India alone accounting for over three-fifths of the world's poor (World Bank Atlas, 1998,
page 14). Also, the problem of poverty is primarily rural. It is therefore
appropriate to look at the success or failure of policies towards poverty
alleviation using India, and South Asia, as examples. Before I do so, let
me make some general remarks.

I will focus primarily on national policies. Rhetoric aside, international policies, other than those that help keep the system of world trade
in goods and services as well as of finance and technology flows open
and free, efficient and stable, have little to do with poverty or its alleviation. International policies such as development aid, debt-relief and so
on, would have little or no impact on poverty unless national policies, and
particularly the opportunity for participation of all socio-economic
groups in political and economic decision making, were conducive to
poverty alleviation. Even if it they are, any realistic increase in financial
aid or debt relief is likely to have only a very modest impact on levels of
poverty. If they are not, it is all too likely that additional aid or resources
released by debt relief will enrich the well-to-do and add to unofficial
capital outflows.

Poverty reduction policies could be grouped into three categories. First
are those that help and empower the poor to climb out of poverty on their
own. These policies enhance the productivity of assets that the poor own,
primarily their own labour, but also of their farms and enterprises. They
may also enable the poor to accumulate assets, particularly their human
capital, as well as improve the quality of such assets. The second category
includes economy-wide policies, such as macroeconomic, foreign trade
and sectoral policies that affect overall economic growth and its impact
on the poor. And third, policies that redistribute income and wealth.

By and large, redistributive policies have had limited, if not perverse,
effects on poverty alleviation. Radical redistribution policies either are
evaded or reduce the effectiveness of policies of the first two categories.
A major source of disparities among males and females is within households: their female members are discriminated against in the allocation of
household resources for education, health and nutrition. Public policy interventions cannot easily correct this discrimination. Of course, for those
who do not own non-labour assets, and whose participation in the labour
force is constrained by their own idiosyncratic situation—for example,
due to physical disability, health or family circumstances, redistributive
transfers are needed. But such individuals are more likely to constitute a
small fraction of a population. For the majority of the poor, the only effective policies are those that enhance their productivity and those that

enable the economy to grow, not only more rapidly, but also ensure that growth is of a character that benefits the poor. In particular, whether the poor benefit from growth will depend on whether rapid growth is brought about by fuller and more efficient utilization of labour. Greater integration to the world economy not only will accelerate growth, but will also make it pro-poor by exploiting to a greater extent the static and dynamic comparative advantage of most poor countries in labor intensive goods and services.

However, success in integrating developing countries with the world trading system depends on its remaining open to labor intensive exports of poor countries without high tariff and non-tariff barriers. Unfortunately, the developing countries as a group have not participated effectively in most of the eight rounds of multilateral negotiations (MTN) under GATT auspices. This was in part because they were pursuing a development strategy that emphasized import substituting industrialization and in part because, nurtured by the early post second World War development thinking, they were pessimistic about their export prospects and did not view trade as an engine of growth. Instead they demanded special and more favorable treatment and preferences from their developed trading partners. Developed countries found it in their advantage to concede to these demands, because it enabled them to get away with their own egregious violations of the principle of non-discrimination and maintaining high and discriminatory trade barriers, such as in the multi-fibre arrangement (MFA) governing trade in textiles and apparel. Their grant of generalized system of preferences (GSP) was conditional and quantitatively small. Thus, by demanding and receiving such crumbs from the rich man's table as the GSP, developing countries lost an opportunity for ensuring a world trading system that is open and fair to them. In November this year, the third ministerial of the World Trade Organization (WTO) is to be held in Seattle. It is likely another round of MTN will be launched at that meeting. It is very important from the perspective of the poor that the world trading system is further liberalized and kept free of barriers. There are a few demands that developing countries should insist on in the new round towards achieving this objective.

The first demand is to bring trade in agriculture fully into the WTO by phasing out the infamous common agricultural policy (CAP) of the European Union, peanut and sugar quotas of the United States, and other such distortions. This is important since the poor who depend on agriculture for their livelihood in most low income countries are likely to benefit from a globally more efficient agriculture.

Second is to ensure that any agreement on the movement of natural persons is liberal. This is important because many developing countries have comparative advantage in labor intensive services, and some in skill intensive services such as computer software.

Third is to decide once and for all, that the issue of labor standards will be kept out of the WTO and put into ILO where it belongs. The demand from many rich countries for the inclusion of a "social clause" relating to labour standards in the WTO is mostly driven by protectionism and not by altruism. If indeed altruism was the driving force, there are other and more efficient ways than trade sanctions for the rich countries to help poor workers, including liberal immigration policies.

Fourth is to wind up the Committee on Trade and Environment in the WTO and put environmental issues in the UNEP or some other suitable forum. Here again, the probability of capture by protectionists of the genuine concern for the environment is much higher if these issues are taken up in the WTO. In any case, much of the environmental pollution in developing countries is non-trade related and is in fact a reflections of their poverty. Protectionism, masquerading as environmentalism, is no different from any other form of protectionism in its adverse impact on poverty.

Fifth, is to make the use of anti-dumping (AD) illegal in the WTO. Since the Uruguay Round Agreement, which mandated the phasing-out of the MFA, some rich countries have resorted to AD measures to circumvent or evade their commitments. Clearly, apparel is a major labour-intensive export of poor countries. This evasion of their Uruguay Round commitments on MFA by the rich hurts the poor. Unfortunately, some developing countries have also begun to use AD measures. This is an undesirable trend.

Sixth, is to try to take Trade Related Intellectual Property Rights agreement (TRIPS) out of WTO if possible, and into WIPO or other such forum.

Seventh and lastly, to amend Article XXIV of WTO relating to preferential trade agreements, to say that any concessions granted preferentially should be extended to all members of the WTO on a MFN basis within 5-10 years of the conclusion of any preferential agreement.

I have not included in this any demand for special treatment of least developed countries (LDCs). In my view, many LDCs are in need of general resource transfer as well as technical assistance, and not trade preference. By asking for and receiving trade preferences, LDCs would in effect absolve the rich of having to make the more politically costly resource transfer.

Turning to the Indian experience, the foundations of India's development strategy that was pursued until the systematic reforms of 1991, were laid in the late thirties and forties prior to independence in 1947. These were articulated in development plans published by groups from the left to the right of the political spectrum. Remarkably, there was a consensus among them that for India, poverty eradication has to be the over-arching objective of development. Long before UNDP's Human Development Reports, these plans defined development broadly to include improvements in life expectancy, health, and education. They did emphasize rapid income growth (at rates exceeding 7 percent per year), but not as and end in itself, but as a means to poverty eradication. Long before the World Bank published its study on redistribution with growth, these pre-second World War plans discussed redistribution along with growth. Clearly, the failure of India's development plans after independence in eradicating poverty did not lie in their objectives, but in their policy content.

Unfortunately, India's pre-independence plans and their immediate post independence counterparts were heavily influenced by what policy makers thought as the success of Soviet Central Planning in transforming a backward agricultural economy. These plans emphasized import substituting industrialization with an emphasis on heavy industry in an overwhelming rural and agricultural economy. The state was to take the lead in taking the commanding heights of the economy through a monopoly on certain key industries and state control over private sector development, in particular foreign trade and investment. Although savings and investment rates doubled during the period 1950–1980, growth rates did not increase. Much of the employment created in this period was in the inefficient public sector, and outside of the heavily controlled private manufacturing sector. Technology flows were strictly controlled. In fact, the authors of India's First Five Year Plan went so far as to claim that to be against controls is to be against rapid development. This dirigiste development strategy did not generate rapid development, but ended up as the source of political and economic corruption.

The growth record of the economy until the eighties was unremarkable, an average annual growth in GDP of 3.5% against a growth in population at 2.2%. During this period, there was no downward trend in poverty. The proportion of the poor in the population fluctuated around 50%. Until the eighties, a conservative macroeconomic policy was pursued along with a severely distortionary microeconomic policy framework with respect to investment and foreign trade. But in the eighties, macroeconomic prudence was abandoned and some micro distortions were reduced. With fiscal expansionism financed by increasingly costly borrowing at home and abroad, the growth rate accelerated to 5. 5% per year. But given that microeconomic fundamentals were unchanged, and macroeconomic imprudence was at the root of it, it was inevitable that a severe macroeconomic crisis would end this growth sooner or later. It did in 1991, with a severe macroeconomic and balance of payments crisis forcing the government to institute reforms.

While it lasted, the growth in the eighties had a significant effect on poverty. The proportion of the poor in the population came down from nearly 51% in 1977–1978 to a little over a third in 1990–1991 prior to the crisis. In the year of the crisis and the next, it crept up to two-fifths, and since then, with growth accelerating to above 6%, it has once again resumed its downward trend.

There are two policy aspects of poverty alleviation that the all-India trends conceal. First of all, rural poverty in the country as a whole has not gone down since the reforms. Also, in the north and eastern states of India, where a large majority of the Indian population and the poor live, poverty has not gone down unlike in other states. The reason for these differential trends in India are not far to seek. First of all, agriculture on which nearly two thirds of India's workers depend directly or indirectly for their livelihood, and whose performance affects rural poverty, has yet to be touched significantly by the reform process. Indian agriculture has been kept insulated from world markets. In fact, even within India, there are restrictions on private trade in agriculture. Second, among Indian states where rural poverty is decreasing, most are in the South, where the population is better educated and disparity between men and women in health or education is much smaller. Some of these states have already reached replacement levels of fertility. They were better placed to avail themselves of the opportunities opened up by reform.

The experience of other South Asian countries such as Bangladesh, Pakistan and Sri Lanka confirm and reinforce the lessons from Indian experience. Policies for poverty alleviation and reducing discrimination against females are not mysterious or new but mundane, tried and tested. They rest on rapid and labor intensive growth, based on a better educated and healthier work force, participatory democracy, and fuller integration with the world economy.

"Openness Plus ODA Equals Development" by Makoto Taniguchi, Waseda University, Japan

The present state of extreme poverty

According to the OECD study mentioned above, there still exists massive extreme poverty despite recent progress with poverty reduction. As you all know, a world total of some 1.3 billion people, roughly 30% of the world population is classified as being in extreme poverty (defined as per capita daily income, at PPPs, of one US dollar or less). Even rapidly growing economies like China and India with large populations still account for a high percentage of the total. Sub-Saharan Africa is the other major area of poverty, amounting to some 220 million. However, the East Asian experience shows that economic growth through linkage-enhancing policies has not only been good for growth, but also for poverty reduction. Emerging developing economies, mainly in Asia, oriented their economies toward dynamic participation in world trade, investment and technology flows over the past three decades. They have made major progress against poverty. When China started its economic reform in 1978, some 60% of its people lived in poverty, but by 1995, it improved to 22% that lived below the poverty line. In sharp contrast, the poverty reduction has been disappointing in those countries which have not integrated themselves into the world economy through trade, investment and technology.

Projections of growth performance

Based on the empirical evidence, it can be said that poverty reduction can be most effectively achieved by rapid economic growth through integrating into the world economy. As I see it now, the major emerging economies that are integrating into the world economy will even grow faster than the present group of OECD economies in the coming decades. The OECD study estimates that China will have the highest annual rate of growth of 8% with a "high growth" scenario (HG) towards 2020 (with the "low growth" scenario (LG), 5.6%). India's growth rates will be 7% (HG) and 4.4% (LG). Whereas Sub-Saharan Africa's growth rates will be 5.2% (HG) and 2.7% (LG). A "high growth" scenario (HG) means a "high performance" scenario, while a "low growth" scenario (LG) means a "business as usual" scenario.

In terms of per capita income (at constant 1992 PPPs), the dynamic Asian Economies (Taiwan, Singapore, Malaysia, Thailand and the Philippines) and some Latin American Economies (Argentina, Brazil, and Chile) will rapidly catch up with OECD economies towards 2020, and some other major emerging economies (China, Indonesia, and India) will be able to moderately narrow the gap with OECD economies. Nevertheless, even a quarter century of high growth would leave the average per capita income of non-OECD economies far below the OECD average, and Sub-Saharan Africa, in particular, would hardly see a narrowing of its per capita income gap. In HG, it would show moderate growth, reversing the decline of the past decade and a half. In LG, the African continent would see almost no improvement compared with its per capita income in 1995, resulting in an even larger gap with OECD economies and with other developing regions.

Under these assumptions, the proportion of extreme poverty would become negligible in China, would fall by three-fourths in India in 2020. For Sub-Saharan Africa, it would be of the utmost importance to attain at least a 5.2% growth rate in order to reduce the present level of extreme poverty to the half by 2015 as the DAC report "Shaping the 21st Century" proposed. However, the policy challenges facing these economies are tremendous, and all efforts to attain these goals should be made not only by their governments but also by international co-operation. In particular, the growth prospects for the least developed countries such as Sub-Saharan Africa, which are lagging behind the integration into the world economy seem to be lower than those of integrated countries. So that, I would like to focus on the issue of extreme poverty for the least developed countries in this panel of ECOSOC as a priority issue, although I do not deny the seriousness of poverty issues of some emerging economies like China, India, Indonesia, and Brazil which are already in the process of being integrated to the world economy.

Problems which the least developed countries are facing

Flows of private capital to developing economies have risen dramatically, while ODA has been declining in recent years. According to the DAC Chairman's Report 1998, private capital flows have increased from US $43.6 billion in 1990 to US $252.1 billion in 1997 (its share of total net resources flows has increased from 33.6% to 77.7%). On the other hand, ODA which has increased from US $50.6 billion in 1990 to its peak of US $60.3 billion in 1994, started to decline in US $49.8 billion in 1997 (its share has declined from 39% of the total net resources flows in 1990 to 15.3% in 1997).

Also, foreign direct investment (FDI) inflows are concentrated on a small number of countries, some of which are becoming capital exporters themselves. In particular, Asian economies attract a significant share of FDI. East and Southeast Asia alone received 62% of FDI to non-OECD economies in 1995. China stands out as by far the major destination of FDI. The cumulative FDI flows into China, 1991–95, were US $ 114 billion, second only to the US (US $198 billion). Among developing economies, Brazil and Indonesia are also major destinations for FDI. Over the past couple of years, annual FDI flows to Africa has been around US $5 billion. Although FDI to the 48 least developed countries rose 29% in 1995, it amounted to only US$1.1 billion out of total flows to developing countries of US $100 billion. So I should say that the least developed countries have been largely by-passed by the surge in private capital flows. No Sub-Saharan African country figures among the largest 20 recipients of the private capital.

As for the flows of ODA, Africa is still overwhelmingly dependent on ODA, but net ODA receipts by Sub-Saharan Africa have decreased from US $17.3 billion in 1993 to US $15.1 billion in 1997.

Strategies for poverty reduction in developing countries, in particular, in the least developed countries

DAC Report "Shaping the 21st Century", sets up a number of specific goals for economic well-being, social development, environmental sustainability and regeneration to reduce poverty in poorer developing countries. Among others, the Report sets up a goal of reducing the proportion or people living in extreme poverty into half by 2015.

To follow up the DAC 21st Century Strategy, I would like to suggest the following strategies:

1. Integration of the Least Developed Countries into the World Economy

All efforts should be made to help reverse the growing marginalisation of the least developed countries, and to integrate their economies into the global economy, linking their economies through trade, investment and technology flows, as was strongly emphasized in the Agenda for Action for African Development of TICAD-II (The Second Tokyo International Conference on African Development, held in Tokyo in October, 1998).

2. Sound Macroeconomic Policies

Through integration, their economic growth rates should be raised to high level. As TICAD-II exactly pointed out, the real GDP of African countries would need to grow more than 5% annually for meaningful poverty reduction (This target coincides with the OECD's HG rate for Sub-Saharan Africa). For this purpose, sound macroeconomic policies should be enforced.

3. Role of ODA in consolidating social and economic
   infrastructure

First, stronger efforts in donor countries to mobilize ODA (official development assistance) are necessary to help assist the self-help efforts by the least developed countries towards the integration of their economies into the world economy. It is true that major emerging economies also need ODA for their further economic development. However, I am of the view that since they are already blessed with large amount of ODA and massive FDI inflows, limited ODA resources should be directed more to the least developed countries. As mentioned before, major emerging economies would be able to reduce their extreme poverty by maintaining high growth rates mainly utilizing fully available FDI. In this respect, I would not share the view of Prof. Paul Kennedy to concentrate ODA mainly on his so-called "pivotal states" like major emerging economies. Second, ODA should be utilized to help support the social and economic infrastructure of the least developed countries. Human resources development through education, training and healthcare should be promoted as a basic measure for poverty reduction. Also, ODA should help support the development of their trade, which can be most conducive to linking their economies to the global economy, in order to catch and ride the tide of globalization. Third, ODA can also support the necessary macro-economic and structural reforms, including through technical co-operation. A growing number of ODA-dependent countries are implementing reforms that are enabling them to mobilize increased domestic resources and attract foreign investment in amounts that are significant for the size of their economies. In this respect, ODA can play a catalytic role ("pump-priming") in helping the least developed countries to build their capacities to create and mobilize domestic resources, in particular attract FDI and become less dependent on aid. As an example, I would like to introduce my own experience in Papua New Guinea (PNG) in the middle of 1980's. It was very difficult for Japanese businesses to invest into PNG's fisheries, timber and other natural resources until PNG's infrastructure such as ports, roads, bridges was developed by Japan's ODA. Since the majority of the least developed countries like Sub-Saharan Africa are still primary commodity producing countries, the catalytic role of ODA to attract FDI to develop their natural resources should be fully utilized.

4. Agricultural development and food security

First, as the TICAD-II Agenda for Action clearly stated, Africa's economic development and poverty reduction are closely linked to agricultural development. The agricultural sector accounts for some 35% of Africa's GDP, 40% of exports and 70% of employment. And it is gratifying to note that African agricultural production has grown and exports increased. However, Africa's agricultural production and productivity for both food and cash crops is still low and food production has not kept pace with a high population growth of 2.6%. So increased efforts should be made both by African countries and the international community.

Second, Africa should aim at economic development primarily through "green revolution" and then agro-industries. In this connection, I cannot forget my sad experience in ECAFE (present ESCAP) in the 1960's. While working in ECAFE secretariat, I wrote an article which emphasized the importance of modernizing the agricultural sector, through which more balanced growth towards industrialization can be effectively attained. However, the Secretariat, which was strongly influenced by the idea of promoting rapid industrialization, severely criticized me as a neo-colonialist trying to keep Asian developing economies as eternal primary commodity producers. Fortunately, after a decade, Asian development policy shifted towards more balanced growth through the "green revolution". At present, even India, which had severe famines in the past decades, turned to be a self-sufficient food producing country feeding its increasing population. The OECD study estimates that India will continue to be a net exporter towards 2020. China may become a large importer of agriculture and food processing in 2020 together with Japan. But I strongly hope that China can reverse this estimate by its effort to attain self-sufficient food production feeding an increasing population in the coming decades. In this connection, I am very much interested in Japan's programme of rice production in Africa in co-operation with WARDA, the West Africa Rice Development Association, and IRRI, the International Rice Research Institute as one of the follow-up measures of TICAD-II.

Third, while working in OECD, I was involved in the work of the Club de Sahel. The Club made a very interesting study entitled "Preparing for the Future: A Vision of Africa in the Year 2020" in 1995. According to the study, West Africa's agriculture is becoming increasingly market-oriented creating a new class of entrepreneurial farmers who can farm more intensively, with more sustainable methods and investing their own savings in increasingly market-oriented ventures. They are producing more varieties of agricultural products and are already trading across their own borders. Through their trade, the regional economy in West Africa is undergoing transformation, and this will give a bright prospect for the future of sub-regional co-operation in Africa.

5. Sub-Regional Co-operation among the Least Developed
   Countries and South-South Co-operation

Since the least developed countries would not be invited to any major regional integration "arrangement", sub-regional co-operation among the least developed countries and South-South co-operation, supported by developed countries can play an important role. In order to promote sub-regional co-operation, it is very important to develop horizontal linkages through exchange of commodities among neighbouring countries as seen in West Africa. It may be a very challenging task for them, but this sub-regional co-operation may lead a way towards reducing regional conflicts which are unfortunately common happenings in Africa. In order to develop sub-regional co operation, communication network, transportation facilities including roads and railways must be developed. This is a field in which South-South co-operation, together with developed countries' co-operation should be implemented.

Conclusion

As I mentioned before, the Japanese government hosted TICAD-II in 1998, following TICAD-I in 1993. As the follow-up of TICAD-II, the Japanese government now set up, among others, a number of supporting programmes for Africa. These are:

- Social Development Grant assistance amounting to Y90 billion in five years in the fields of education, healthcare and water supply.
- Economic Co-operation
- Establishment of Asia-Africa Investment Information Service Centre
- Rice project in Africa
- South-South Co-operation
- Assistance for the training of 2000 Africans in 5 years under South-South Co-operation Training programmes for Africans in Malaysia by Japan, France and Malaysia

I believe that these programmes are good initiatives and I earnestly hope that many other countries both developed and developing will follow suit. Finally, I conclude my speech by expressing my strong hope that Africa can eradicate its poverty through dynamic economic development.

"The limits of openness" by Dariusz Rosati,
Warsaw School of Economics and National Bank of Poland

The development of the global economy over the past 50 years has been impressive: world GDP increased six times since 1950 while world population increased only 2.5 times, thus implying substantial per capita GDP growth. But not everybody has benefited from this remarkable economic advance; nor was it without several important negative implications. First, the progress has not been equally distributed. Important social groups in many countries and regions still suffer from hunger, poverty and exclusion. Second, in many instances economic growth has inflicted substantial damage to the natural environment. Third, it has not contributed sufficiently to building strong, integrated societies with solidarity.

Inequalities in incomes and wealth are particularly striking. The richest 20% of people consume 86% of total consumption, while the poorest 20% consume only 1.3%. Three billion people live on less than 2 dollars per day and 40,000 children die every day because of hunger-related diseases. At the same time, the combined wealth of the 200 richest people is equal to almost 1 trillion US dollars—equivalent to the annual income of 2,5 billion people living in developing countries.

The key to solving the problems of poverty and exclusion is sustained and balanced economic growth. In the long run, only economic growth can provide the means to satisfy social needs and systematically raise living standards. But growth is neither automatic nor equally distributed, it requires specific resources and good policies. And even sustained and balanced growth should not be considered an end in itself, but rather as an essential means for the fulfillment of important human and social objectives, such as improved living standards, eradication of poverty, and a better society, one with less conflicts, healthier, educated people, providing fair and equal opportunities for everybody, including equal opportunities for women.

Recent years have offered us important lessons on how to secure sustained economic growth while putting it in a broader social context. These lessons stem primarily from three important developments that have been taking place in the course of the last decade: the market transformation in central and eastern Europe, the financial crisis in east Asia and the uneven and hesitant economic progress in developing countries in general. The first lesson is that macroeconomic stability, liberalization and privatization are necessary but not sufficient to secure economic growth and social justice—other important elements are indispensable, such as good institutions and social capital. The second lesson emphasizes the pivotal role of good public governance in socio-economic development. The third lesson is that development involves all segments of the society and requires broad social participation in order to be successful.

The market transformation of post-communist economies has been based on the standard prescriptions of liberal economies—or the so-called "Washington consensus". Almost all central and east European countries adopted similar stabilization-cum-reform programmes designed jointly with the IMF. And yet, the results obtained are strikingly different in different countries. The pattern seems to be clear; the more advanced the countries were at the outset of transition, the more successful they became in terms of growth and integration with Western Europe. In fact, this regularity can be rephrased in an even more compelling way: the more distant the transition countries are from Brussels, the more problems they have with going ahead with transformation. Obviously, this regularity has little to do with geography, but simply reflects the extent of influence of Western European institutions on the level of institutional development in individual transition countries: the rule of law, market and democratic institutions and social capital have been generally better developed in central European countries than in southern and east European countries, and in some more remote CIS countries they were simply non-existent. After ten years of transition experiences from Prague to Ulan Bator and from Tallinn to Tirana, one has to admit that the initial reform programmes largely ignored the vast differences in the initial endowments of institutions and social capital in individual countries. The result has been the uneven progress of reforms, continued economic decline and growing social inequalities in many transition countries. This in turn has led to rapidly falling support for market reforms in those countries.

The phenomenal rates of economic growth observed in east Asian countries over the last several decades have clearly demonstrated the inherent assets of east Asian societies, such as high propensity to work, save and innovate, as well as social discipline. They have also demonstrated that active and strong governments can be very helpful in providing conducive environment for rapid and sustained growth. But the recent series of financial crises in that region have also shown the limitations of the east Asian model of development: strong governments seem to be particularly prone to certain risks such as arbitrariness, cronyism and corruption, they tend to distort the behaviour of investors, and they are not always able (or willing) to maintain effective and transparent regulatory frameworks in the economy. The events in east Asia have also shown that not all capital inflows are beneficial and that liberalization of capital transactions may result in macroeconomic instability.

The rate of economic growth in developing countries has not lived up to expectations and needs. The process of catching up with the industrialized world is slow, and for some regions such as Africa or West Asia, does not take place at all. As a result, wide gaps exist between rich and poor countries. This does not only show the deficiencies of national economic policies, but also demonstrates the inability of international organizations to effectively assist poor countries to elaborate and implement good development strategies.

The lessons of the last decade suggest that there is a need to find a new formula for what should be an effective development strategy. First, it should be a strategy oriented towards explicit social and human development goals, rather than towards technocratic considerations only. This implies a more prominent role for goals such as education, social and natural environment, poverty reduction and equal opportunities. Second, it should be a strategy based on a comprehensive and balanced development of all the necessary foundations of growth, including especially institutions and social capital. Third, governments have an important role to play as market-makers, efficient and impartial regulators and in establishing and enforcing the rule of law. Fourth, a development strategy should not be imposed from outside but rather reflect a joint commitment and effort and be based on broad social participation and understanding.

Economic growth requires traditional factors of production such as capital and labour. But growth will not be sustained if some other essential resources are neglected, such as efficient institutions, honest and effective governments and social capital. The acute shortage of these non traditional factors calls for a shift in emphasis and priorities within the framework of national policies and international cooperation. There is a need to restore balance in development. Much more effort and resources, both from national sources and from international organizations should be spent on non-traditional factors of growth. An efficient market economy can function only under the rule of law and within a properly designed and developed institutional and regulatory framework.

Over the past fifty years, the dominant development paradigm evolved from central planning to industrialization through import-substitution to liberal policies based on the "Washington consensus". However, there is a growing consent that contemporary challenges cannot be confronted effectively without going beyond the traditional approach. Recognizing the need for macroeconomic discipline, liberalization and openness, the agenda for national governments and international organizations should also include priorities in four broad areas: first, attaining important social goals such as education for all, health care services, and social protection systems, including active programmes to eliminate unemployment and ensure gender equality; second, building honest and competent governments at all levels; third, establishing open, transparent and effective legal, regulatory and justice systems; and fourth, developing important components of physical infrastructure, especially in transport communications and communal services, including water supply and sanitation.

III. Fighting poverty: the role of social policy

"A safety net in the transition to capitalism: the example of China,"
     by Fan Gang
"Ensuring access to fundamental social services," panel summary
"Eradicating poverty by managing natural resources,"
     by Indira Khurana
"Empower the policy-makers," by Louka Katseli

Note of Introduction

While economic policy provides a necessary basis for poverty alleviation, such as remunerative employment, it is often insufficient to rely on "trickle down" for providing public goods such as health, education, social peace or a sustainable environment. This is where social policy comes in. In "A safety net in the transition to capitalism: the example of China," Fan Gang illustrates how China is managing to keep social cohesion while undergoing market reform. The program described protects people that are laid off by state-owned enterprises and helps them find a new livelihood in the private sector with minimal disruption in their incomes or entitlements.

"Ensuring access to fundamental social services" summarizes one of the panels, entitled "Ensuring access to fundamental social services and putting vulnerable people first." It provides a "bird's eye view" of three essential social services—education, health, and income for the elderly, analyzes the issues currently facing policy makers in these areas and provides recommendations for national governments and international organizations.

In "Eradicating poverty by managing natural resources," Indira Khurana notes that most poverty is rural, and therefore, most poor people today are heavily dependent on natural resources. Managing these resources to make them sustainable is therefore a key objective. Once sustainability is achieved, products and by-products can be traded outside the village for more income, and people can join a more mainstream path to development that involves credit, enterprises, and the consumption of modern goods—without emigrating to urban areas.

Altogether, the three panelists in this section provide examples of the various social policies that exist for developing economies (India), transition economies (China), and developed economies (i.e. pension systems covered in the panel summary). Louka Katseli wraps up by examining the new governance patterns that are required to make both economic and social policies work against poverty.

"A safety net in the transition to capitalism: the example of China" by Fan Gang, National Economic Research Institute, China Reform Foundation and Graduate School of the Chinese Academy of Social Sciences

The current situation of China's unemployment

There are three type of unemployment or under-employment in China, concerning about 300 million people:

Type 1: Unemployment of the urban labour is reflected by the official "urban unemployment rate"(about 3.5% a year in recent years), mainly referring to the new comers to the labor force, the people in transition to new jobs, and the people who have been laid off by the private sector. The registered urban unemployed are covered by an unemployment insurance managed by the social welfare department of the government. Currently, there are about 6 million urban unemployed.

Type 2. Rural under-employment. The rural population is never considered totally unemployed because all are entitled to a piece of farming land, no mater how small the land is. The rural sector suffers huge "surplus labour" of perhaps 200 million, and its per capita income remains low. That is why rural people are emigrating or moving out of agriculture to look for better paid jobs in other industries. If they find new jobs and they are better-off, they stay; if not, they may return to their piece of land, which serves as the ultimate social safety net. From the point of view of politics, the employment of rural people has never been the responsibility of government. They have never been covered by government-run social security programs, even not under the previous socialist welfare system. From this point of view, rural under-employment is in principle not a political issue, and rural people in fact do not go to the government when they have problems finding or keeping a job. However, the government takes the responsibility for providing incentives to farmers to increase their agricultural products and to take responsibility for income equality.

Type 3. Laid-off former state employees. Workers in State-Owned Enterprises (SOEs) were guaranteed by the government life time employment under the previous socialist "social contract." They are still protected under a special status as "off-duty workers" (Xia-gang Zhigong). With this special status, they are entitled to receive a certain amount of minimum payment higher than the unemployment insurance allowance, plus the continuation of their pension program, medical care, housing, and so on. That is why they are not and should not be put in the same category as the "urban unemployed". At the moment, there are about 8 million people with the status of "off-duty worker".

The special problem of laid-off state employees

Many ongoing reforms of state-owned enterprises involve laying off workers.

Under the best scenario, 30% of about 110 million state workers should go. But no one should assume that this could happen overnight. If the restructuring were to be carried out using a "gradualist approach" over ten years, you would still need to lay off on average 3 million people a year. Roughly speaking, this has been the case in the past five years. In total, about 12 million people have been laid off since 1994 and 3 million in 1998.

Why would this be accepted by the workers and how can the government avoid major social unrest while this is happening? First of all, the overall economic conditions have changed. The SOEs in concern are already troubled with financial difficulties and many are not able to pay their workers anyway. The largest social protests by workers in the past years were mainly caused by the delay (of 6 months, 10 months, etc.) in wage payment. With not much hope of improvement, people are starting to realize that SOEs are no longer reliable for job security or income growth. In short, staying with SOEs becomes a less and less attractive choice.

Meanwhile, after twenty years of development, the non-state sector now contributes to over 70% of output and 80% of growth. The possibility of finding a new job in the non-state sector (or simply of starting self-employment) while still getting some income out of the SOEs are both increased. In other word, leaving the SOEs becomes a more and more attractive option.

As mentioned earlier, the compensation package for redundant workers normally enable them to keep most of the benefits they enjoyed in the SOEs. They can keep their pension programs and housing. With the "off-duty worker" status, they are still entitled to medical care and minimum wages (above the urban poverty line) for at least 2 years. Upon finally leaving after this transition period, a lump-sum compensation is normally provided. The key issue here is, whether the minimum wage can be paid and paid on time, and whether the government or SOEs can provide help in finding a new job within a reasonable time. In 1998, a new program was introduced by the central government, the "Urban Re-employment Center"(URC). The key new element of the URC is that unemployment benefits and re-employment programs should be financed by three parties, i.e., the central government, the local government, and the company concerned, instead of only the company as before. This apparently has improved the situation of laid-off people. According a report of the Ministry of Labour, the percentage of laid-off workers who got paid in time increased to 97% in 1998, from 12% in the previous year. That may be the major reason why much less incidents of labour unrest were reported in 1998, compared to the previous year. In addition, the URC also provides re-training programs and job offers (three to five times in two years before final separation).

Eighteen billion RMB—2% of total budgetary revenue or 0.2% of GDP, were spent on these programs. In the next two years, this expenditure may be doubled, but that would still remain within a manageable range.

The success of the URC program encouraged the government to pursue further lay-offs. Lay-offs by themselves can not solve all the problems of SOEs and may not guarantee a successful restructuring, but they are definitely one of the necessary conditions for it.

Retraining and re-employment

Although financial security is absolutely necessary, the most important thing for unemployed people is re-employment.

There have been various re-training and job consulting programs offered to laid-off workers since the early 1990s, when lay-offs started. Several lessons can be drawn from the experiences to date.

First, re-training programs should be run by government agencies, rather than by the companies themselves. At the beginning, these retraining programs were mainly organized by the companies that lay off workers. This was due to the previous company-linked social security system. At the beginning, the government encouraged it in order to reduce the social impacts of unemployment, but did not take the responsibility financially and administratively. As a result, the following problems occurred:

(1) The companies that laid off workers were mainly the companies that were in a bad financial situation and might lack adequate financial means to run the retraining programs. (2) A company, particularly a small company, may be in a position to lay off only a small number of workers.

It seems too costly for the company to offer a wide variety of retraining programs, which could meet different needs and lead to a wide range of job opportunities As a result, the workers either stayed unemployed with the companies, or just returned to a job in the company later.

With the progress of social security reform, the municipal governments started to take responsibility for job consulting and then retraining. It began with the retraining programs conducted by the local industrial bureaus. Later on, with the establishment of the Urban Re-employment Centers, the retraining programs became more institutionalized and associated with job offer-consulting. A laid-off worker is currently offered two retraining programs and three to five job opportunities in 2 years. Afterwards, he or she graduates from the Center and registers with the unemployment welfare schemes, also run by the government.

While the government should take the main responsibility, other parties such as NGOs should also be welcome. But due to the weak development of NGOs in China, the only active player in this regard is the official trade unions in the companies.

A second lesson is that retraining does not have to be for more sophisticated jobs, but is usually just for jobs, particularly in the service sectors. In developed countries, new jobs may require retraining for higher technologies, such as computers. But for a developing country like China, technology may indeed cause unemployment rather than help it. Conversely, the new positions may be found everywhere else—cooks, tailors, barbers, craft, sales clerks, etc. Training agencies should encourage people to take simpler jobs rather than high-skill jobs, which are more difficult to bid for against younger and better educated competitors in the job market. As most needy people are those in their forties and fifties who have most difficulties in learning high tech, this training-for-low-end-jobs approach may be important.

Third, training should include a knowledge of market forces. Many people from either SOEs or rural areas have no experience with the market place or market forces. State workers used to be protected by the state welfare and by the promise of life-time employment. They normally have no idea how to find a job in the labour market. For example, they may not know how to take a job interview, how to write a resume, or how to show their capabilities. Others may not know how to run a small business or become self-employed.

While it is not necessary to set up formal courses, some retraining centers provide people with consulting personnel that teach how to register a new business, how to apply for a loan, how to do the book-keeping, and how to pay tax.

Fourth, most people who have been laid-off by the public sector are able to pursue a "second income" while they earn their unemployment benefits, thus allowing them some practice with the labour market before they immerse themselves into it. During their two years with the Re-employment Center, many state workers are able to find some job to do. Some are temporary, some are long term, at least on a long term track; some are part time, some are full time. Legally speaking, in such cases, most of them are actually no longer unemployed by definition or in terms of their income, and they should be removed from the re-employment center. But local governments normally allow people to "moonlight," as it were. This two years' transition becomes very helpful to get used to new circumstances and to get confident at the new jobs. Re-training by practice may be the best way to understand the market. And the "first income" allows you to make mistakes with the "second income" during these two years.

In conclusion, during significant economic and social transformation, massive un-employment and re-employment are inevitable, creating potential economic and social problems. From this point of view, retraining and safety nets are worth all our best efforts.

"Ensuring access to fundamental social services"

Summary of the panel held in preparation of the high-level segment of ECOSOC, entitled "Ensuring access to fundamental social services and putting vulnerable people first" [1]
(New York, 12 May 1999)

Poverty eradication is an overarching objective of the United Nations, encompassing the different sectoral areas which emerged from the recent major United Nations conferences and summits. The recent process of globalization has impacted considerably on the delivery of social services at the national level, and this has further increased the exclusion of the poor. Thus there is a need to call for increased efforts to make fundamental social services available to all, especially the poor and those most vulnerable. These essential services include education, health and social services for the elderly, women and the youth as vulnerable groups.

---

1   The panel was moderated by Dr. Richard Jolly of UNDP and included four panellists: Mrs. Rebecca Grynspan, former Vice-President of Costa Rica, Professor Franco Modigliani, Nobel Laureate in Economics and Professor Emeritus at the Massachussets Institute of Technology, Dr. Ismail Serageldin, Vice-President for the Special Programs Group of the World Bank and Dr. Lincoln Chen, Executive Vice President of the Rockefeller Foundation

Education

There are an estimated one billion teenagers in the world, representing the largest population group. Most of them are in developing countries whose population pyramid is a flat one. Against this background the goal of education for all seems difficult to achieve, as 120 million children are not in school and another 130 million young people, in particular girls, have dropped out of school.

While several countries have invested in education, with positive impacts on the development process (such as Costa-Rica, Korea, Malawi for primary education), others have reduced their expenses or transferred their responsibilities to the local level, with accompanying negative results in terms of access to education by the poor. Therefore, strong political will is needed to ensure that the education sector is provided with the necessary resources to meet the needs. Training has to be provided at several levels at the pre-elementary, elementary, and secondary levels as well as for vocational training. The latter two are crucial if Governments are to be able to provide some hope for a decent future for their youth, thus preventing juvenile delinquency and avoiding other social problems such as early pregnancies.

As the structure of employment changes with an increased percentage of the active population working in the service sector, the modalities of education are also changing accordingly. Education has come to be seen as a continuing means for individuals to acquire the skills necessary to adapt to changing work requirements throughout life. Therefore, innovative approaches are needed, not only to accommodate new students, but also to determine the kind of educational systems to put in place. However, lack of flexibility in some education systems makes it difficult for many developing countries to adapt to these changes. The new opportunities for the young, e.g. through increased access to information via the Internet mostly benefit the rich and powerful segments of the world population, and this also needs to be reversed.

Basic social services, including health, for the most vulnerable

Most population growth occurrs in the urban context, where traditional family ties have already weakened and social problems are acute. In Latin America, population growth has not even given rise to the quality and quantity of jobs needed. According to ECLAC, 84% of newly created jobs were in the informal sector. The process of globalization (including structural reform and the opening of markets) has not been accompanied by appropriate social protection schemes, thereby generating new groups of vulnerable people. Therefore, a process of quality economic growth, which would generate employment opportunities with adequate salaries, should be promoted.

There is also great inequality in the achievement of health goals, as indicated by the differences in life expectancies both between countries and within countries. The globalization process had eroded Governments' capacities in tackling health issues. This is a factor for the so-called third wave of health challenges, namely the diseases of the poor such as malnutrition, infectious diseases among children, women's reproductive health problems, and environmental health diseases. HIV/AIDS is so widespread in some countries that it has become a development problem as much as a health problem.

Providing a solution to health concerns in poor areas requires the implementation of social security systems that could be adapted to the informal sector. Since it is difficult to mobilize the private sector in support of programmes and services for the poor, state interventions continue to be needed. Health and social security services have to be based on a solidarity-financing compact, to be properly assessed and implemented, taking into account the efficiency of the services provided and transparency in the regulation and supervision of social services.

In brief, globalization is characterized by a simultaneous social inclusion and exclusion process. While many people are becoming members of a transnational middle class, increasingly inter-connected and inter-dependent, others in virtually every neighbourhood and in each country are left behind. This situation in turn threatens the very process of globalization. However, alleviating poverty is an attainable goal when it is considered, for example, that the costs of providing basic infrastructures for water and sanitation in developing countries is estimated at US $ 80 billion, while transactions on the capital market are in the order of US $ 1.4 trillion per day. Several speakers stressed, in such a context, the need for securing the necessary resources for providing basic social services, although it was difficult to find solutions that applied everywhere.

Social services for the elderly

The life cycle theory of savings, elaborated by Prof. Modigliani, is based on the behaviour of rational economic agents. According to this theory, people make provisions for retirement based on the theory of the life cycle; that is, they save money when they are young and productive and spend it when they are old. The cessation of earning capacity is due to institutional rules (e.g. retirement age, set by law). As a result, consumption depends less on current income than on life income.

However, in spite of this rational behaviour, poverty is still a crucial problem, including among older persons. The factors that explain old-age

poverty include: lack of rational planning, lack of appropriate investments protected from inflation, and a reliance on traditional family ties,
with young people maintaining support for the elderly who had themselves supported them when they were younger.

Social security systems were created to replicate such rational behaviour and make it more systematic, and pension systems forced people
to save when they were young. Although such systems have achieved relative success, particularly in terms of removing old people from poverty,
drawbacks still exist. One of the reasons is that rational behaviour by individuals is preferable to pension systems as they exist. Life cycle seeks
to maximize consumption over all while social security systems, through
the principle of forced savings, does not promote optimal consumption,
nor does it allow one to use the accumulated funds to bridge periods of
real financial need.

Although national systems of social security have contributed to alleviating poverty, they are encountering difficulties almost all over the
world. People receive the same amount of pension regardless of the size
of their contributions. In addition, pension systems are dependent on the
population structures, particularly the ratio of young to old, which has
been changing in recent years. As a result, it is no longer possible to rely
on the capital accumulated during one's lifetime to finance one's pension. There is therefore a need for reforms to be carried out in this area,
failing which contributions for pensions will have to rise significantly.

States therefore need to move to a fully funded system, in which contributions are used for investing in financial assets. This should be done
in a collective way, and special efforts should be made to cover unfunded
liabilities during the transition period. Since such systems rely on the
capital that is built up on the basis of the life cycle, they are not vulnerable to population structures and do not depend on a favourable ratio of
young to old in the population.

Recommendations

At the national level, Member States should:

- maintain a high level of public expenditures in the educational sector on a fixed long-term basis;
- build up public infrastructures and social services that are more participatory;
- create social observatory systems for assessing and evaluating social
  needs and public policies in this field;
- adopt fully funded pension systems, based on investments of life
  savings in financial assets.

At the international level, Member States and International Organizations should:

- strengthen the 20/20 initiative, while reversing the decline of ODA;
- adopt incentive measures for the private sector to undertake research and development to fight new diseases;
- reexamine the role of the States and of the international community and define a new global compact for health, drawing upon past achievements;
- create new taxes at the international level to provide additional resources for basic social services for the poor (for example taxation on airline tickets).

The United Nations Economic and Social Council should:

- include health in its areas of work;
- continue its work on the elaboration of basic indicators to measure social development at the global level;
- be increasingly used as a forum for a comprehensive (rather than sectoral) debate on these matters, where national experiences in the economic and social field could be addressed in practical terms. ECOSOC, in view of the collegiality of the United Nations, its "renaissance" and increased collaboration with specialized agencies, constitutes the appropriate body for that purpose.

"Eradicating poverty by managing natural resources" by Indira Khurana, Centre for Science and the Environment, New Delhi, India.

Most of the poor live in rural areas, surviving on subsistence economy, and are therefore dependent on natural resources—fodder, fuel wood, fibre and crops. As degradation of these resources increases, so does poverty. Thus, overcoming economic poverty requires, first of all, overcoming *ecological* poverty. In the process, it is possible to boost employment by tapping the rural unemployed to regenerate the natural environment. This can provide both short-term employment and sustainable livelihoods. Two case studies are presented, where exceptional results were obtained with community management of water. Food security has naturally followed.

Redefining poverty

Rural people largely survive in a subsistence economy—on the biomass, products obtained from plants and animals. About 70% of Indians (700 million) live in rural areas, in villages that sustain themselves on a biomass-based economy. In other words, there are about 700 million people in India alone, that depend on plant and animal products—food, fuel, animal feed, building materials and healthcare needs are met through locally available resources. The degradation of the environment—deforestation, destruction of grasslands, soil erosion, water depletion—therefore all lead to a direct increase in poverty and destitution.

There is a thus strong need for economists to redefine poverty, away from measurement by per capita earnings, to a shortfall in the quantity and quality of the biomass that is needed for basic survival. In other words, in order to measure the survival economy of the rural poor, we need a concept like gross *natural* product, instead of gross national product. The poor, caught in their daily struggle for survival on diminishing natural resources, eventually turn into ecological refugees. The story is the same everywhere—from the barren hills of the Himalayan highlands, through the degraded slopes of the Andes, to the drought devastated soils of the Sahel and the waterlogged and flood affected plains of Bangladesh. As for those who stay behind, their struggle for survival hampers them from rebuilding their devastated ecological capital.

Ecological poverty, therefore, is the lack of an ecologically healthy natural resource base needed for the survival and development of a human society. High levels of ecological poverty today prevent a large part of the world's poor from helping themselves to improve their economic condition.

Ecological poverty is different from economic poverty—which modern economists concentrate on. Economic poverty is largely measured in terms of cash income and is almost totally irrelevant in a biomass-based, subsistence economy. The approaches needed to deal with the two kinds of poverty are also drastically different. While the policies to tackle economic poverty tend to concentrate on welfare schemes, tackling *ecological* poverty requires institutional, legal and financial empowerment, with a strong emphasis on community-based property rights over ecological resources.

Creating win-win solutions for sustainable development

To overcome economic poverty, one has to overcome ecological poverty and generate ecological wealth through employment creation, which will then generate food security, nutrition security and bring about a social transformation. What is needed is to provide the rural poor with the necessary infrastructure in terms of finances, training, etc, so that economic security today becomes the basis of ecological security tomorrow.

The experience worldwide has shown that community participation is essential for the management and regeneration of natural resources. The experience of India throughout the 1970s and 1980s have repeatedly shown that outstanding economic change in rural communities can occur wherever these communities have reorganised themselves to manage their own natural resources. Bureaucratic resource management systems, on the other hand, have invariably failed or have been cost-ineffective. This disqualifies them in a world where financial resources for development are limited.

In turn, the vast numbers of unemployed people in the rural South provide us with an extraordinary opportunity: that of greening the world by creating sustainable livelihoods. The poor— even those who are living at the margins of survival in the world's most ecologically degraded regions—can be put to work in a massive enterprise for the regeneration of the natural capital.

Understanding the village ecosystem

Villages in India, like elsewhere in the developing world are highly integrated micro-systems. The entire village ecosystem is in fine ecological balance. Each village has its own croplands, grasslands, and tree or forest lands, and each of these land-use systems interact with each other. Developments in one will naturally impact on the others. The trees or forest lands provide firewood. This prevents the villagers from consuming cow dung as fuel. Cow dung can instead be used to fertilise the lands and maintain their productivity. Cattle graze on the grasslands and, when grasslands dry off in the dry seasons, crop residues are available as fodder, as are leaves from the trees. This system can easily be ripped apart. Natural resources thus need to be managed and regenerated.

Two case studies of successful policies in two Indian villages will illustrate this argument. There, the transformation came from the management of a precious natural resource—water, which in turn cannot be separated from land and living resources. And this enhances food security. In both cases, the most important factor is local water management and rain water harvesting, the key to a sustainable biomass based economy. In other words, these communities learnt the value of raindrops and collected it.

Case 1: Sukhomajri

This village has the distinction of being the first village in India to be levied income tax on the income it earns from the ecological regeneration of its degraded watershed.

In 1976, Sukhomajri was a small hamlet with a population of 455— with sparse vegetation, poor agriculture and high levels of soil erosion and run off. Even though the average rainfall was 1,137 mm, ground water was not available at practical depths. Soil erosion and gully formation was increasing and consequently, arable land was declining. Subsistence for survival was the norm. The livestock grazed on whatever was available, making regeneration impossible. The surrounding hills were therefore bare—only 5 % had a vegetation cover of sorts.

In 1979, India faced a severe drought. The villagers built a small tank to capture rainfall and agreed to protect their watershed in order to ensure that this tank did not get silted up. This started a process that would have vast implications for the village and beyond. The villagers continued building more tanks. They protected the heavily degraded forest around the catchment area of the tanks. The protected forest increased the availability of fodder and grass, and this allowed a shift in livestock pattern from the lowly goat to the more rewarding and environment friendly cattle.

Between 1977 and 1986, wheat productivity increased from 0.61 tonnes per hectare to 1.22 tonnes per hectare. Grass production increased from 40 kg per hectare to 11.43 tonnes per hectare. This grass has traditionally been used to make ropes for beds all over north India. The grass is also very good pulping material for paper mills when mature. The number of goats went down from 246 to 10 and the number of buffaloes from 79 to 291. The tree density went up from 13 to 1,292 per hectare. The worth of these trees in terms of wood increased to Rs 900 million (US$ 21.08 million). If the forest is harvested on a sustainable basis, the forest will yield Rs 30 million annually (US $ 0.7 million). The trees also produce a valuable condiment used with betel leaves. If these villagers were to set up a small village enterprise to harvest and sell this condiment, they could hope to earn Rs 36 million (US $ 0.84 million).

As a result, household incomes have gone up. Instead of a thatched mud house, villagers now live in birch and cement dwellings. Most households now boast of bicycles, radio sets, electric fans, sewing machines and TV sets.

A study indicates that the return on investment for this project has been of the order of 19 % annually. One of the impressive savings has been on desilting operations, since the flow of sediment has come down by 90%. This saves the government Rs 7.56 million ($ 0.2 million) annually in dredging operations.

Lessons for governance

A lesson to remember arises from the role of government in this success. The main incentive for people to protect their watershed was the assurance they got from the forest department that they would have the right to the usufruct of the degraded forest land. If this assurance had been missing, the entire experiment would have collapsed. A crucial role in this entire exercise was played by the village level institution that was specifically created for the purpose of watershed protection. The Hill Resource Management Society consists of one member from every household in the village. This provides a common platform to all. A framework was also agreed on for the fair distribution of the resources thus generated—water, grass and wood, amongst all the households.

Today the village is capable of withstanding even the most serious of droughts.

Case 2: The Ralegan Siddhi experience: from alcoholism to affluence

This village is situated in a drought-prone area where the villagers were not assured of even one crop a year. In the summer, these villagers regularly took state-sponsored drought relief measures.

In 1975, the village was in the grip of poverty. Each family had hardly one acre of land to itself. The yields from agriculture were poor—the village barely met 30% of its requirements. Fifteen to 20% of the families were undernourished and men migrated to look for work. The village was thus in the grip of chronic poverty, money lenders and country-made liquor.

Enter K. B. Hazare, a retired jeep driver from the Indian army. He began work in the village by constructing storage ponds, reservoirs and gully plugs. Due to the steady percolation of water, the groundwater table began to rise. Simultaneously, governmental social forestry schemes were utilised to plant 300,000–400,000 trees in and around the village. Because of the availability of irrigation water, the land that was lying fallow came under cultivation and the total area under farming increased from 630 hectares to 950 hectares. The average yields of millets, sorghum and onion increased substantially.

Every effort was made to ensure equitable access to the resources generated. Water was distributed equitably. Initially, as water availability was low, only crops requiring little water were planted. All farmers got water in turn, and a second irrigation was possible only after the first round was over. Now, since the commons belong to all, even the landless families, about five in all, get their share of water. Water conservation has led to the development of community wells.

The results speak for themselves. Farmers now grow 2–3 crops per year, yielding fruits and vegetables, which are now exported to places as far as the Middle East. Today, not a single inhabitant of the village depends on drought relief. Incomes have increased substantially.

By Indian standards, Ralegan Siddhi is a very rich village now. Over

25% of the households earn over half a million rupees a year. The village is so rich that a major bank was set up in it. The total savings of the village is Rs 30 million (US$ 0.7 million). For a village that was less than two decades ago riddled with alcoholism and a badly degraded environment, this is indeed a miracle.

Mobilizing a wide range of actors

A new system for decision making was created in the village. Some fourteen committees now operate to ensure people's participation. A democratic institution called the Gram Sabha was created to take community decisions. In other words, the village of Ralegan gave greater importance to participatory, rather than representative democracy. Watershed decisions are undertaken only after they are discussed in the Gram Sabha. People have contributed with their labour, as well as financially.

In addition, other organisations, registered as societies, have been established for different activities. They are all independent but report to the Gram Sabha. This united social action has so far succeeded in preventing outlawed activities, such as grazing in open grasslands or encroaching on common lands.

Efforts should be made to promote the involvement of people in natural resource management. A sense of ownership will go a long way towards reducing the misuse of government funds. A sense of ownership also means that the resources will be judiciously allocated. International agencies such as the World Bank and the United Nations should work towards ensuring a global right to survival for the world's poor. Local and national governments can spur these efforts by striving toward a national right to work, or a "right to survival", all the while strengthening community organizations.

The role of civil society is to publicise success stories; help the poor to help themselves by ensuring transparency and democracy; form networks to provide intellectual leadership, as well as a forum to community groups to lobby for policy changes.

The global right to survival will naturally require funds. These funds should be given by the various donor agencies to programmes on the condition that the recipient countries set up institutional and legal frameworks for community resource management. Money would have to be transferred in a transparent manner to village level institutions and not remain in national capitals. New village institutions would need to be established on the principle of participatory rather than representative democracy.

In India, it is estimated that a nation-wide, legally guaranteed right to work would require about US$ 4–6 billion every year. World-wide, the cost should not work out to be more than US$ 30–40 billion per year for about 10 years. Detailed studies are however needed.

Global benefits

In conclusion, the vast numbers of unemployed people in the rural South provide us with an extraordinary opportunity: that of greening the world by creating sustainable livelihoods. The poor, even those who are living at the margins of survival in the world's most ecologically de-graded regions, can be put to work in a massive enterprise for the regeneration of the natural capital. In other words, a problem can be turned into an asset. Additional benefits include: reducing the work burden of women; creating conditions where the girl child can go to school and where a child will not be seen simply as a pair of working and earning hands; and generate better family conditions to reduce population growth rates.

"Empower the policy-makers"
by Louka T. Katseli, University of Athens, Greece

To promote growth, employment and gender equality, most analysts recommend policies to empower people and improve their capabilities, as well as policies to strengthen social safety nets and governance. Reforms are needed in this direction. But even if we can agree on what to do, can we agree on how to do it?

All these goals—employment generation, gender equality and the elimination of poverty—require not only good policies but *the empowerment of policy making and policy makers themselves.*

In the era of liberalization and deregulation, markets have expanded but market outcomes are not always socially acceptable or desirable. If we are to make markets work for all, we need to reinstate the legitimacy of policy making and of pro-active governments and institutions, to strengthen their capacity to decide, to integrate and implement policies, to restructure institutions accordingly and to monitor and evaluate the effectiveness of policy making both at the national and international level.

To empower policy making we need to discuss more explicitly the processes by which we set priorities and decisions, by which we implement them and by which we monitor outcomes. Let me identify some important challenges ahead of us:

Policies must be integrated

Liberating commodity, capital and labor markets, achieving fiscal consolidation or appropriate monetary and exchange rate policies will not automatically guarantee more employment and less poverty. Employment generation and poverty alleviation require integrated policies and an integrated approach to policy. The provision of social-safety nets for example, or the expansion of employment through public-works programmes, have direct fiscal implications which need to be evaluated in the context of fiscal policy. Does it still make sense to leave the employment question entirely to labour or social affairs ministries, while fiscal policies are delegated to ministries of finance? We will soon have to reopen this discussion. The same holds true at the international level. Let us explore innovative ways to coordinate and integrate the policies of international institutions and maybe go as far as instituting an Economic and Social Security Council to monitor coordination and effectiveness of international policies and assistance programmes.

Policies must be attuned to women's needs

Gender equality requires that the priorities of women be taken into account in policy making. These are partly manifested through their expenditure patterns, which are more oriented to human priorities such as employment, health and education, their needs to combine child-bearing and child-rearing with their participation in labour markets and their preferences for networking, for more flexible and less hierarchical organisational structures. A first step in this direction would be to evaluate the gender dimension of every policy as we do with environment.

Policies must be in the right sequence

We need to develop guidelines as to what to do first and what to leave last. In democratic societies, short-term success is important in building support for reforms that produce longer-term benefits but face greater opposition. Shock therapy works in some cases but not in many others. Regulatory frameworks should be established before liberalisation. FDI should probably be liberalised before trade, and liberalisation of short-term capital flows should be done later in the reform process. The pace of reforms should be determined by the adaptive capacity of political and economic systems.

Find the optimal regulatory areas

In a global world order, we should develop guidelines as to what should be decided globally, regionally, nationally and locally. The present situation reflects the ability of special interests, mostly financial interests, to organize effectively at the international level, rather than the careful selection of optimal regulatory areas. Is there any fundamental economic reason why, for example monetary policies or exchange rate policies are to be decided regionally or internationally, while employment or educational policies are left to the local or national level? If externalities are important in assigning policies to the supra-national level, I cannot think of an area which creates more externalities than education or training.

We must create and strengthen institutions to correct market failures and meet institutional deficits.

To meet market failures, we need to strengthen oversight and regulatory frameworks. These are extremely weak at the international level. To promote employment and alleviate poverty, we need to develop intermediate, flexible, institutions which act as development catalysts to support local entrepreneurial activities.

Effective networking can enhance the legitimacy of policy

Finally, we all agree that community participation is essential at the national or supra-national levels. Tripartite arrangements between industrial employers, unions and governments were very useful in the 1960s and 1970s. They are not suitable for the new realities of the 1990s and the 21st century. NGOs and community organisations having to deal with the grim reality of poverty, unemployment and marginalisation at the local level, should have a voice in the formulation of economic policy. Financial managers should meet occasionally with government officials and social partners to review the societal environment and social effects of portfolio decisions. Building effective networks of policy makers, market actors and development agents is a precondition for sound policies and their effective implementation. As we approach the 21st century, let us learn from our successes and our failures and bring closer together academics, practitioners and policy makers to resolve actual policy problems. We might not be able to pursue first-best policies, but let us at least implement effectively what we all sense are reasonable policies.

IV. "Ten strategic priorities"
Statement by the President of ECOSOC on Poverty Eradication, Geneva, 30 July 1999

Note of Introduction

To enhance the policy relevance of the substantive session of ECOSOC devoted to poverty, the President issued a call to action, on the basis of "Ten strategic priorities", in the form of the concluding Presidential statement that follows.

"Poverty eradication has been the major focus of this Session of ECOSOC. We acknowledge that the major challenge facing the world in the new millennium is the eradication of poverty. This should be based on the promotion of an accelerated pace of growth and development in the developing countries with the support of the international community. 1.3 billion human beings still remain deprived of the most basic necessities of life. Based in part on the uneven impact of globalisation, there is growing income inequality. This is underlined by the fact that the income disparity between the richest one fifth and the poorest one fifth of the world's population has doubled during the past three decades. This is a moral outrage in an age of plenty. Poverty generates conflicts, violence and an array of social evils. It compels the people living in poverty, especially women and children, to live in destitution and stifles their human potential. It is a permanent threat to the most basic of all human rights—the right to a life in dignity and freedom.

People everywhere, governments, international organisations, civil society and the business world are invited to join hands with the United Nations in an all out campaign to fight the scourge of poverty in our world. In order to succeed, we must empower the people living in poverty and ensure that they participate fully in this fight. This world-wide campaign must and can be won within our life time. It requires renewed national efforts vigorously supported by an enhanced international cooperation for development and an enabling environment for sustained economic growth, which promotes social development, trade and investment.

It has been estimated that 40 billion $ a year are needed to achieve the international goals related to poverty eradication. This is one tenth of the illegal traffic in drugs. As a first step, the proportion of people living in abject poverty (with an income of less than a dollar a day) should be reduced by half by 2015.

To achieve this goal, mutually supportive actions are needed at the national and international level around ten immediate and interdependent priorities that have emerged from the ten global conferences of the 1990's.

1. Eradication of poverty cannot be brought about by charity. It is unacceptable that 1.3 billion people live in abject poverty. They have little access to income and social services. They must be in-

tegrated into social and economic life. We need first and foremost to **empower the poor**, focussing on women, and tap their tremendous potential.

Poverty must be fought on many fronts; national actions for equity and grass-roots participation and enhanced international co-operation to reduce the gap between the rich and the poor.

2. **Women** fall into poverty more easily and more frequently than men. They constitute the majority of people living in poverty. Ending discrimination against women and girls and promoting gender equality are critical for poverty eradication. Women rights are human rights: they are indivisible.

The strengthening of existing and emerging microcredit institutions, which proved so successful in some developing countries, should be pursued with the support of international financial institutions.

3. **Productive employment**, including self-employment, plays a central role in poverty eradication. In the face of rising urbanisation, job opportunities must be created for the young people entering the labour market in the next generation.

Access of the poor to land, capital and other productive resources must be improved. Small and medium enterprises, cooperatives and informal businesses, especially for women, should be encouraged.

Poverty eradication requires economic growth that generates employment. Sound policies at the national level must be supported by strong international cooperation.

4. **Hunger and malnutrition** are the worst manifestations of poverty. The chronically hungry cannot grow out of poverty. This is morally reprehensible and economically wasteful. Efforts should be redoubled to reduce the proportion of the under-nourished by half by 2015. Immediate steps should be taken to promote sustainable food security for the poor and to improve food self-sufficiency by enhancing the productivity of agriculture.

Action should be taken to provide agricultural services to achieve higher yields of food crops, reduce waste and improve post-harvest management, through storage facilities and rural access roads.

5. **Sufficient supply of safe water and a clean environment** are necessary for life. Poverty eradication and environment protection should be mutually supportive. People have the right to adequate housing, to protect their well-being and dignity.

Action must be taken to provide safe drinking water, improved sanitation and to conserve fresh water supplies for irrigation and other economic activities for the poor. The use of renewable sources of energy and reduced recourse to perishable sources such as wood is of paramount importance.

6. **Good health** is essential for an active and productive life. Primary health care, including reproductive health care, must be available to all. Balanced nutrition is fundamental for present and future generations. With even limited but wise investments and the right policies, we can achieve major breakthroughs to improve the health of the poor.

   In particular, comprehensive programs of preventive medicine, including immunisation and control of communicable diseases should be implemented. Campaigns that tackle the social causes of diseases, like the "roll back malaria" initiative, and the program to fight HIV/AIDS should be strongly supported and implemented at a faster pace.

7. **Education** is the key to development. Universal access must be assured to basic education and literacy. Quality basic education, as well as secondary and higher education, vocational training, and skill acquisition throughout life are indispensable tools to eradicate poverty. In particular, action should be taken to ensure enrolment and completion of school by all children, especially girls, as it is among the highest return investments available.

   We cannot afford to squander the enormous potential of young people by neglecting their intellectual growth and development.

8. **Social services** must be developed with more social investment by Governments and less military expenditure, if poverty is to be defeated.

   National and international efforts should be directed to improve economic opportunities and social safety nets for those in need, who often include: children, women, indigenous people, the elderly, disabled, migrants and the unemployed. Furthermore, since poverty is the main cause of social exclusion and in almost all societies threatens the ability of families to meet the needs of their members, policies should be adopted to strengthen the role of the family in poverty-eradication strategies.

9. **Good governance** and effective administration are prerequisites to effectively fight poverty. Public policy should aim at preserv-

ing social cohesion and promoting social stability, especially through democracy, the rule of law and the respect for human rights and fundamental freedoms.

In particular, governments' capacity to carry out effective policies and programmes for those living in poverty, to ensure transparency and accountability and to fight corruption, needs to be strengthened.

We must prevent drugs trafficking and organized transnational crime from flourishing due to the lack of alternative livelihoods for the poor.

10. **A global alliance** must be forged by the entire international community, with Governments, United Nations, International Financial Institutions, Regional Organisations, Civil Society and Private Sector joining hands to make poverty eradication a central goal of humanity. Poverty should be dealt with simultaneously at the national and international levels. Improving market outcomes for those living in poverty is essential at the national level. Poorest countries must benefit from a more fair international trade regime.

Wider, deeper and faster debt relief for the poorest countries, coordinated with increased international aid, is needed for successful anti-poverty policies and programmes. Developed countries should strengthen their efforts to achieve, as soon as possible, the agreed target of 0.7% of their gross national product for overall official development assistance and within this target earmark 0.15–0.20% for the least developed countries. Poverty eradication is not a utopian goal. It can be done. Never before has there been such great awareness of the need to do it. Never before has there been such technological innovations, such expansion in trade, such flows of new investments. Never before have conditions been more favourable for a massive attack on poverty. All that is needed is real political will by all partners to act, and act now.

5

Are we making a difference? Measuring social progress worldwide

Informal meeting of the Economic and Social Council on Basic Indicators for the Integrated and Coordinated Implementation and Follow-up of the Major United Nations Conferences and Summits May 1999

CONTENTS

Overview

Overview

Everyone is familiar with standard measurements in the economic sphere, such as the Gross National Product. But there is no such coherent system of indicators to measure the social reality world-wide. Or at least, analysts often resort to compiling data of uneven quality, originating from various agencies, and generated with different methodologies.

This gap in our knowledge is becoming increasingly obvious as world leaders are trying to assess progress made in implementing the goals of the UN Conferences of the 1990's. Several challenges exist. In recent years, statistics have suffered from budget cutbacks both at the national and international levels. Statistics are decidedly un-glamorous, yet require a sustained, multi-year effort, dedication, professionalism and independence. They are also a public good, which may explain the difficulty that exists in securing adequate financial support for them. And, if statistics are to be made internationally compatible, a high degree of coordination is needed, not only between national offices, but between international agencies as well. In addition to improving the quality of the data, coordination can also make it more cost-effective to obtain this data, by preventing duplication and by avoiding to burden national offices with multiple requests.

The United Nations has always been regarded as the "natural" home for collecting and coordinating statistics world-wide. In the 1990's, the United Nations finalized the System of National Accounts, which records official financial statistics in a comparable form. But several recent developments are generating a renewed interest in setting up a solid and comprehensive system for gathering social indicators: the follow-up effort to the UN Conferences; the implementation, in the field, of the Common Country Assessments and the United Nations Development Assistance Framework, along with the World Bank's Comprehensive Development Framework; and the enhanced HIPC debt relief initiative, which requires measurable improvements in poverty. Adding to this renewed interest, the IMF concluded that part of the reason for the Asian crisis was faulty statistics, or insufficient dissemination of available statistics. It is therefore carrying its own effort at improving financial statistics with the Special Data Dissemination Standard and the General Data Dissemination Standard initiatives.

The Economic and Social Council, which is charged with coordinating the efforts of the UN system in implementing the Plans of Action of global conferences, decided in 1998 to initiate a comprehensive process of evaluation of the statistical tools at hand, with a view to identifying the gaps and duplication that may exist.

On 10–11 May 1999, ECOSOC held an informal meeting on "Basic indicators for the integrated and coordinated implementation and follow-up of the major United Nations conferences and summits". The summary of the meeting is included here, along with the President's opening speech and the ECOSOC resolution that ensued. That event was followed in November 1999 by a joint meeting in Paris with the World Bank and the Organization for Economic Cooperation and Development, which launched the Partnership In Statistics for Development in the 21st Century.

I. Opening speech by the President of the Economic and Social Council

Last year, we discussed extensively the integrated and coordinated implementation and follow-up of the major UN conferences and summits. We are preparing the "+ 5" review of the Cairo, Beijing and Copenhagen conferences and the 10 year mark is approaching rapidly. The importance of a comprehensive information system that indicates in a reliable manner whether and how much progress we have made in reaching the many goals reflected in the conference documents becomes apparent. That is the reason why the Council decided in 1998 to devote this informal two-day meeting exclusively to the topic of development indicators in the context of conference follow-up.

The area of development indicators is a particularly complex one as many players are involved. At the national level, policy decision-makers in government and analysts in public and private national organizations formulate their demands for indicators and statistics in the light of the country context. The national statistical apparatus, which is also often composed of various elements (such as a national statistical office, central bank, specialized ministries and institutes and possibly non-governmental providers of information) tries to satisfy this demand for information as best as its often-limited resources permit. The same user/producer pattern is replicated at the international level. On the one hand decision-makers, such as our body, and analysts request information on development that is comparable and uniform despite the considerable social-economic differences across countries. On the other hand, there is the global statistical system, a network consisting of many statistical entities of national and international organizations, including departments, agencies funds and programmes inside the UN system as well as outside.

In this context many questions arise: Are national statistical systems as the primary providers of information sufficiently empowered to respond to the varied demands? How are the priority areas determined at the national, and in particular at the international level? Are there information gaps in high priority policy areas? And given the many players involved is there effective coordination, or are there instances of duplication, which is not only wasteful given increasingly scarce resources, but also misleading in those cases where duplication leads to data inconsistencies?

This forum will not be concerned with the more technical aspects of development indicators, but rather with the political aspects related to creating an effective international system which continuously produces high-quality and relevant development indicators.

II. Summary by the President of the Council

The Economic and Social Council, pursuant to decision 1998/290 of 31 July 1998, taken at its substantive session of 1998, held a two-day informal meeting on basic indicators for the integrated and coordinated implementation and follow-up of the major United Nations conferences. In this decision, the Council also commissioned a report of the Secretary-General which was to consider in a comprehensive manner the work being carried out by the United Nations system and other relevant international and national institutions on basic indicators to measure progress towards the implementation of the integrated and coordinated follow-up of all aspects of major United Nations conferences and summits, including means of implementation, in the economic, social and related fields at all levels, with a view, as a first step, to taking stock and identifying overlapping duplication and gaps (Council decision 1998/290, para. (e)).

In accordance with the above decision, the meeting was organized in the format of an interactive dialogue with panels of experts so as to encourage dialogue among the participants and delegations. For the panel discussions, 15 high-level experts in the area of basic indicators were invited; they covered the broad spectrum of users and producers of information from both the national and the international level. The panel discussions were organized around four themes: (a) reviewing progress in conference implementation: difficulties and achievements; (b) international collaboration: major initiatives and gaps; (c) strengthening national statistical capacity and collaboration; and (d) means of implementation and looking forward.

The presentation of the panellists led to a rich and wide-ranging dialogue and a productive exchange of views on basic indicators for confer-

---

*   E/1999/100 and Add.1.

ence follow-up. This interactive dialogue represented an encouraging further step in the Economic and Social Council's efforts to ensure coherence and cooperation in the multifaceted conference implementation efforts.

In the course of the dialogue, the analytical report of the Secretary-General on a critical review of the development of indicators in the context of conference follow-up (E/1999/11), prepared on the basis of a collaborative effort, was welcomed. It was stressed by both panellists and delegates that the report provided a solid foundation for a comprehensive and fruitful discussion of the issues involved. It was also stated repeatedly that the proposals for the follow-up contained in the report were a valid starting point for further action of the Economic and Social Council. It was suggested by many delegations that the Council should continue addressing the subject of basic indicators at its substantive session of 1999 in Geneva in July. In particular, speakers highlighted two key areas where Council guidance and involvement were believed to be needed: (a) strengthening of national statistical capacity and (b) more effective coordination of international organizations in their indicator initiatives within the framework of follow-up to global conferences.

The following summary presents the main issues raised in the debate. They are grouped into six categories: importance of indicators; strengthening national statistical capacity; coordination at international level; core set of common indicators; means of implementation; and role of the Economic and Social Council.

Importance of indicators

Indicators and statistics are vital to assessing progress towards concrete policy goals as formulated by recent global conferences and national development policies. Indicators also permit the evaluation of whether public resources are being spent efficiently and transparently. Indicators and statistics, if policy-relevant, accurate and timely, are also a powerful tool for raising awareness, thus facilitating effective implementation of the development agenda. To effectively advocate a development programme and to mobilize the necessary resources, good data are indispensable. However, it was also stressed that not all development phenomena can be reflected by numbers.

Strengthening national statistical capacity

A key theme of the meeting was the need to build national statistical capacity in such a way as to ensure that progress achieved would be irreversible: in brief, the objective must be a sustained development of national statistical systems. This must be done in relation to all stages of the information process, from data collection to analysis and dissemination. A collaborative effort of the United Nations system, including the World Bank and the International Monetary Fund (IMF) as well as the Organisation for Economic Cooperation and Development (OECD), is called for in order to build capacity. Panellists stated that, given the heightened awareness of the importance of development information, the moment was opportune for advocating the building of national statistical capacity now.

There is a need at the national level to establish effective coordination mechanisms among all information-producing units. In this context, the central role of national statistical offices in the coordination of national departments involved in data collection and dissemination and in the development of methodological and operational standards was noted. The status and the independence of statistical offices need to be strengthened in line with the Fundamental Principles of Official Statistics.[1]

The national dialogue between producers and users of information has to be intensified. Policy makers need to involve statisticians in the identification of the information that they require for policy decision-making, and statisticians need to respond in a flexible manner to these information demands.

There is a need to establish clear priorities so as to address the problem of data gaps which continue to persist, even for such traditional basic indicators as gross domestic product/gross national product (GDP/GNP) and literacy, but particularly for the newer areas identified by world conferences. In this context, it was underlined that traditional income indicators were not sufficient to capture the multidimensionality of sustainable human development. The challenge is to construct an information system for the social and environmental areas that is similar to the existing information system for economics. Therefore, closing the gaps in respect of data availability of "newer indicators" in the areas of environment, nutrition, housing, health care, the informal sector, women's work and social integration is an urgent necessity. Social integration was cited as a good example of an area with a need for adequately disaggregated data (by relevant social groups and gender). There is also a need for the development of subnational disaggregation to address social issues at the local and regional levels. On the other hand, with respect to globalization, it also appeared increasingly important to compile statistics and indicators addressing global, transnational aspects, such as global warming, multinational corporations and information flows.

---

[1] See *Official Records of the Economic and Social Council, 1994, Supplement No. 9* (E/1994/29), para. 59.

In addition to coverage, data quality needs to be improved in terms of timeliness, reliability and relevance. A number of programmes exist in the area of capacity-building and should be strengthened.

Regional or subregional collaborative networks need to be encouraged to share experiences and to develop common methodologies and practices which suit specific regional and subregional needs. Donors could be invited to support these subregional networks through appropriate training activities so as to create a critical mass of expertise within such subregions.

Coordination at the international level

There is the sense that overlap among international organizations, both in the creation of indicators and in the collection of information, has become more acute. This may be partly a result of the comprehensive approach, which was encouraged by all international conferences. Proliferation of indicators used by international organizations in relation to conferences has led, in some cases, to overburdening national statistical offices. In others, the data needs of conferences may be ignored. International agencies should make efforts to better coordinate their data requests to countries, avoid duplicative requests and share the data collected. The Economic and Social Council could provide stronger guidance in this endeavour.

Coordination must start within international agencies, where often more than one unit is producing statistical information and requesting data.

Existing coordination mechanisms, such as the Administrative Committee on Coordination (ACC) Subcommittee on Statistical Activities, need to be strengthened and active participation of all members needs to be encouraged.

The proposal to create a high-level working group on donor coordination in support of national statistical development strategies required further clarification on participation as well as on its value beyond that of existing mechanisms. It was suggested that the working group secure and maintain a strong link to policy and funding, including bilateral funding. Full involvement of the regional commissions and recipient countries was stressed as being indispensable. One panellist saw the Department of Economic and Social Affairs of the United Nations Secretariat as a possible convener. The working group could review funding for statistical programmes in a proactive rather than a reactive manner.

The World Bank announced a plan to constitute a special trust fund for statistical capacity-building.

Core set of common indicators

The development of a set of common indicators by the multilateral system is important to permit global analysis of progress in implementing conference goals. It can also lessen the burden on member States in providing data. The list of universally accepted and relevant indicators would necessarily have to be limited. Countries and regions will have to add individual indicator sets, in a flexible manner, that are relevant in their development context. Perhaps a hierarchical structure of sets, with national, regional and/or sector extensions could be envisaged. In any event, such a structure would not be a short-term goal: it would need to be developed as a continuously evolving and broadly based consultative process.

The Common Country Assessment (CCA) indicator list was seen as a good starting point for working towards a core set of indicators. However, there was still need for more direct involvement and ownership by countries, including through their national statistical offices. It was suggested that careful analysis at the country level of the availability of data for the CCA indicator list should lead to the formulation of statistical programmes supported by the United Nations funds and programmes. Specialized agencies, including the World Bank and IMF, as well as OECD/ Development Assistance Committee (DAC), should participate more fully with their specific sector expertise in the process of further developing and implementing the CCA indicator list.

Indicators and data collected internationally must be of value for domestic policy-making. New indicators should be designed through a dialogue process taking into account the existing databases and statistical capacities of countries. Statisticians could advise on the feasibility and costs of certain indicators. The Statistical Commission and the ACC Subcommittee on Statistical Activities could review newly formulated indicators.

Means of implementation

Conferences have established goals both for socio-economic development and for resource commitments, which are applicable for all countries. Basic indicators are needed to evaluate progress towards conference goals in creating an enabling environment for development. Many stated that the Economic and Social Council should discuss in a more comprehensive manner indicators on the means of implementation of major conferences. More work had to be done in this area, including monitoring the volume and effectiveness of official development assistance (ODA).

A number of delegations also underscored that further deliberations on the issue of basic indicators should focus on conference implementation, rather than on development per se, in accordance with earlier decisions of the Economic and Social Council. In this regard, the emphasis should be on partnership relationships, rather than on donor/recipient relationships.

Data collection and statistical capacity-building are expensive. Too often, statistical activities are not adequately funded. It was stressed that development programmes needed to allocate sufficient resources to the generation of adequate information bases which would allow evaluation of the programme implementation. The shortage of financial and human resources makes it even more vital to ensure that maximum use is made of already collected statistics and to eliminate overlap in the creation of new indicators by international organizations.

Role of the Economic and Social Council

It was stated repeatedly by delegations that the Economic and Social Council is the appropriate forum in respect of taking the lead in the indicator debate, particularly because of its holistic perspective as well as its overall coordination function, especially for the follow-up and implementation of major United Nations conferences. It is the forum where all concerned parties can come together, including the Bretton Woods institutions, the regional commissions and other international institutions like OECD/DAC.

In addition, it was stressed, that regarding specific, more technical decisions on indicators, the Economic and Social Council is supported by those of its functional commissions that are responsible for the follow-up of conferences and the Statistical Commission.

III. ECOSOC Resolution 1999/55: Integrated and Coordinated Implementation of and Follow-up to Major United Nations Conferences and Summits

The Economic and Social Council,

Recalling its agreed conclusions 1995/1,15[1] its resolutions 1996/36 of 26 July 1996, 1997/61 of 25 July 1997 and 1998/44 of 31 July 1998 and its decision 1998/290 of 31 July 1998,

Taking note of the reports of the Secretary-General on an integrated and coordinated implementation of and follow-up to major United

---

1 *Official Records of the General Assembly, Fiftieth Session, Supplement No. 3* (A/50/3/Rev.1), chap. III, para. 22.

Nations conferences and summits,[2] on a critical review of the development of indicators in the context of conference follow-up[3] and on the possible modalities of a review by the Economic and Social Council in 2000 of progress made within the United Nations system in promoting an integrated and coordinated implementation of and follow-up to major United Nations conferences and summits,[4]

Ways to enhance an integrated and coordinated implementation of and follow-up to major United Nations conferences and summits

Calls upon Governments, at the national and international levels, to renew their efforts to implement the commitments they have undertaken and make more tangible progress towards the targets, goals and objectives set by the United Nations conferences and summits;

Decides to transmit to the General Assembly, as inputs for the five-year reviews of the Fourth World Conference on Women and of the World Summit for Social Development, the Council's outcomes on (a) the role of employment and work in poverty eradication: the empowerment and advancement of women, (b) operational activities, in particular poverty eradication and capacity-building, and (c) coordination of implementation and coordinated follow-up by the United Nations system of initiatives on African development;

Urges its functional commissions and other relevant bodies of the United Nations system to enhance coordination and complementarity among the five-year reviews and, to that effect, encourages the bureaux of the preparatory committees for the forthcoming five-year reviews of the Fourth World Conference on Women and of the World Summit for Social Development to consult with one another to avoid duplication and ensure cross-fertilization of ideas;

Recommends that the end-of-decade assessment of progress towards the goals of the World Conference on Education for All be taken into account in the five-year reviews of other conferences;

Reaffirms the importance of ensuring the policy guidance of the General Assembly and the coordination role of the Economic and Social Council on the follow-up to United Nations conferences and summits and calls for further cooperation between the functional commissions and the rest of the United Nations system in order to complement United Nations

---

2 E/1999/65.
3 E/1999/11.
4 E/1999/63.

conferences and summits in a coherent way and recalls in this context that adoption of multi-year thematic programmes for the functional commissions responsible for follow-up to major conferences can be helpful;

Encourages the functional commissions, in their outcomes, to identify more clearly actions that require a coordinated United Nations system-wide response as well as to highlight recommendations specifically addressed to organizations of the United Nations system and to identify areas in which the Council could provide guidance to the programmes, funds and agencies regarding the decisions and recommendations of the functional commissions addressed to them;

Invites the regional commissions to further strengthen their active participation relating to the implementation at the regional level of the results of major United Nations conferences and summits and the five-year reviews;

Welcomes the efforts made by some of the governing bodies of the programmes, funds and agencies to address relevant aspects of themes from conferences to ensure greater coherence and complementarity in their work, including at the country level, and requests that further efforts be made in this regard and that the results of their deliberation be brought to the attention of the Council;

Invites concerned specialized agencies to advise the Council on how to improve the way in which the outcomes of the Council, together with proposed follow-up actions, can be brought to the attention of their governing bodies, particularly concerning conference follow-up;

Welcomes the efforts of the Administrative Committee on Coordination and its standing machinery to assist the work of the Council and the functional and regional commissions, in particular in coordinating the follow-up to major United Nations conferences and summits, and encourages them and the United Nations system to pursue and deepen their efforts in this area;

Decides to review the follow-up by the functional commissions of the decisions and recommendations of the Council addressed to them and invites the commissions to discuss follow-up to the Council's outcomes under a specific agenda item at their sessions;

Invites the functional commissions, in accordance with their rules and regulations, to consider innovative modalities for further engaging non-governmental organizations and other actors, as appropriate, in conference follow-up;

Basic indicators for the integrated and coordinated implementation of and follow-up to major United Nations conferences and summits at all levels

Requests the Secretariat, in particular the Statistics Division, to serve as a focal point to promote networking among national and international institutions in the area of statistics and indicators relating to the follow-up to United Nations conferences and summits so as to facilitate the exchange of relevant information and metadata;

Recognizes the importance of relevant, accurate and timely statistics and indicators for evaluating the implementation of the outcomes of the United Nations conferences and summits at all levels;

Also recognizes the progress made in the development of basic indicators in developing countries which require international support for national efforts to build national statistical capacity in data collection, analysis and dissemination;

Stresses the need to further develop indicators on means of implementation to evaluate progress towards conference goals in creating an enabling environment for development;

Welcomes the efforts already undertaken by the various bodies of the United Nations system, including the Administrative Committee on Coordination, to harmonize and rationalize the basic indicators used in the context of follow-up to United Nations conferences, and encourages them to continue their efforts in order to lessen the burden on Member States;

Invites the Statistical Commission, with the assistance of the Statistics Division and in close cooperation with other relevant bodies of the United Nations system, including the Administrative Committee on Coordination, and, as appropriate, other relevant international organizations, to review, with a view to facilitating future consideration by the Council, the work undertaken in harmonizing and rationalizing basic indicators in the context of follow-up to United Nations conferences and summits, taking fully into account the decisions taken in other functional and regional commissions and, in that process, to identify a limited number of common indicators from among those currently accepted and widely used by the States Members of the United Nations, in order to lessen the data provision burden on Member States, bearing in mind the work done so far in this area;

Reaffirms the important role that the functional commissions have to play in the integrated and coordinated follow-up and the evaluation of the implementation of the outcome of major United Nations conferences and summits;

Urges countries, United Nations programmes and funds, the Secretariat, bilateral funding agencies, the Bretton Woods institutions and regional funding agencies to work together closely in order to mobilize the required resources to support national statistical capacity-building in developing countries and coordinate their statistical capacity-building programmes;

Requests the Secretary-General to prepare a progress report on the implementation of this section of the resolution for consideration by the Council at its substantive session of 2000;

Modalities for a review by the Council in 2000 of progress made in the promotion of an integrated and coordinated implementation of and follow-up to major United Nations conferences and summits

Decides to assess, at the coordination segment of its substantive session of 2000, the progress made within the United Nations system, through the conference reviews, in the promotion of an integrated and coordinated implementation of and follow-up to major United Nations conferences and summits in the economic, social and related fields as a possible contribution to the Millennium Assembly;

Invites the functional and regional commissions, programmes, funds, and specialized agencies, and encourages non-governmental organizations, to make substantive contributions to the review by the Council;

Requests the Secretary-General to prepare a report to support the review by the Council in collaboration with organizations of the United Nations system.

46th plenary meeting
30 July 1999

6

Coordination at work:
Putting Haiti back on track

C ONTENTS

Overview

Overview

With the end of the Cold War, security concerns have become more and more intertwined with development issues in countries that have been affected by conflict. Rather than spurred by ideology, conflicts now tend to reflect economic desperation or crises of governance. Conversely, development programmes can no longer ignore the special needs of war-torn societies or post-conflict reconstruction.

Because of these inter-related dynamics, the actions required to re-build societies range from prevention and mediation to rehabilitation, reconstruction and long-term development.

At the United Nations one aspect of this new, integrated approach is visible in the reactivation of article 65 of the United Nations Charter, which gives the Economic and Social Council a mandate to assist the Security Council, in particular by providing it with information.

In its resolution 1212 of 1998, the Security Council invited ECOSOC to contribute in the design of a long-term programme of support for Haiti. In 1999, ECOSOC created the Ad Hoc Advisory Group on Haiti, to take stock of the work being done in helping Haiti achieve sustainable development, and to provide recommendations for its long-term development.

The Report, reprinted here, evaluates the combined efforts of the international community and makes recommendations for further improvements, in particular the creation of a long-term strategy and programme of support for Haiti. The resolution of ECOSOC that follows endorses many of its recommendations and urges the international community to continue its efforts on behalf of peace and development in Haiti.

I. Report of the Ad Hoc Advisory Group on Haiti

General economic and national context

As noted in the last report of the Secretary-General to the Security Council on the situation in Haiti (S/1999/579), the country has been slowly recovering from its most recent political crisis since April 1997. In March 1999, a new Prime Minister was appointed, and in April 1999 a new transitional Government was formed. A new Provisional Electoral Council has also been created, and has started work on preparations for legislative and local elections, which are expected to take place by December 1999, with a new Parliament scheduled to be in place by 11 January 2000. Legislative elections will be followed by Presidential elections, which are planned for November 2000.

The Secretary-General has characterized as encouraging the steps taken so far by the Haitian political leadership in its efforts to resolve the protracted political crisis through elections, and has called on all Haitian political leaders to participate constructively in the electoral process to ensure its success. In recognition of the fact that the forthcoming legislative and local elections are the only viable way to resolve the present crisis, the transition Government, in its recently issued plan of action, announced plans to work closely with the Provisional Electoral Council to ensure free, fair and transparent elections, and to seek to revive the interest in participation of the Haitian population in the democratization process. For their part, the donor community and the United Nations system have pledged to actively support the electoral process through direct financial, logistical and technical support, on the provision that the Government takes adequate measures to ensure security and transparency. This support is being provided in conjunction with the role of political facilitation being played by the "Friends of Haiti" Group of Ambassadors, the representative of the Secretary-General, and a number of personalities, including the former President of Costa Rica, Oscar Arias.

Haiti continues to be a least developed country, the only one in the western hemisphere. Its indicators on situational development compare poorly at both regional and interregional levels. Haiti's annual per capita income of US$ 250 is significantly below the average of US$ 3,320 for Latin America and the Caribbean region. Based on its assessment in March 1998 of poverty in Haiti, the World Bank estimates that about 80 per cent of the approximately two thirds of the population that live in the rural areas are poor, with about two thirds of those considered to be extremely poor. In addition to the low gross domestic product (GDP) per capita, Haiti also has serious wealth distribution issues to address. It is estimated that about 4 per cent of the population own 66 per cent of the country's entire resources, 16 per cent own 14 per cent, 70 per cent own barely 20 per cent, while 10 per cent of the population is considered to be entirely destitute.

Despite these negative social indicators, trends in overall economic performance since the return from exile of the constitutional Government in 1994 show some positive achievements. The latest IMF economic performance review mission conducted in March 1999 highlighted some of these achievements.

The current IMF-monitored economic programme put in place in November 1998 as a follow-up to the 1997/98 programme is designed to maintain macroeconomic stability and make further progress in the area of structural reform while the political situation settles, and while a possible new enhanced structural adjustment facility programme is being considered. The 1998/99 programme was formulated taking into consideration the negative effects of hurricane Georges. It aims to promote output growth, contain inflation and central government budget deficits, strengthen international reserves and continue support for structural reforms in the public enterprise sector. The programme also takes into account and endorses donor-supported sectoral policies to improve efficiency in the areas of education, health, justice, infrastructure rehabilitation and maintenance.

These relatively positive trends must however be viewed within the framework of enormous development challenges, particularly the need to combat extreme mass poverty while uniting the country around a shared, positive and long-term vision of its future. This challenge is compounded by the protracted political crisis that has further eroded the authority of the State and its already diminished capacity to deliver basic social services to the population. At another level, the challenge is that of managing the development process to ensure that immediate national and international actions to alleviate extreme and massive poverty do not lose sight of the need to build strong national governance institutions in the medium and long term.

Beyond the fundamental requirement to reinstate and significantly improve upon the basic functions of the State and the institutions of government, the World Bank poverty assessment report (1998) also recommended a number of measures that would need to be taken to ensure sustainable economic and social development in Haiti. These include (a) strengthening macroeconomic stability and reducing distortions so as to encourage private sector investment; (b) improving the quality of government spending in order to invest in basic social services and raise the level of human capital; and (c) rationalizing the assistance provided by external donors.

The mandate of the newly formed transitional Government, installed in April 1999, is limited to facilitating the organization of the upcoming general elections and identifying short- and medium-term priorities that a subsequent government could start to address on a more sustainable basis. Given the present situation in which the Government is called upon to operate, its actions at the time can only be of a short-term nature, with its first priority being given to organizing free and fair elections as soon as possible to help guarantee institutional stability. Its action in the above-mentioned sectors will thus consist of short-term projects and policy reflections to identify viable approaches for subsequent governments.

Role of the United Nations system

The United Nations system in Haiti is made up of:

- Two missions, MIPONUH, in charge of the civilian police, and MI-CIVIH, a human rights observation mission. These missions report through the Department of Peacekeeping Operations and the Department of Political Affairs, respectively, to the Security Council and the General Assembly;
- Seven agencies (UNDP, the United Nations Children's Fund (UNICEF) the United Nations Population Fund (UNFPA), the World Food Programme (WFP), the Food and Agriculture Organization of the United Nations (FAO), the United Nations Educational, Scientific and Cultural Organization (UNESCO), the Pan American Health Organization/World Health Organization), who report through their respective governing bodies and the Economic and Social Council to the General Assembly;
- The Bretton Woods institutions (World Bank and IMF).

In addition, the International Organization for Migration (IOM) is permanently associated with all United Nations system activities in Haiti.

Unlike the bilateral and other multilateral institutions represented in Haiti, the United Nations agencies have a degree of flexibility that has enabled them to work closely with both the Government and NGOs in assisting the population at the grass-roots level, both during and after the embargo that followed the 1991 military coup. The areas of assistance include the following:

- Good governance, including support to the democratization process, police mentoring, judicial system reform, human rights, state modernization and reforms, decentralization, participatory local governance and electoral support;
- Universal health care, including the fight against human immunodeficiency virus/acquired immunodeficiency syndrome (HIV/AIDS) and population issues;
- Disaster prevention, preparedness and management;
- Promoting productive employment;
- Basic education for all;
- Protection and restoration of the environment;
- Food security;
- Cultural development and tourism;
- Culture of peace and migration;

- Support for coordination mechanisms of Governments, donors, and the United Nations system.

Excluding the World Bank and IMF, the United Nations system's disbursements in Haiti in support of socio-economic development objectives stand at US$ 127.8 million since the return of the constitutional Government. During this period, UNDP has been the largest United Nations system donor, with US$ 54 million disbursed between 1995 and 1998. Since 1998, however, UNDP disbursements have greatly diminished, due in part to an overall drop in UNDP resources at the central level. Other important United Nations system donors include WFP, WHO and UNICEF, with disbursements of more than US$ 10 million each between 1995 and 1998.

At a meeting held in April 1999 chaired by the resident coordinator, who also acts as the UNDP resident representative and deputy representative of the Secretary-General, it was agreed that progress achieved in the field of inter-agency coordination be further consolidated through the preparation of a common country assessment by the end of 1999. This is a key step under the Secretary-General's reform programme as it will lead to the formulation of a United Nations development assistance framework in 2000, as well as harmonized programming cycles by 2002. It should also complement the World Bank's country development framework. Thanks to the common country assessment, the United Nations agencies will have the elements necessary to define a long-term United Nations development assistance programme for Haiti, and to further harmonize and integrate their operations.

In response to the more urgent requirements for disaster preparedness, regular meetings of the disaster management team have been held in order to prepare for the hurricane season. In 1999, such activities by the United Nations system in Haiti will benefit from a newly approved UNDP-financed technical assistance project, which in collaboration with the Office for the Coordination of Humanitarian Affairs will reinforce the capacity of the Haitian authorities to prevent and manage disasters.

Adequacy, coherence, effectiveness and coordination of the international community's assistance to Haiti

Adequacy of assistance

The international community, including the United Nations system, responded to the return of the constitutional Government from exile at the end of 1994 with a resumption of official development assistance, beginning in 1995. The total volume of aid, however, has been dropping quite significantly. Ongoing programmes are currently limited to levels formulated and approved before the June 1997 electoral controversy and subsequent resignation of the Government. As shown in table 1, total bilateral and multilateral assistance to Haiti has dropped by about 35 per cent between 1995 and 1998. Far from signifying a deliberate decision by donors to reduce aid to Haiti, this drop is directly linked to absorptive capacity constraints and non-approval of available loans by the Haitian Parliament. As of December 1998, IDB and the World Bank alone has a combined total of over US$ 570 million worth of new programmes and projects awaiting approval by the Haitian Parliament or finalization by the formulation missions. As a result of the discords between the executive and legislative branches, these new programmes have still not been approved and will not be until a new Parliament is in place. Many other partners are in a similar situation, which has had a very negative impact on the rate of resource flows to Haiti. It is hoped that the upcoming elections will provide the institutional framework required to ensure that aid flows to Haiti can again become adequate.

Although Haiti's foreign assistance needs are enormous, it should be said that despite this significant drop, Haiti is still a major recipient of de-

TABLE 1
Volume and main sources of aid, 1995–1998
(Thousands of United States dollars)

Sources	1995	%	1996	%	1997	%	1998	%
United States	100 179	18.7	48 780	11.5	85 625	24.4	94 564	26.8
Canada	44 263	8.3	28 621	6.8	32 535	9.3	30 241	8.6
France	52 859	9.9	23 815	5.6	25 146	7.2	17 762	5.1
Japan	31 548	5.9	15 798	3.7	5 979	1.7	8 336	2.4
Taiwan Province of China	31 260	5.9	8 642	2.0	12 000	3.4	4 400	1.2
Other bilateral aid	4 447	0.8	19 860	4.8	12 223	3.4	15 356	4.3
Total bilateral	264 556	49.5	145 516	34.4	173 508	49.4	170 659	48.4
Multilateral sources								
IDB	87 855	16.4	49 777	11.8	57 362	16.3	68 565	19.4
World Bank	67 451	12.6	66 219	15.6	39 366	11.2	28 752	8.1
IMF	25 774	4.8	22 486	5.3	551	0.2	828	0.2
European Union	55 344	10.4	92 384	21.8	39 197	11.2	55 439	15.7
Other multilateral	923	0.2	77	0.0	1 953	0.5	990	0.3
UNDP	12 858	2.4	16 855	4.0	16 948	4.8	8 153	2.3
Other United Nations system	16 816	3.1	21 611	5.1	14 523	4.2	19 966	5.6
Total multilateral aid	267 021	49.9	269 409	63.6	169 900	48.4	182 693	51.6
Assistance from NGOs	2 868	0.5	8 449	2.0	7 830	2.2	NA	
Total external aid	534 445	100.0	423 374	100.0	351 238	100.0	353 352	100.0

Source: UNDP, 1997 *Development Cooperation Report* and preliminary data for 1998.

velopment assistance, with a per capita aid of $74 in 1995, $57 in 1996 and $47 in 1997, compared to an average $12 per capita for the developing world at large.

Sectoral concentration

Balance of payment disbursements made up the largest share (29.8 per cent) of total disbursements for the 1995–1997 period, followed by governance (13.7 per cent), humanitarian assistance (8.5 per cent), transport (7.08 per cent), health (6.5 per cent), water and urban infrastructure (6.2 per cent) and agriculture (5.3 per cent). Together, health and education account for only 14.65 per cent of total disbursements and the environment for 1.1 percent; 70 percent of these disbursements were grants while 30 per cent were loans. External aid financed approximately 86 percent of all public investment in Haiti during this period. Preliminary disbursement figures for 1998 show a different configuration of sectoral priorities, with education and health accounting for 18 percent, at the same level as humanitarian assistance, transport receiving 12 percent, and agriculture, social development and governance each accounting for 8 per cent of total disbursements for the year. These variations are indicative of the shifting priorities and trends in Haiti's development needs.

Coherence of assistance

On the whole, it can be said that external assistance to Haiti since the return of the constitutional Government has sought to respond to national development needs identified by the Government and the international community. The framework within which most of these needs were identified at the time was the emergency recovery programme to which donors pledged funds. So far, the areas of concentration of foreign assistance have addressed the priority areas contained in this programme, as well as in other jointly formulated bilateral and multilateral programmes. However, the aid policies of some partners have required them to work directly at the grass-roots level, using international NGOs as executing agents. While this approach has helped achieve significant results at this level, it has not helped the Government's efforts to improve upon its coordination role and enhance overall coherence of development assistance.

To harmonize its programming cycles starting, beginning in 2002, in line with ongoing United Nations reform objectives, the United Nations system aims, through its resident coordinator mechanism, to support national efforts to ensure greater coherence of external assistance. As indicated above, the planned common country assessment will also constitute an important input to these efforts.

Effectiveness of assistance

Although no formal evaluation has been made of the impact of aid to Haiti over the past five years, it is clear that substantial foreign assistance has made a significant contribution to the functioning of the Government. This was a period that followed three years of centralized authority from 1991 to 1994, during which official foreign aid disbursements were suspended and economic activity slowed down considerably. A major problem facing the delivery of foreign assistance is that of insufficient coordination by the Government and slow disbursements due to diminishing absorptive capacity.

Another factor affecting the effectiveness of aid to Haiti is the concentration of donor resources on humanitarian activities. There is now a need to shift it towards support for sustainable development objectives, including capacity-building and institution-building. Given the present evolution of Haiti's development needs, it is important to focus more on building capacities for measuring both the impact of aid on the country and the impact of specific national and donor-sponsored programmes on the overall development situation. To this end, the United Nations system in Haiti, under the leadership of the resident coordinator, has launched a number of initiatives aimed at strengthening the country's capacity to produce socio-economic statistics that are vital for monitoring its development progress. In addition to the internal harmonization of approaches referred to above, the United Nations system is also about to launch a 20/20 initiative[1] for Haiti aimed at encouraging increased government and donor attention to the social sectors. By focusing aid and national resources on these sectors, it will be possible to target the most needy sections of the population.

Coordination of assistance

Coordination by the Government

Strengthening the leadership role of the Government in aid coordination is key to making Haiti's cooperation with its international development partners more effective. Decades of institutional instability have adversely affected the coordination capacities of the Government accumulated in previous years. The situation steadily further worsened

---

[1] The 20/20 initiative, launched at the World Summit for Social Development, suggests that interested developed and developing countries partners agree on mutual commitments to allocate, on average, 20 per cent of official development assistance and 20 per cent of the national budget respectively to basic social programmes.

following the 1991 military coup, when the constitutional Government went into exile and the void in development was filled by international donors and NGOs. Since the return of the constitutional Government in October 1994, the institutions officially charged with aid coordination have found it increasingly difficult to effectively coordinate the activities of most external partners. This is partly due to donor-driven initiatives and the fact that many of these partners, including some non-governmental organizations, have not yet shed the isolated operational practices adopted during the embargo years.

Since the return of the constitutional Government, the implementation of donor-financed projects at the operational level has been the responsibility of two special government agencies, namely the Unité centrale de gestion and the Fonds d'assistance économique et sociale. These were set up to facilitate project implementation under emergency circumstances. Each of these entities has a Board of Directors, including representatives of the Ministry, other government agencies and NGOs. The Office of the President has also received and managed donor project support, and has been involved in monitoring the implementation of a variety of urban infrastructure projects. An implementation unit tracks the progress of these and other donor-supported efforts.

Starting from 1995, project/donor coordination units were set up in each sectoral ministry, with funding from the European Union and other partners. This reflected a policy, subsequently confirmed by the Government in 1996, to give sectoral ministries responsibility for managing and coordinating donor contributions to their respective sectors. The purpose of these units was to ensure that project duplication was eliminated, and that procedural and reporting requirements were more easily and promptly met. In this way, the technical units of the ministries concerned were freed to address the technical aspects of the programmes involved. A World Bank consultative group-related assessment of these units in 1997 found their track record to be mixed. At least two ministries had instituted a donor coordination unit that was attempting to harmonize existing projects by bringing donors together, identifying programme gaps and seeking new project funding on the basis of an ongoing strategic planning process. The major problems facing these units involved communication with donors, government administrative procedures, donor-imposed procedures at the project identification level, design and implementation stages, and the lack of adequate information regarding ongoing and planned projects.

The Government recognizes the importance of effective donor coordination, and has recently launched a number of initiatives to strengthen its leadership in this area. With the support of UNDP and other donors, a number of workshops on coordination and decentralized planning have been organized to help clarify its policies and expectations in this area. In the newly issued plan of action of the Government, the Office of the Prime Minister plans to formulate new policies in a number of areas, including international cooperation and human resource development, in order to help it accomplish its coordination functions. Emphasis will be placed on the creation of effective information flows, documentation systems, and the harmonization of management and coordination procedures through the elaboration of a procedures manual.

Coordination within the donor community

The consultative group process facilitated by the World Bank remains the framework for inter-donor coordination and for donor-government consultations on development priorities and policies, as well as on issues of funding. The first formal consultative group meeting on Haiti took place in Paris in January 1995, at which over US$ 1 billion were pledged by the donor community. A second meeting was held in April 1997, at which, among other things, consensus was reached on the critical components of a comprehensive poverty alleviation strategy. A message was also sent to the Haitian Parliament to advance legislative action required to ensure that the population benefit from the reform programme. The major sectors covered during these meetings included agriculture, education, the environment, health, justice reform, roads and transportation, water and sanitation, governance and poverty alleviation.

The political crisis has hampered formal follow-up of the sectoral issues raised during these consultative group meetings. Given this situation, donors have been undertaking informal consultations among themselves through monthly meetings in Haiti. These meetings were attended by the donor community and the United Nations system agencies. More formal meetings were convened on an ad hoc basis by the World Bank in Washington, D.C., and informal working groups have been created in the areas of justice reform, environmental protection, health, agriculture and rural development, education and support for the police. The purpose of these consultations has been to enable donors to identify areas of complementarity and avoid duplication among their programmes, as well as to maintain dialogue and to harmonize their views and approaches on aid policy issues.

Through these consultation mechanisms, the donor community and the United Nations have succeeded in maintaining development policy dialogue while efforts continue at the political level to resolve the crisis. It has also been possible to pursue donor-funded programmes approved prior to the current crisis, thus enabling the population to continue to benefit from vital development support. The most recent donor meeting, held in Washington, D.C., in March 1999, reviewed progress in all these sectors and resolved to pursue and strengthen related consultations. Given its transitional nature, the newly installed Government has not sought a formal consultation group meeting. The implications, once again, are that all long-term policy dialogue between the Haitian authorities and its major development partners will have to wait till governmental institutions are renewed through the upcoming elections.

Coordination within the United Nations system

While MIPONUH and MICIVIH are responsible for the police mentoring and human rights observation programmes respectively, the rest of the United Nations system, under the leadership of the resident coordinator, is actively engaged in socio-economic development activities in the relevant sectors of the different agencies. Since the beginning of 1998, very important progress has been made in the areas of United Nations coordination. In his last report (November 1998) on MIPONUH, the Secretary-General noted that Haiti offers an excellent example of the way the different United Nations organizations can work together efficiently.

Following a first coordination workshop held in May 1998, seven thematic working groups were established in mid-1998, addressing the issues of population and environment, gender equity, food security, local governance, health, education and productive employment. The mandate of these groups was to: (a) undertake situation analyses in each of the sectors identified; (b) assess ongoing United Nations activities; and (c) make recommendations for improved coordination. An eighth working group was also established for common services. The groups presented their findings and recommendations during a second inter-agency coordination workshop held in November 1998. The main recommendations were: (a) to proceed rapidly with the formulation and implementation of concrete joint actions; (b) to focus United Nations assistance on national priorities identified by the working groups in consultation with the Haitian Government and in areas where the United Nations system has clear comparative advantages; and (c) start preparations to undertake a common country assessment that would pave the way for long-term programming of United Nations assistance to Haiti.

The terms of reference for the common country assessment working group are being finalized. The target date for its finalization has been set for December 1999, and it will take into account the recently published

TABLE 2
Thematic areas: responsible agencies

Thematic area	Responsible agency
Economic context	World Bank/IMF/UNDP
Governance (including the democratization process/consolidation of the rule of law)	UNDP/World Bank
Human rights	MICIVIH/UNICEF
Employment	UNDP/ILO
Population	UNFPA
Rural development/food security	FAO/WFP
Education	UNESCO
Health	WHO/PAHO
HIV/AIDS	UNAIDS/UNFPA
Environment	UNDP
Culture/culture of peace	UNESCO
Migration	IOM

action plan of the Government. Responsibilities have been assigned to agencies concerning (a) the collection of necessary data and information and for the completion of the common country assessment indicator framework (see table 1); and (b) the preparation of a status report on the major conventions, declarations and international conferences (see table 2). A preliminary list of common country assessment themes has been established, and their respective focal points and three cross-cutting themes (gender equity, human rights and poverty) have also been identified. The division of labour among the agencies with regard to data collection and analyses in the different thematic areas is described in table 2.

As has already been noted, in compliance with General Assembly resolutions, the agencies of the United Nations development group in Haiti (UNDP, UNICEF, UNFPA and WFP) have pursued their efforts towards the harmonization of their respective programme cycles by the year 2002. This will have been preceded, in 2001, with the formulation of a United Nations development assistance framework for Haiti.

United Nations representation in Haiti

In order to ensure the smooth integration of United Nations development system activities with the United Nations political and peacekeeping role in Haiti, the UNDP resident representative, in addition to being resident coordinator of the United Nations development system, is also deputy representative of the Secretary-General and deputy head of MIPONUH.

The unique combination has enabled:

- Close complementarity between MIPONUH and UNDP, in particular with regard to:
  - Coordinated assistance provided to the Haitian National Police;
  - Assistance with the electoral process, where both the representative of the Secretary-General and UNDP play a key coordination role, respectively, on the political and technical sides;
  - Assistance in the resolution of the institutional crisis and facilitating the reconciliation process;
- Direct continuous reporting to the United Nations, including through the quarterly reports of the representative of the Secretary-General to the Secretary-General, on the United Nations system development activities and progress made in terms of United Nations coordination and implementation of the Secretary-General's reform programme.

Supplementary observations

Much has yet to be done in order to ensure that ongoing and future international assistance in support of the Government of Haiti for achieving sustainable development continues to be adequate and coherent, and that the main problems related to the coordination and effectiveness of the assistance are addressed. As has been reported, capacity-building is of paramount importance and a critical objective for assisting Haiti in all sectors. This would enable both the Haitian Government and civil society to effectively coordinate and absorb international economic cooperation.

Given that about 86 per cent of development investments in Haiti are funded from external resources, it is vital that the flow of such resources to the country is not only maintained but is also increased over the next few years, as the country seeks to strengthen its institutions and to accelerate its economic and social development. At the same time, however, the Government will have to address the weakest link in the development aid chain, that of inadequate aid management and coordination. Unfortunately, capacity-building within those national institutions that have a mandate for aid coordination is being hampered by the political stalemate, which has made it difficult to approve new technical cooperation projects, some of which would have strengthened managerial and coordination capacity. The first step towards reinstating institutional stability and ensuring that the Government effectively plays its leadership role in formulating and implementing development policy is through holding the forthcoming elections to renew Parliament and local council assemblies and enable a new government to be formed.

The consultative group led by the World Bank constitutes the formal aid coordination mechanism among the bilateral donor community, and between the donors and the Haitian Government. Despite the willingness of the donors to strengthen and support this process, a formal consultative group meeting to address long-term development objectives with Haiti's partners will not be possible before a new Parliament is elected. In the meantime, the donor community and the United Nations system have instituted informal coordination and consultation mechanisms that have already succeeded in minimizing duplications and in developing synergies within their programmes. These include working groups and regular donor meetings within Haiti and in Washington, D.C.

It is recognized that there is a vital link between national stability and economic and social development, and that the provision of adequate and sufficient assistance to Haiti is largely subject to a return to political stability. It is therefore of the utmost importance that all political forces support the forthcoming elections and agree on appropriate modalities for the full participation of the people.

Recommendations

Need for a long-term programme of support for Haiti

There is a recognized need to develop, in collaboration with the "Friends of Haiti" group of countries and other donors, intergovernmental and non-governmental organizations, a strategic framework and comprehensive approach for a long-term United Nations programme of support for Haiti to cover such areas as education, peace-building, poverty eradication, durable recovery and sustainable development. The Government of Haiti must take a leading role in defining the objectives and priorities of this long-term strategy and programme of support, in accordance with paragraph 17 of Economic and Social Council agreed conclusions 1998/1.

Concerted efforts have been deployed by the agencies of the United Nations system engaged in assisting Haiti through the resident coordinator mechanism, as well as by the other multilateral and bilateral donors who have coordinated their actions and contributions through the consultative group led by the World Bank, in consultation with the Haitian authorities.

However, there is a great need for capacity-building and strengthening the leadership role of the Government of Haiti in providing orientation and coordination for all development activities, including the coordination of aid at the recipient end, the development of absorptive capacity and the promotion and creation of employment. Capacity-building has proven to be a critical factor for enabling Governments and civil society to manage their own affairs and effectively absorb international cooperation in post-crisis situations.

The Ad Hoc Advisory Group on Haiti recommends that:

- The Council request the Secretary-General to establish, in consultation with the Government of Haiti and making use of the existing United Nations presence in Haiti, the necessary mechanisms to develop a long-term strategy and programme of support for Haiti in such areas as education, peace-building, poverty eradication, durable recovery and sustainable development, aimed particularly at reinforcing capacity-building objectives both in governmental and civil society institutions;
- The United Nations specialized agencies, funds and programmes, the World Bank, the Inter-American Development Bank, other multilateral institutions and regional organizations, bilateral donors, including within the consultative group meetings led by the World Bank, and non-governmental organizations continue to support and to work in very close collaboration with the Haitian Government and the rest of the donor community for the purpose of elaborating and supporting the long-term strategy and programme for Haiti, including prioritizing sustainable development and capacity-building objectives;
- The coordination of the work of the agencies of the United Nations system in Haiti continue to function through the resident coordinator mechanism since it has proven to be a very adequate means for effective coordination. Such coordination should be further strengthened through the completion of the common country assessment and subsequent preparation of a United Nations development assistance framework for Haiti, which will provide the elements to define an effective long-term United Nations development assistance programme for the country. UNDP should provide increased financial and technical resources to this mechanism in order to further strengthen it;
- The long-term development programme of support for Haiti address the issues of capacity-building of governmental institutions, especially in such areas as governance, the promotion of human rights, the administration of justice, the electoral system, law enforcement, police training, and other areas of social and economic development,

which are critical for enabling the Haitian Government to adequately and effectively coordinate, manage, absorb and utilize international assistance and development aid;
- The long-term strategy and programme of support for Haiti also address the issue of capacity-building in civil society institutions.

Need for national stability

The Group emphasized that there is a vital link between national stability and economic and social development. In addition, in the case of Haiti, certain multilateral and bilateral aid flows have been put on hold until the new parliamentary and governmental authorities are constituted through the forthcoming elections.

The Government of Haiti has requested international electoral assistance for its plans to organize and hold these legislative, local and presidential elections.

The Ad Hoc Advisory Group on Haiti recommends that:

- The Council urge the United Nations system to continue to support the preparations for legislative, local and presidential elections in Haiti, including contributing funds to the ongoing efforts of the Haitian Government to organize these elections;
- The Council invite the General Assembly to renew the mandate of the International Civilian Mission in Haiti (MICIVIH), taking into account the need to review the mandate to reflect the challenges of the next two years;
- The Council request the Secretary-General to coordinate with the Government of Haiti other modalities under which reinforced support from the international community can be ensured for the electoral processes.

Need for a secure domestic environment

Recognition has been made of the importance of a peaceful, secure and stable environment as a precondition for free and fair elections and of its link with sustainable development efforts.

Similarly, recognition has been made of the importance of a professional, self-sustaining, fully functioning national police for the consolidation of democracy and the revitalization of Haiti's system of justice, and for the maintenance of a secure and stable environment necessary for the conduct of development and democratic activities.

The United Nations Civilian Police Mission in Haiti (MIPONUH) has been active in the area of police training programmes and MICIVIH has been active in promoting human rights.

The Ad Hoc Advisory Group on Haiti recommends that:

- The Council urge the United Nations system to continue to work in the areas of consolidation of democracy, training and professionalization of the national police force of Haiti, and to that end invite the General Assembly to consider devising a United Nations special training and technical assistance programme for the Haitian National Police;
- The Council invite the General Assembly to request the Secretary-General to continue his good offices in Haiti through his representative and to maintain the existence of the political office there headed by him, which would also have the responsibility of managing any new civilian mission mandated by the United Nations.

Need for a synthesis report on United Nations activities in Haiti

A periodic synthesis report on United Nations system activities in Haiti is needed so as to enable the members of the Council to closely follow developments in Haiti.

The Ad Hoc Advisory Group on Haiti recommends that:

- The Council request the Secretary-General to submit an integrated annual synthesis report on the elaboration and implementation of the long-term programme of support for Haiti, including observations and recommendations on the work of the relevant United Nations bodies in their respective areas of competence;
- In preparing that report, due account be taken of the Haitian Government's development plans and programmes for the country, as well as of the United Nations system common country assessment for Haiti and, when completed, the United Nations development assistance framework for Haiti;
- Similarly, in preparing that report, due attention be paid to a systematic evaluation of the impact of the various programmes of assistance to Haiti with a view to enhancing their overall effectiveness.

II. Resolution 1999/11: Long-term strategy and programme of support for Haiti

The Economic and Social Council,

Recalling paragraph 17 of its agreed conclusions 1998/1,[1] in which the Council noted the need to develop, through a strategic framework, when

---

1 *Official Records of the General Assembly, Fifty-third Session, Supplement No. 3* (A/53/3), chap. VII, para. 5.

appropriate, a comprehensive approach to countries in crisis, in which key aspects of durable recovery, peace-building, all human rights, sustained economic growth and sustainable development, in accordance with the relevant resolutions of the General Assembly and recent United Nations conferences, were included,

Recalling also that the development of such a comprehensive approach must involve national authorities as well as the United Nations system, donors and intergovernmental and non-governmental organizations, and that national authorities must take a leading role in all aspects of the recovery plan,

Recalling further its resolution 1994/4 of 7 May 1999, by which it created an Ad Hoc Advisory Group on Haiti, with the mandate of submitting to the Council, at its substantive session of 1999, for its consideration, its recommendations on how to ensure that international community assistance to the efforts to support the Government of Haiti in achieving sustainable development is adequate, coherent, well coordinated and effective,

Reaffirming the leading role of the Government of Haiti in all aspects of the recovery plans for Haiti,

Having examined the report of the Ad Hoc Advisory Group on Haiti,[2]

Emphasizing the need to develop a strategic framework and a comprehensive approach for a long-term United Nations programme of support for Haiti,

Emphasizing also that capacity-building is a key element to enable Governments and civil society to manage their affairs and effectively absorb international assistance in post-conflict situations,

Stressing the vital link between national stability and economic and social development,

Taking note of the request by the Government of Haiti for international electoral assistance for its plans to organize and hold the forthcoming legislative, local and presidential elections,

Bearing in mind the importance of the role of the United Nations High Commissioner for Human Rights with regard to human rights issues in Haiti and of the work of the independent expert on Haiti of the Commission on Human Rights,

---

2 E/1999/103.

Notes with appreciation the report of the Advisory Group on Haiti and welcomes its recommendations;

Requests the Secretary-General, in consultation with the Government of Haiti and making use of the existing United Nations presence in Haiti, to take the necessary steps to develop on a priority basis a long-term strategy and programme of support for Haiti in such areas as education, peace-building, poverty eradication, social integration, productive employment, trade, durable recovery and sustainable development, aimed particularly at reinforcing capacity-building objectives in both governmental and civil society institutions;

Requests the programmes, funds and agencies of the United Nations system, the World Bank, the Inter-American Development Bank, other multilateral institutions and regional organizations, bilateral donors, including within the Consultative Group meetings led by the World Bank, non-governmental organizations and the rest of the donor community to continue to support and to work in close collaboration with the Government of Haiti for the purpose of elaborating and supporting the long-term strategy and programme for Haiti, including prioritizing sustainable development and capacity-building objectives;

Urges that the coordination of the work of the organizations of the United Nations system in Haiti continue to function through the Resident Coordinator mechanism, since it has proved to be an adequate means for effective coordination, and that such coordination should be further strengthened through the completion of the common country assessment and subsequent preparation of a United Nations Development Assistance Framework for Haiti, which will provide the elements to define an effective long-term United Nations development assistance programme for the country;

Recommends that the long-term programme of support for Haiti address the issues of capacity-building of governmental institutions, especially in areas such as governance, the promotion of human rights, the administration of justice, the electoral system, law enforcement, police training and other areas of social and economic development, which would enable the Government of Haiti to adequately and effectively coordinate, manage, absorb and utilize international assistance and development aid;

Also recommends that the long-term strategy and programme of support for Haiti also address the issue of capacity-building in civil society institutions, particularly community-based organizations, labour unions and professional associations;

Urges the United Nations system to continue to support the preparations for legislative, local and presidential elections in Haiti, including supporting financially the ongoing efforts of the Government of Haiti to organize these elections;

Recommends to the General Assembly to review all aspects of the mandate and operations of the International Civilian Mission in Haiti in the light of the situation in Haiti and to consider renewing the mandate of the United Nations component of the Mission;

Requests the Secretary-General to coordinate with the Government of Haiti other modalities under which reinforced support from the international community can be ensured for the electoral processes;

Urges the United Nations system to continue to work in the areas of consolidation of democracy and training and professionalization of the national police force of Haiti, and, to that end, recommends to the General Assembly to consider devising a United Nations special training and technical assistance programme for the Haitian National Police;

Recommends to the General Assembly to consider requesting the Secretary-General to continue his good offices in Haiti through his Representative and to maintain the existence of the office there, which would also have the responsibility of managing any new civilian mission mandated by the United Nations;

Requests the Secretary-General to submit to the Economic and Social Council, at its substantive session of 2000, and to the appropriate United Nations intergovernmental bodies, an integrated synthesis report on the elaboration and implementation of the long-term programme of support for Haiti, including observations and recommendations on the work of the relevant United Nations bodies in their respective areas of competence.

41st plenary meeting
27 July 1999

Index of documents

Index

223